MW00816752

THE COLD AND DREARY EVENING SET
FORTH A MOST UNFORGIVING WIND,
THAT DECEMBER.YOU COULD HEAR THE
DEAD LEAVES RUSTLING PAST, AS EACH
GUST CHILLED YOU TO THE BONE.

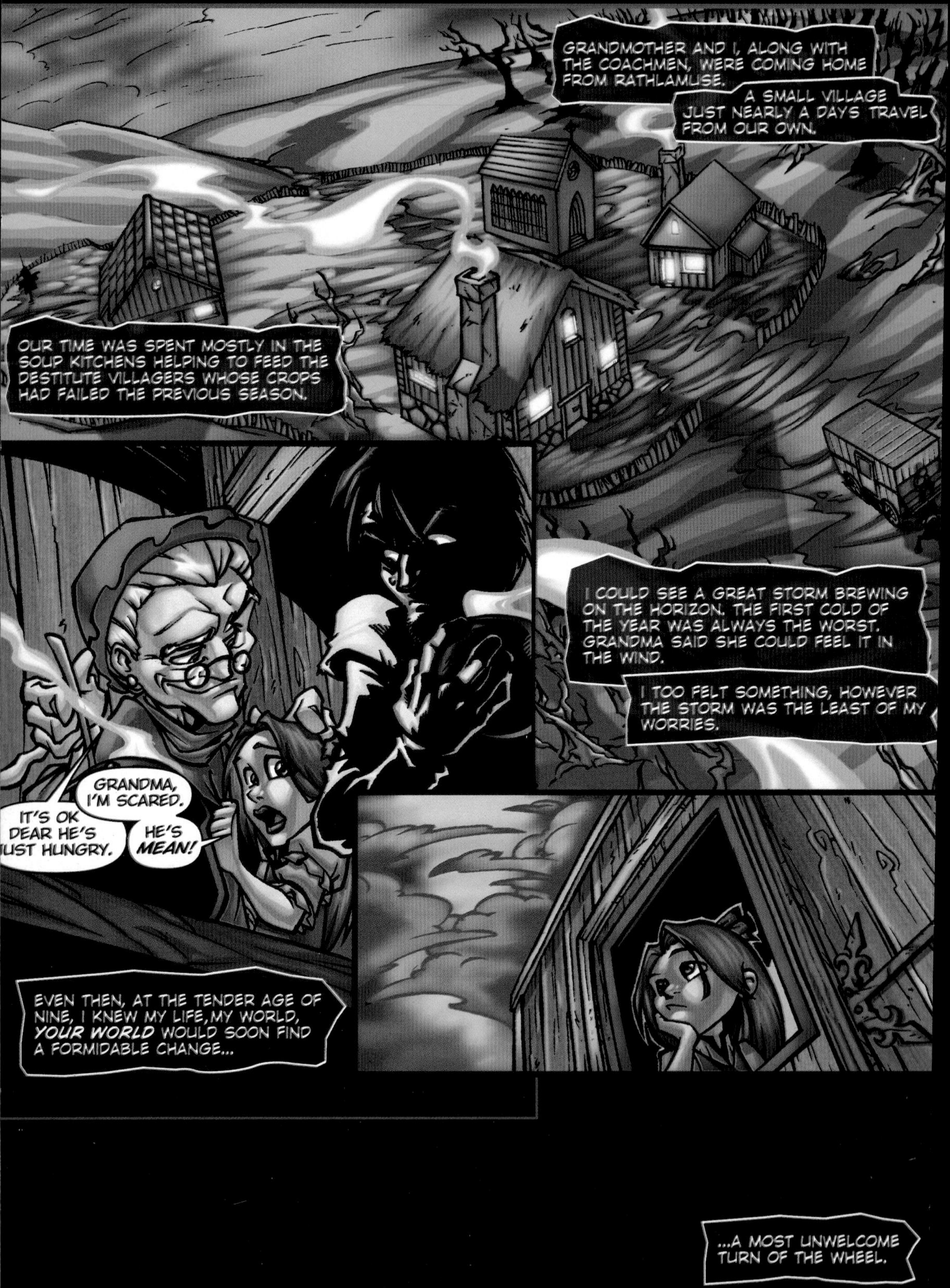
GRANDMOTHER AND I, ALONG WITH THE COACHMEN, WERE COMING HOME FROM RATHLAMUSE.
A SMALL VILLAGE JUST NEARLY A DAYS TRAVEL FROM OUR OWN.
OUR TIME WAS SPENT MOSTLY IN THE SOUP KITCHENS HELPING TO FEED THE DESTITUTE VILLAGERS WHOSE CROPS HAD FAILED THE PREVIOUS SEASON.
I COULD SEE A GREAT STORM BREWING ON THE HORIZON. THE FIRST COLD OF THE YEAR WAS ALWAYS THE WORST. GRANDMA SAID SHE COULD FEEL IT IN THE WIND.
I TOO FELT SOMETHING, HOWEVER THE STORM WAS THE LEAST OF MY WORRIES.
GRANDMA, I'M SCARED.
IT'S OK DEAR HE'S JUST HUNGRY.
HE'S *MEAN!*
EVEN THEN, AT THE TENDER AGE OF NINE, I KNEW MY LIFE, MY WORLD, *YOUR WORLD* WOULD SOON FIND A FORMIDABLE CHANGE...
...A MOST UNWELCOME TURN OF THE WHEEL.

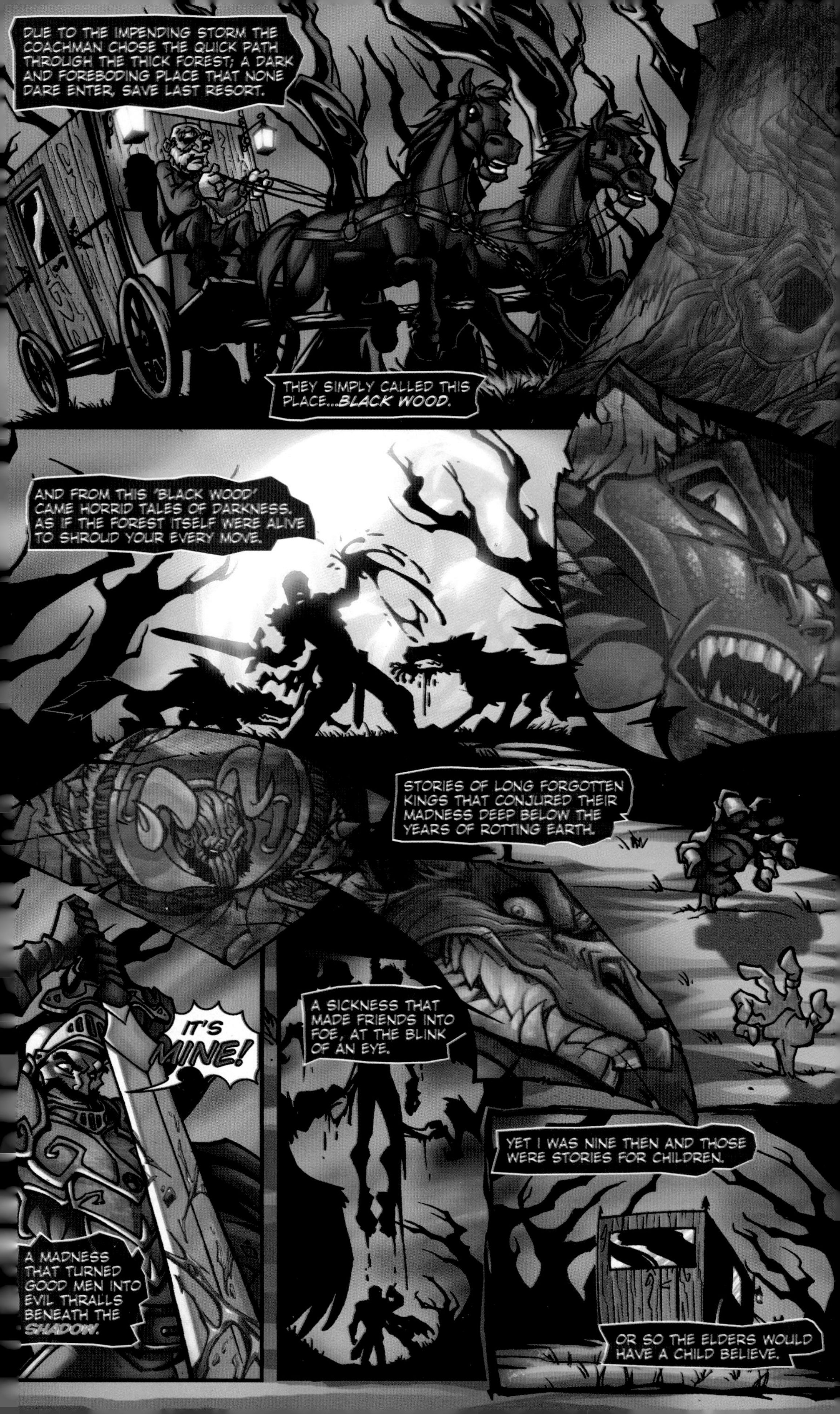
DUE TO THE IMPENDING STORM THE COACHMAN CHOSE THE QUICK PATH THROUGH THE THICK FOREST; A DARK AND FOREBODING PLACE THAT NONE DARE ENTER, SAVE LAST RESORT.
THEY SIMPLY CALLED THIS PLACE...BLACK WOOD.
AND FROM THIS 'BLACK WOOD' CAME HORRID TALES OF DARKNESS. AS IF THE FOREST ITSELF WERE ALIVE TO SHROUD YOUR EVERY MOVE.
STORIES OF LONG FORGOTTEN KINGS THAT CONJURED THEIR MADNESS DEEP BELOW THE YEARS OF ROTTING EARTH.
IT'S MINE!
A MADNESS THAT TURNED GOOD MEN INTO EVIL THRALLS BENEATH THE SHADOW.
A SICKNESS THAT MADE FRIENDS INTO FOE, AT THE BLINK OF AN EYE.
YET I WAS NINE THEN AND THOSE WERE STORIES FOR CHILDREN.
OR SO THE ELDERS WOULD HAVE A CHILD BELIEVE.

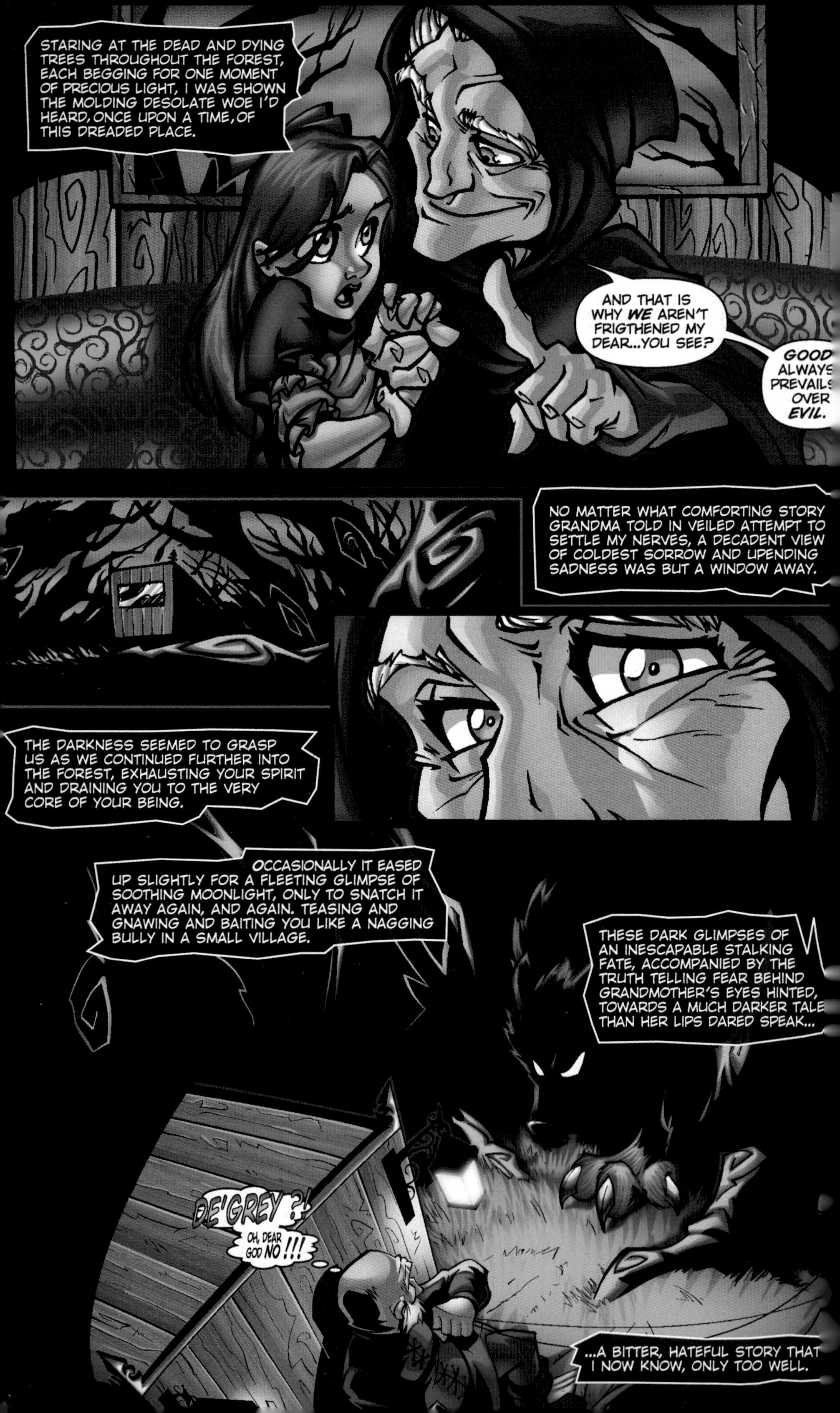

STARING AT THE DEAD AND DYING TREES THROUGHOUT THE FOREST, EACH BEGGING FOR ONE MOMENT OF PRECIOUS LIGHT, I WAS SHOWN THE MOLDING DESOLATE WOE I'D HEARD, ONCE UPON A TIME, OF THIS DREADED PLACE.
AND THAT IS WHY *WE* AREN'T FRIGTHENED MY DEAR...YOU SEE?
GOOD ALWAYS PREVAILS OVER ***EVIL.***
NO MATTER WHAT COMFORTING STORY GRANDMA TOLD IN VEILED ATTEMPT TO SETTLE MY NERVES, A DECADENT VIEW OF COLDEST SORROW AND UPENDING SADNESS WAS BUT A WINDOW AWAY.
THE DARKNESS SEEMED TO GRASP US AS WE CONTINUED FURTHER INTO THE FOREST, EXHAUSTING YOUR SPIRIT AND DRAINING YOU TO THE VERY CORE OF YOUR BEING.
OCCASIONALLY IT EASED UP SLIGHTLY FOR A FLEETING GLIMPSE OF SOOTHING MOONLIGHT, ONLY TO SNATCH IT AWAY AGAIN, AND AGAIN. TEASING AND GNAWING AND BAITING YOU LIKE A NAGGING BULLY IN A SMALL VILLAGE.
THESE DARK GLIMPSES OF AN INESCAPABLE STALKING FATE, ACCOMPANIED BY THE TRUTH TELLING FEAR BEHIND GRANDMOTHER'S EYES HINTED, TOWARDS A MUCH DARKER TALE THAN HER LIPS DARED SPEAK...
DE'GREY ?!
OH, DEAR GOD NO !!!
...A BITTER, HATEFUL STORY THAT I NOW KNOW, ONLY TOO WELL.

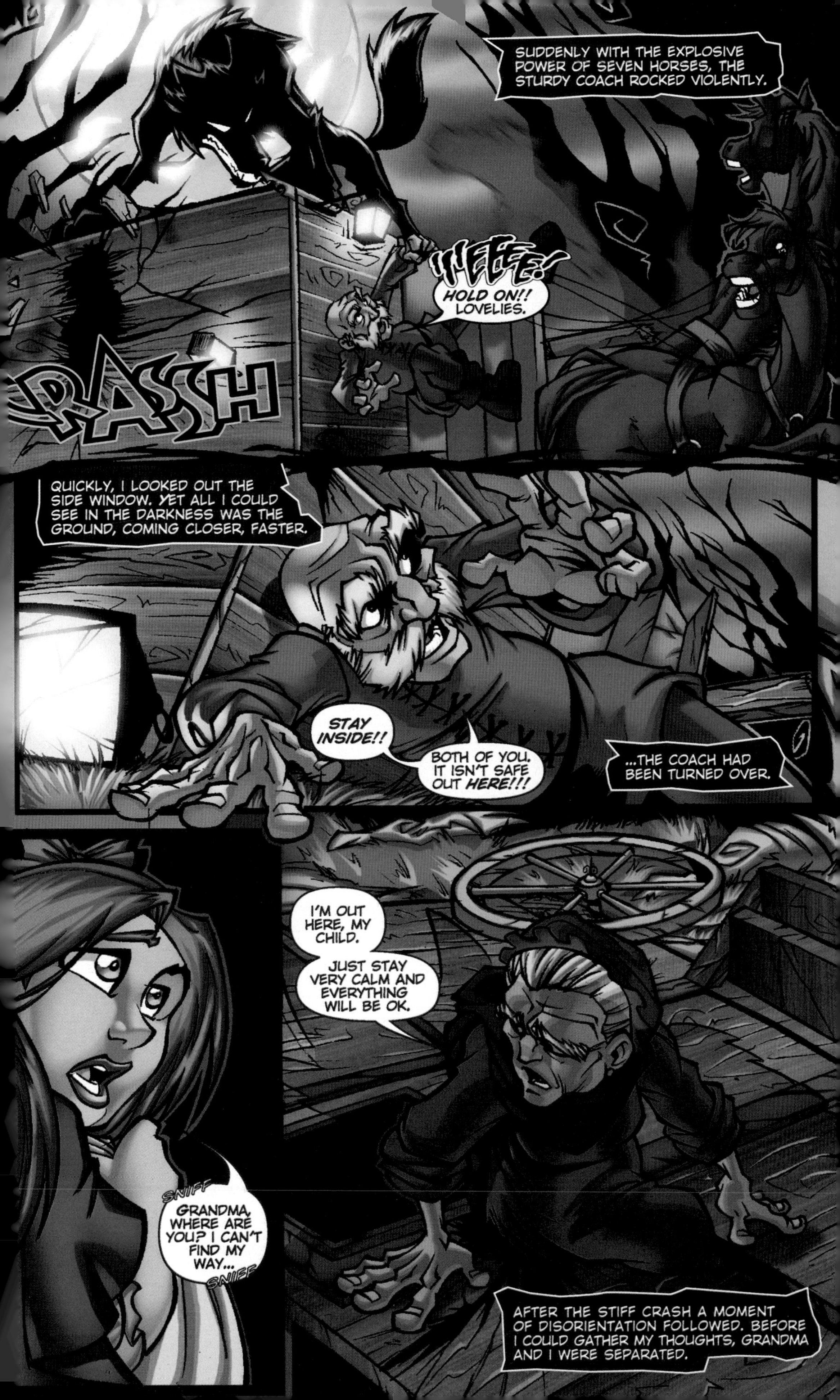
SUDDENLY WITH THE EXPLOSIVE POWER OF SEVEN HORSES, THE STURDY COACH ROCKED VIOLENTLY.
WEEEE!
HOLD ON!! LOVELIES.
CRASH
QUICKLY, I LOOKED OUT THE SIDE WINDOW. YET ALL I COULD SEE IN THE DARKNESS WAS THE GROUND, COMING CLOSER, FASTER.
STAY INSIDE!!
BOTH OF YOU. IT ISN'T SAFE OUT HERE!!!
...THE COACH HAD BEEN TURNED OVER.
I'M OUT HERE, MY CHILD.
JUST STAY VERY CALM AND EVERYTHING WILL BE OK.
SNIFF
GRANDMA, WHERE ARE YOU? I CAN'T FIND MY WAY...
SNIFF
AFTER THE STIFF CRASH A MOMENT OF DISORIENTATION FOLLOWED. BEFORE I COULD GATHER MY THOUGHTS, GRANDMA AND I WERE SEPARATED.

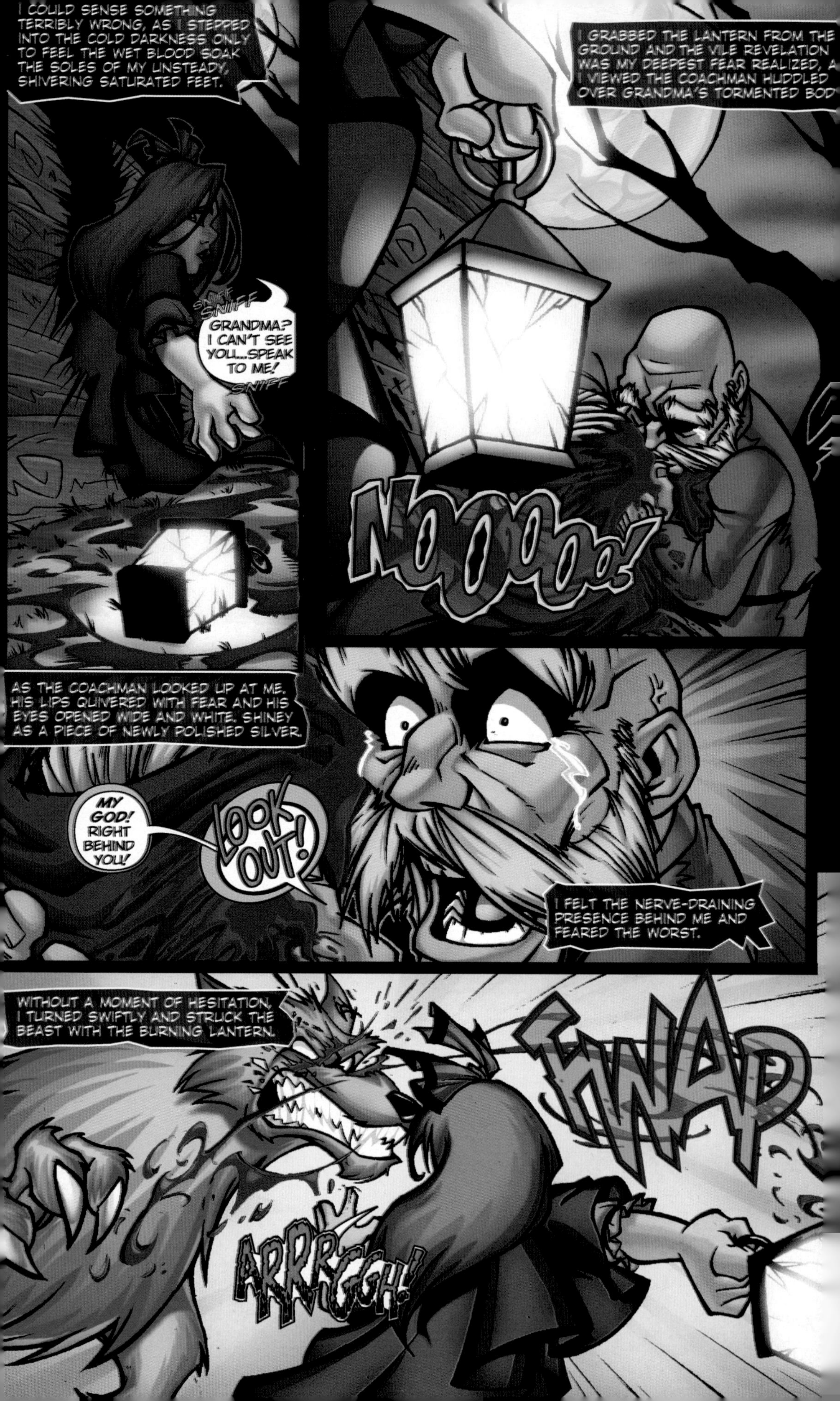
I COULD SENSE SOMETHING TERRIBLY WRONG, AS I STEPPED INTO THE COLD DARKNESS ONLY TO FEEL THE WET BLOOD SOAK THE SOLES OF MY UNSTEADY, SHIVERING SATURATED FEET.
SNIFF SNIIFF
GRANDMA? I CAN'T SEE YOU...SPEAK TO ME!
SNIFF
I GRABBED THE LANTERN FROM THE GROUND AND THE VILE REVELATION WAS MY DEEPEST FEAR REALIZED, A I VIEWED THE COACHMAN HUDDLED OVER GRANDMA'S TORMENTED BOD
NOOOOoo!
AS THE COACHMAN LOOKED UP AT ME, HIS LIPS QUIVERED WITH FEAR AND HIS EYES OPENED WIDE AND WHITE, SHINEY AS A PIECE OF NEWLY POLISHED SILVER.
MY GOD! RIGHT BEHIND YOU!
LOOK OUT!
I FELT THE NERVE-DRAINING PRESENCE BEHIND ME AND FEARED THE WORST.
WITHOUT A MOMENT OF HESITATION, I TURNED SWIFTLY AND STRUCK THE BEAST WITH THE BURNING LANTERN.
WHAP
ARRRGGH!

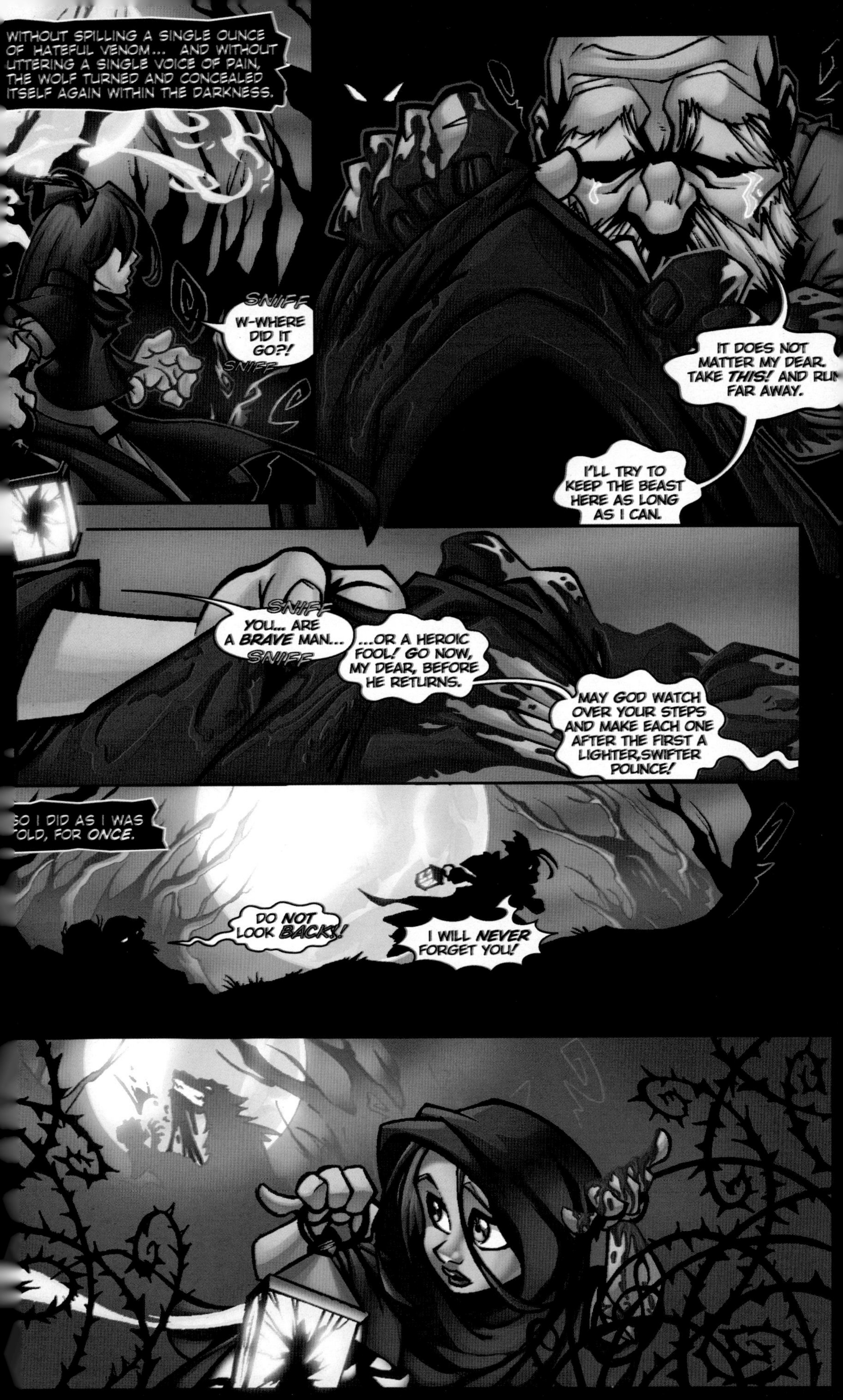
WITHOUT SPILLING A SINGLE OUNCE OF HATEFUL VENOM... AND WITHOUT UTTERING A SINGLE VOICE OF PAIN, THE WOLF TURNED AND CONCEALED ITSELF AGAIN WITHIN THE DARKNESS.
SNIFF
W-WHERE DID IT GO?!
SNIFF
IT DOES NOT MATTER MY DEAR. TAKE THIS! AND RUN FAR AWAY.
I'LL TRY TO KEEP THE BEAST HERE AS LONG AS I CAN.
SNIFF
YOU... ARE A BRAVE MAN...
SNIFF
...OR A HEROIC FOOL! GO NOW, MY DEAR, BEFORE HE RETURNS.
MAY GOD WATCH OVER YOUR STEPS AND MAKE EACH ONE AFTER THE FIRST A LIGHTER,SWIFTER POUNCE!
SO I DID AS I WAS TOLD, FOR ONCE.
DO NOT LOOK BACK!
I WILL NEVER FORGET YOU!

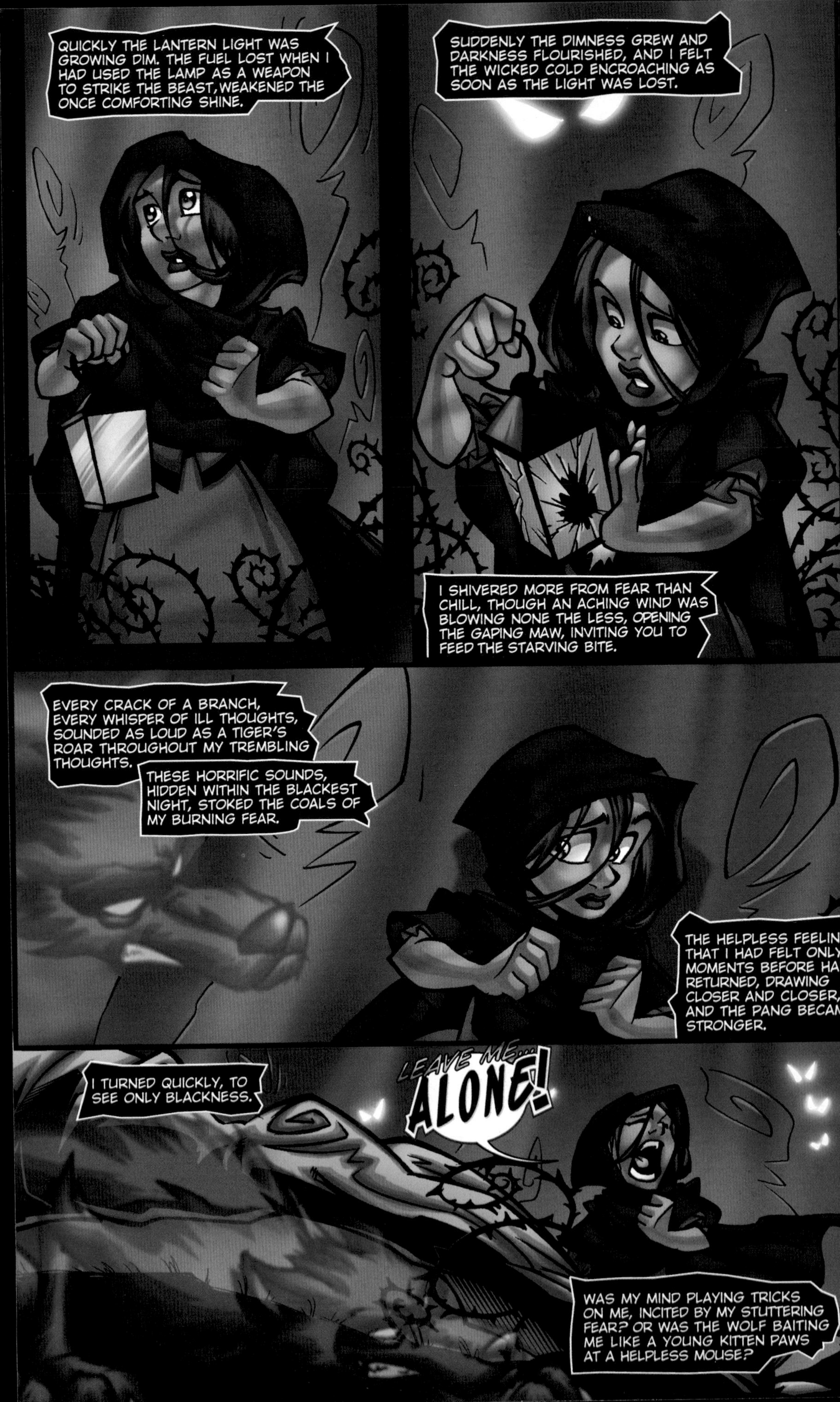
QUICKLY THE LANTERN LIGHT WAS GROWING DIM. THE FUEL LOST WHEN I HAD USED THE LAMP AS A WEAPON TO STRIKE THE BEAST, WEAKENED THE ONCE COMFORTING SHINE.
SUDDENLY THE DIMNESS GREW AND DARKNESS FLOURISHED, AND I FELT THE WICKED COLD ENCROACHING AS SOON AS THE LIGHT WAS LOST.
I SHIVERED MORE FROM FEAR THAN CHILL, THOUGH AN ACHING WIND WAS BLOWING NONE THE LESS, OPENING THE GAPING MAW, INVITING YOU TO FEED THE STARVING BITE.
EVERY CRACK OF A BRANCH, EVERY WHISPER OF ILL THOUGHTS, SOUNDED AS LOUD AS A TIGER'S ROAR THROUGHOUT MY TREMBLING THOUGHTS.
THESE HORRIFIC SOUNDS, HIDDEN WITHIN THE BLACKEST NIGHT, STOKED THE COALS OF MY BURNING FEAR.
THE HELPLESS FEELIN THAT I HAD FELT ONLY MOMENTS BEFORE HA RETURNED, DRAWING CLOSER AND CLOSER, AND THE PANG BECAM STRONGER.
I TURNED QUICKLY, TO SEE ONLY BLACKNESS.
LEAVE ME... ALONE!
WAS MY MIND PLAYING TRICKS ON ME, INCITED BY MY STUTTERING FEAR? OR WAS THE WOLF BAITING ME LIKE A YOUNG KITTEN PAWS AT A HELPLESS MOUSE?

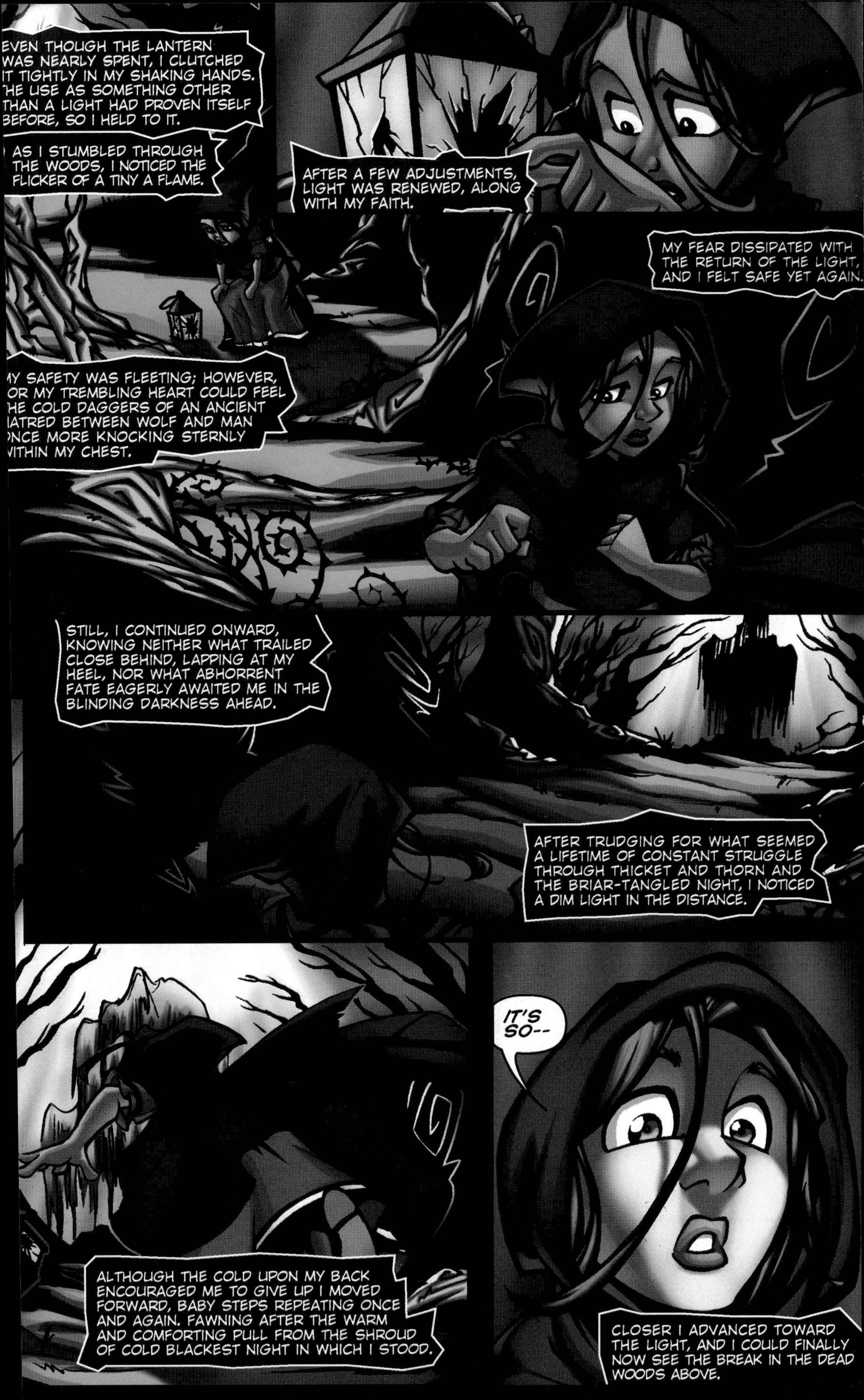
EVEN THOUGH THE LANTERN WAS NEARLY SPENT, I CLUTCHED IT TIGHTLY IN MY SHAKING HANDS. THE USE AS SOMETHING OTHER THAN A LIGHT HAD PROVEN ITSELF BEFORE, SO I HELD TO IT.
AS I STUMBLED THROUGH THE WOODS, I NOTICED THE FLICKER OF A TINY A FLAME.
AFTER A FEW ADJUSTMENTS, LIGHT WAS RENEWED, ALONG WITH MY FAITH.
MY FEAR DISSIPATED WITH THE RETURN OF THE LIGHT, AND I FELT SAFE YET AGAIN.
MY SAFETY WAS FLEETING; HOWEVER, FOR MY TREMBLING HEART COULD FEEL THE COLD DAGGERS OF AN ANCIENT HATRED BETWEEN WOLF AND MAN ONCE MORE KNOCKING STERNLY WITHIN MY CHEST.
STILL, I CONTINUED ONWARD, KNOWING NEITHER WHAT TRAILED CLOSE BEHIND, LAPPING AT MY HEEL, NOR WHAT ABHORRENT FATE EAGERLY AWAITED ME IN THE BLINDING DARKNESS AHEAD.
AFTER TRUDGING FOR WHAT SEEMED A LIFETIME OF CONSTANT STRUGGLE THROUGH THICKET AND THORN AND THE BRIAR-TANGLED NIGHT, I NOTICED A DIM LIGHT IN THE DISTANCE.
ALTHOUGH THE COLD UPON MY BACK ENCOURAGED ME TO GIVE UP I MOVED FORWARD, BABY STEPS REPEATING ONCE AND AGAIN. FAWNING AFTER THE WARM AND COMFORTING PULL FROM THE SHROUD OF COLD BLACKEST NIGHT IN WHICH I STOOD.
IT'S SO--
CLOSER I ADVANCED TOWARD THE LIGHT, AND I COULD FINALLY NOW SEE THE BREAK IN THE DEAD WOODS ABOVE.

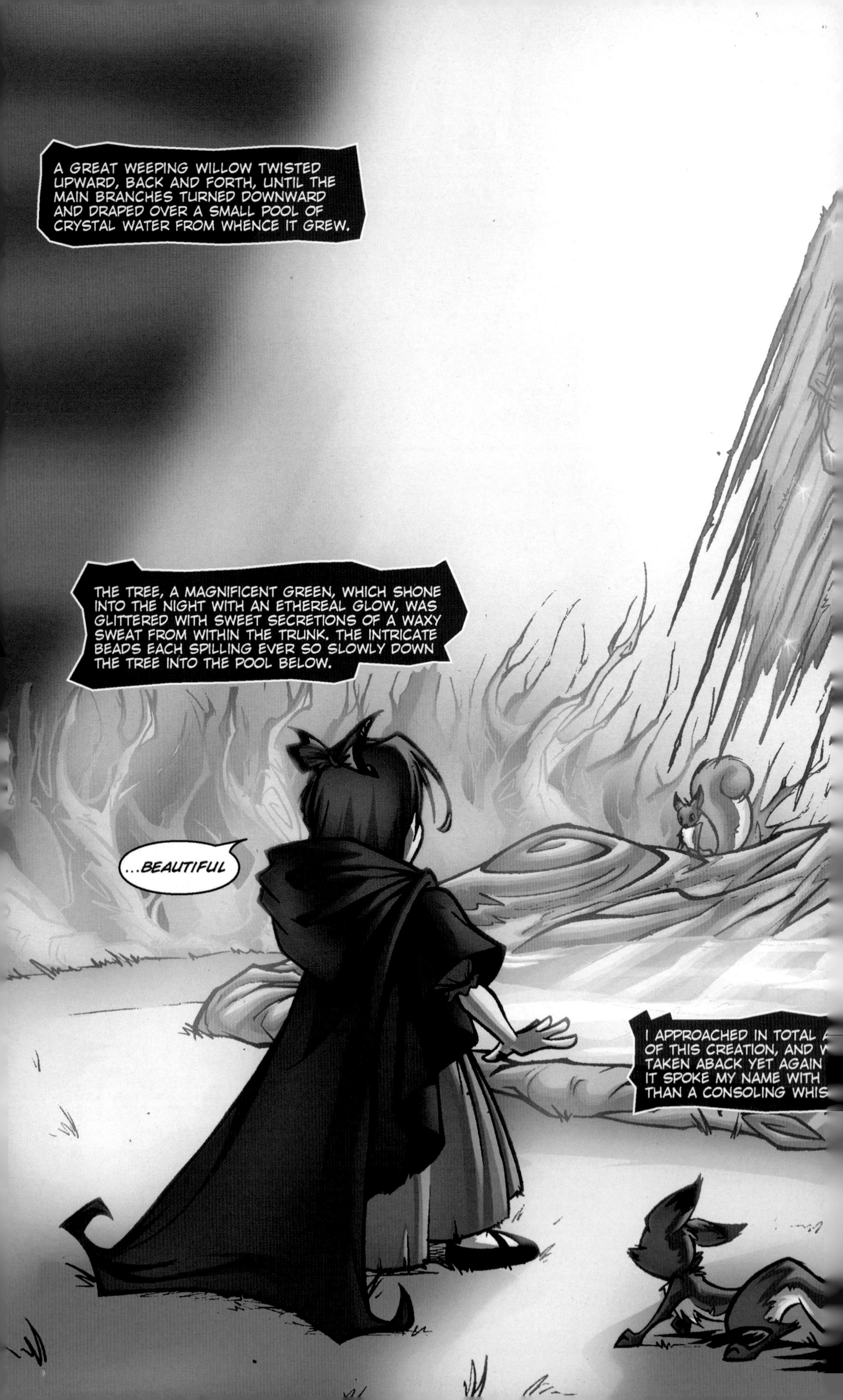
A GREAT WEEPING WILLOW TWISTED UPWARD, BACK AND FORTH, UNTIL THE MAIN BRANCHES TURNED DOWNWARD AND DRAPED OVER A SMALL POOL OF CRYSTAL WATER FROM WHENCE IT GREW.
THE TREE, A MAGNIFICENT GREEN, WHICH SHONE INTO THE NIGHT WITH AN ETHEREAL GLOW, WAS GLITTERED WITH SWEET SECRETIONS OF A WAXY SWEAT FROM WITHIN THE TRUNK. THE INTRICATE BEADS EACH SPILLING EVER SO SLOWLY DOWN THE TREE INTO THE POOL BELOW.
...BEAUTIFUL
I APPROACHED IN TOTAL
OF THIS CREATION, AND
TAKEN ABACK YET AGAIN
IT SPOKE MY NAME WITH
THAN A CONSOLING

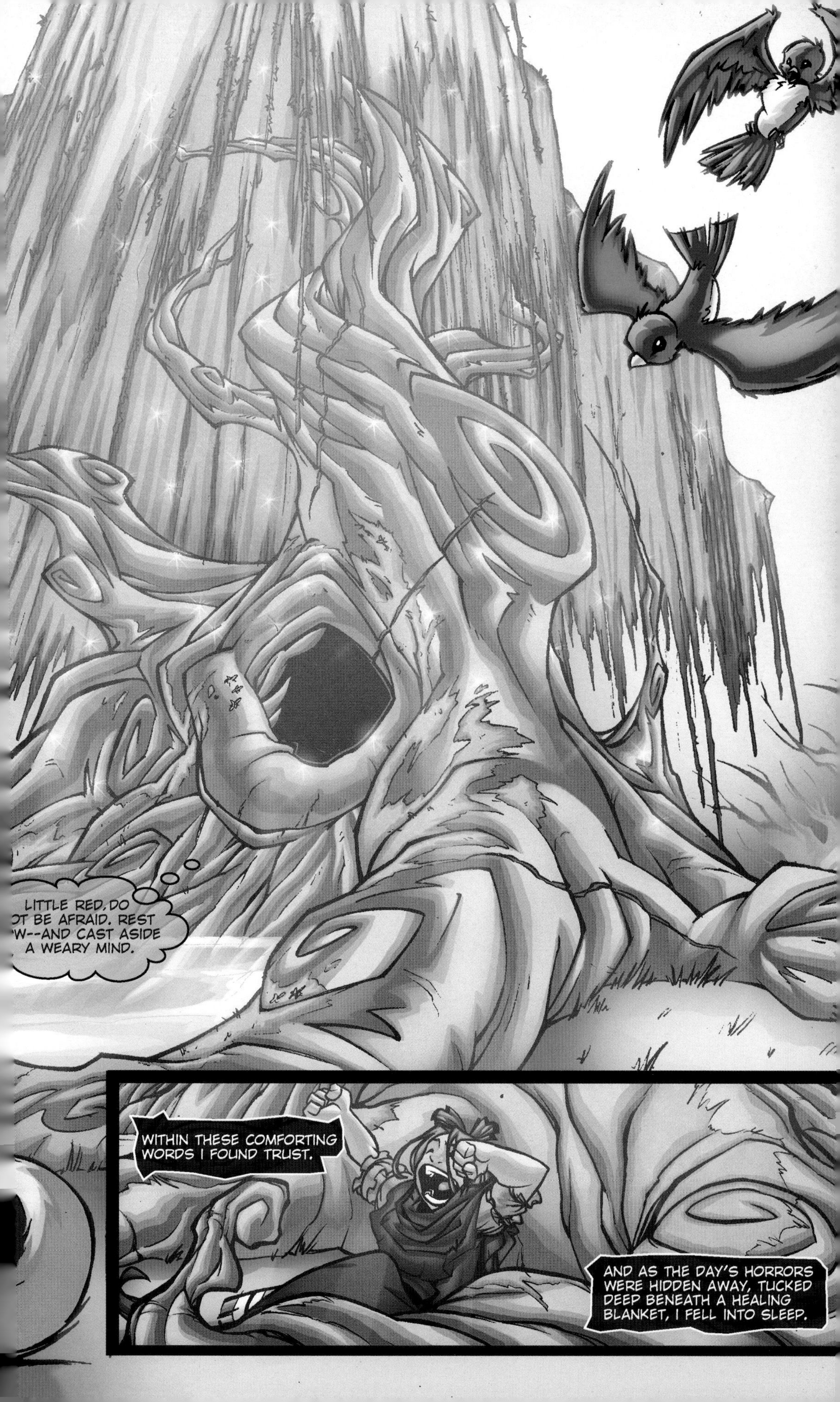

LITTLE RED, DO OT BE AFRAID. REST W--AND CAST ASIDE A WEARY MIND.
WITHIN THESE COMFORTING WORDS I FOUND TRUST.
AND AS THE DAY'S HORRORS WERE HIDDEN AWAY, TUCKED DEEP BENEATH A HEALING BLANKET, I FELL INTO SLEEP.

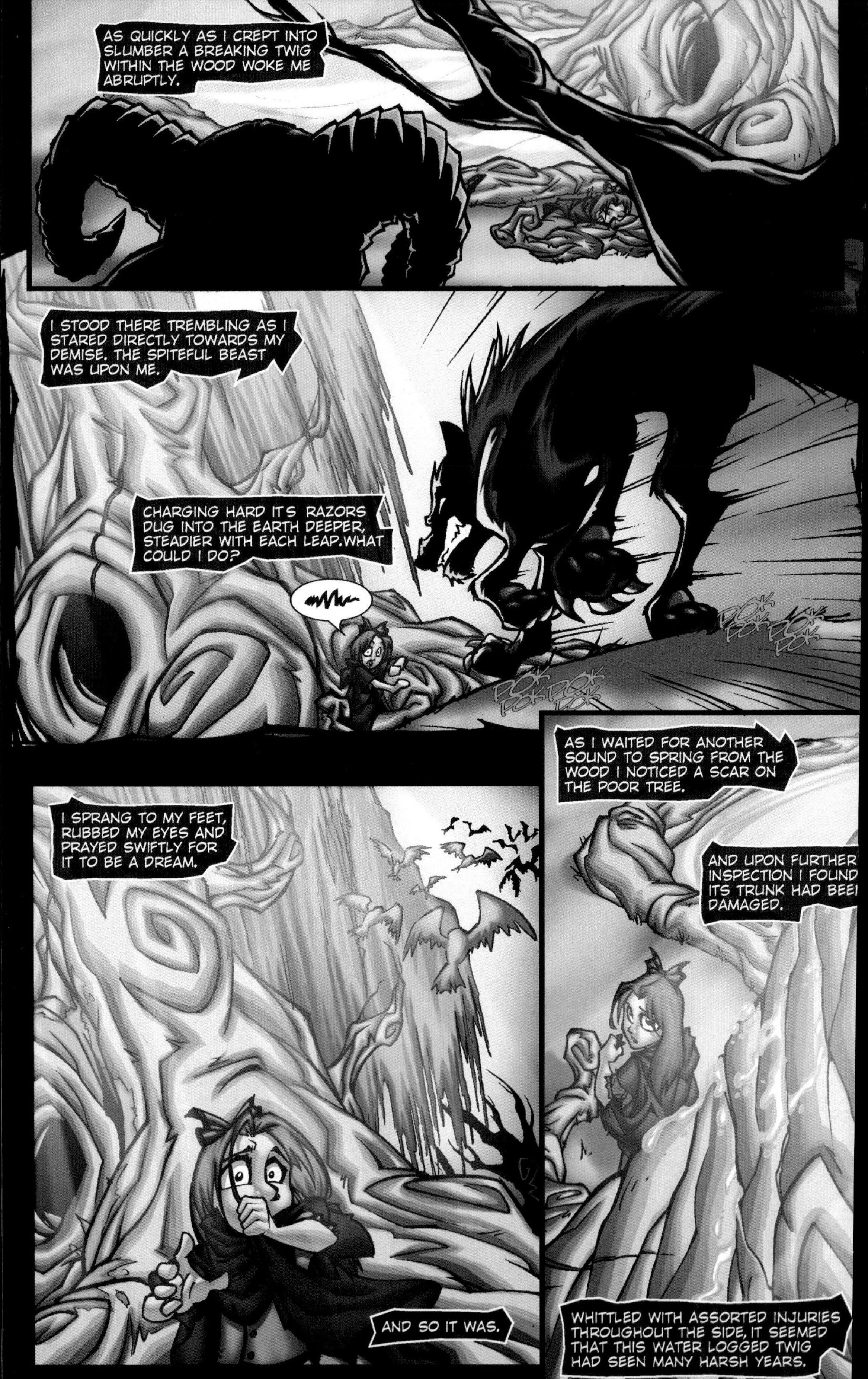
AS QUICKLY AS I CREPT INTO SLUMBER A BREAKING TWIG WITHIN THE WOOD WOKE ME ABRUPTLY.
I STOOD THERE TREMBLING AS I STARED DIRECTLY TOWARDS MY DEMISE. THE SPITEFUL BEAST WAS UPON ME.
CHARGING HARD ITS RAZORS DUG INTO THE EARTH DEEPER, STEADIER WITH EACH LEAP.WHAT COULD I DO?
I SPRANG TO MY FEET, RUBBED MY EYES AND PRAYED SWIFTLY FOR IT TO BE A DREAM.
AND SO IT WAS.
AS I WAITED FOR ANOTHER SOUND TO SPRING FROM THE WOOD I NOTICED A SCAR ON THE POOR TREE.
AND UPON FURTHER INSPECTION I FOUND ITS TRUNK HAD BEE DAMAGED.
WHITTLED WITH ASSORTED INJURIES THROUGHOUT THE SIDE, IT SEEMED THAT THIS WATER LOGGED TWIG HAD SEEN MANY HARSH YEARS.

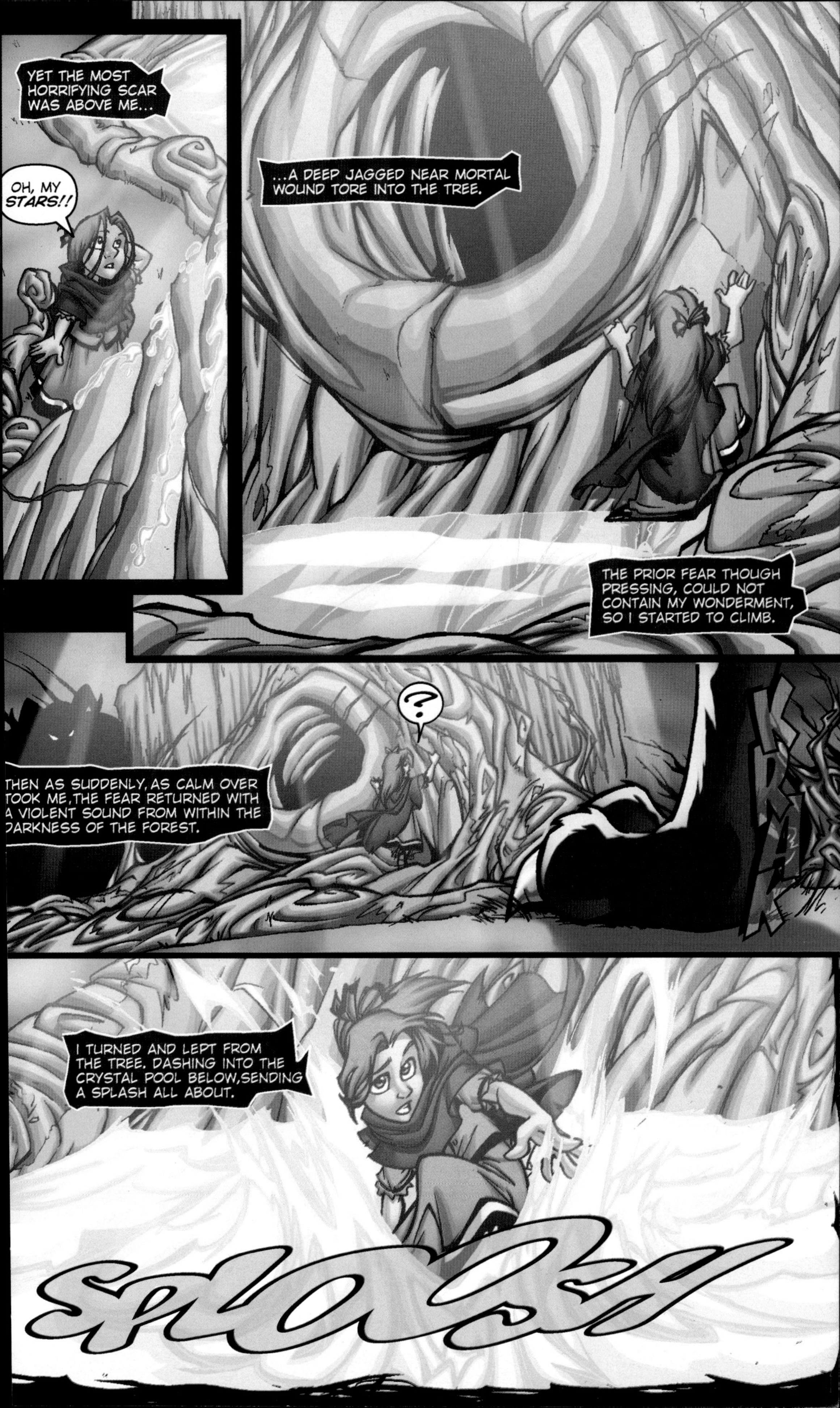
YET THE MOST HORRIFYING SCAR WAS ABOVE ME...
OH, MY STARS!!
...A DEEP JAGGED NEAR MORTAL WOUND TORE INTO THE TREE.
THE PRIOR FEAR THOUGH PRESSING, COULD NOT CONTAIN MY WONDERMENT, SO I STARTED TO CLIMB.
?
THEN AS SUDDENLY, AS CALM OVER TOOK ME, THE FEAR RETURNED WITH A VIOLENT SOUND FROM WITHIN THE DARKNESS OF THE FOREST.
I TURNED AND LEPT FROM THE TREE. DASHING INTO THE CRYSTAL POOL BELOW, SENDING A SPLASH ALL ABOUT.
SPLASH

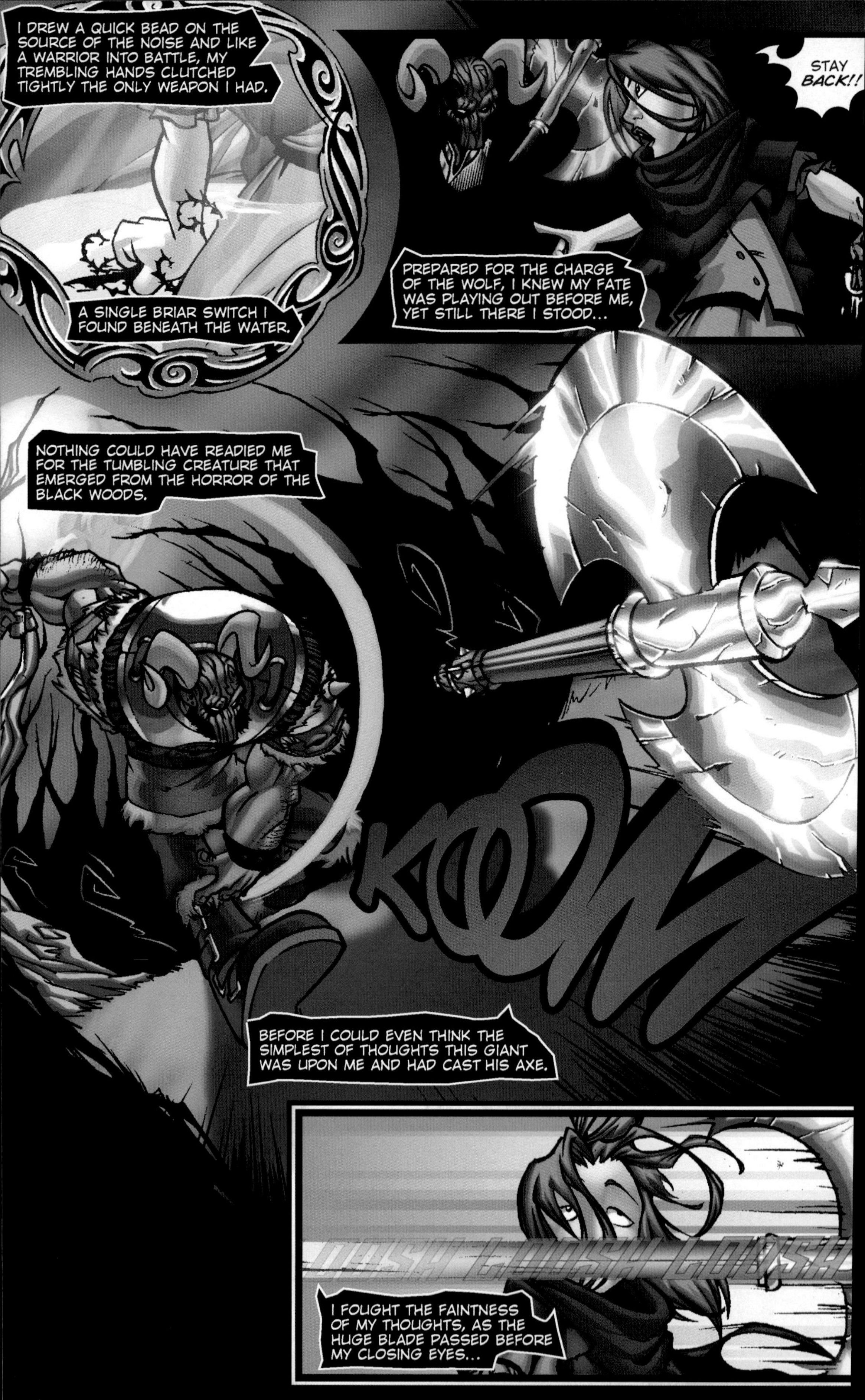
I DREW A QUICK BEAD ON THE SOURCE OF THE NOISE AND LIKE A WARRIOR INTO BATTLE, MY TREMBLING HANDS CLUTCHED TIGHTLY THE ONLY WEAPON I HAD.
A SINGLE BRIAR SWITCH I FOUND BENEATH THE WATER.
STAY BACK!!
PREPARED FOR THE CHARGE OF THE WOLF, I KNEW MY FATE WAS PLAYING OUT BEFORE ME, YET STILL THERE I STOOD...
NOTHING COULD HAVE READIED ME FOR THE TUMBLING CREATURE THAT EMERGED FROM THE HORROR OF THE BLACK WOODS.
KOOM
BEFORE I COULD EVEN THINK THE SIMPLEST OF THOUGHTS THIS GIANT WAS UPON ME AND HAD CAST HIS AXE.
GOOSH GOOSH GOOSH
I FOUGHT THE FAINTNESS OF MY THOUGHTS, AS THE HUGE BLADE PASSED BEFORE MY CLOSING EYES...

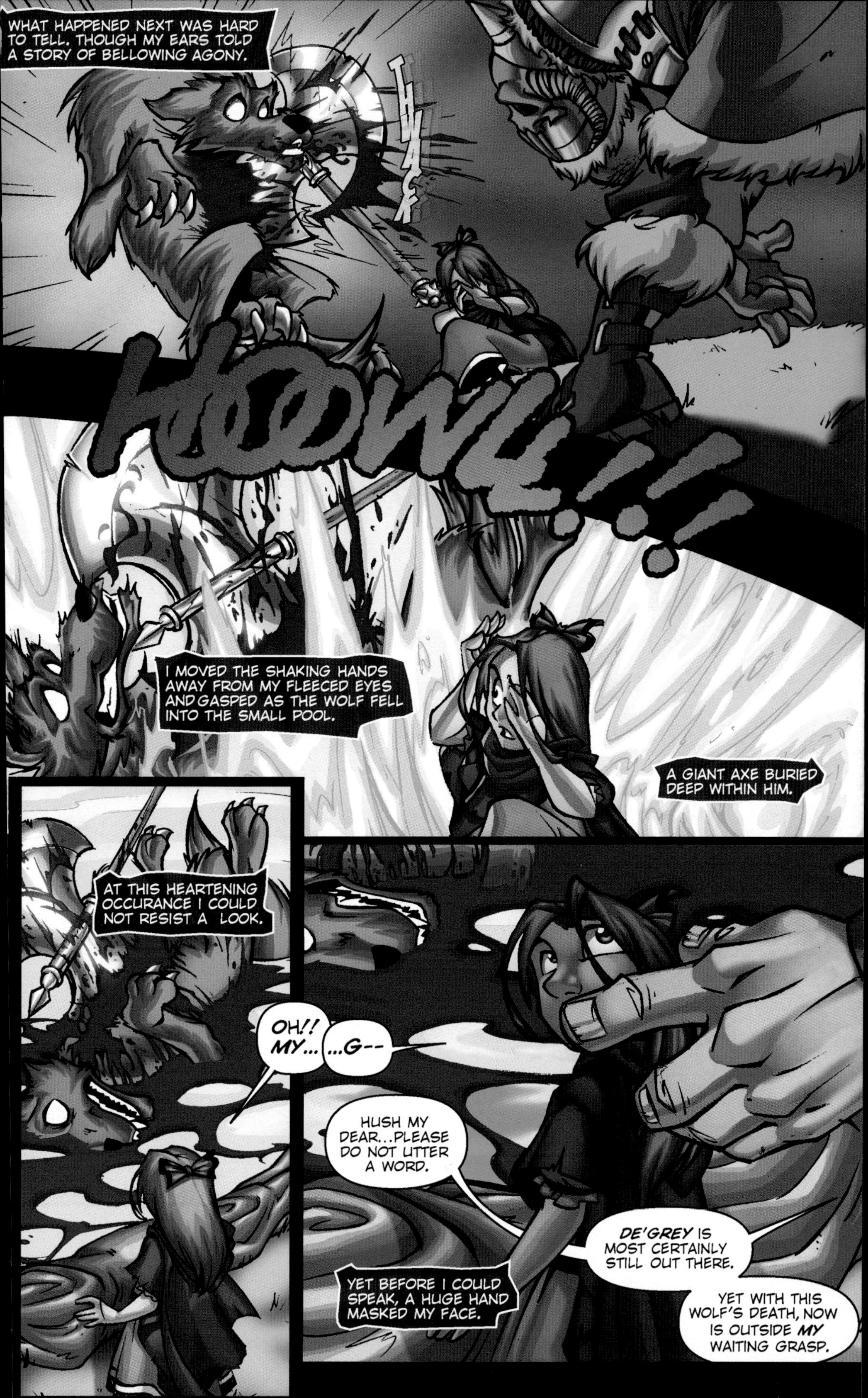
WHAT HAPPENED NEXT WAS HARD TO TELL. THOUGH MY EARS TOLD A STORY OF BELLOWING AGONY.
THWACK
HOOWL!!!
I MOVED THE SHAKING HANDS AWAY FROM MY FLEECED EYES AND GASPED AS THE WOLF FELL INTO THE SMALL POOL.
A GIANT AXE BURIED DEEP WITHIN HIM.
AT THIS HEARTENING OCCURANCE I COULD NOT RESIST A LOOK.
OH!! MY...
...G--
HUSH MY DEAR...PLEASE DO NOT UTTER A WORD.
DE'GREY IS MOST CERTAINLY STILL OUT THERE.
YET BEFORE I COULD SPEAK, A HUGE HAND MASKED MY FACE.
YET WITH THIS WOLF'S DEATH, NOW IS OUTSIDE MY WAITING GRASP.

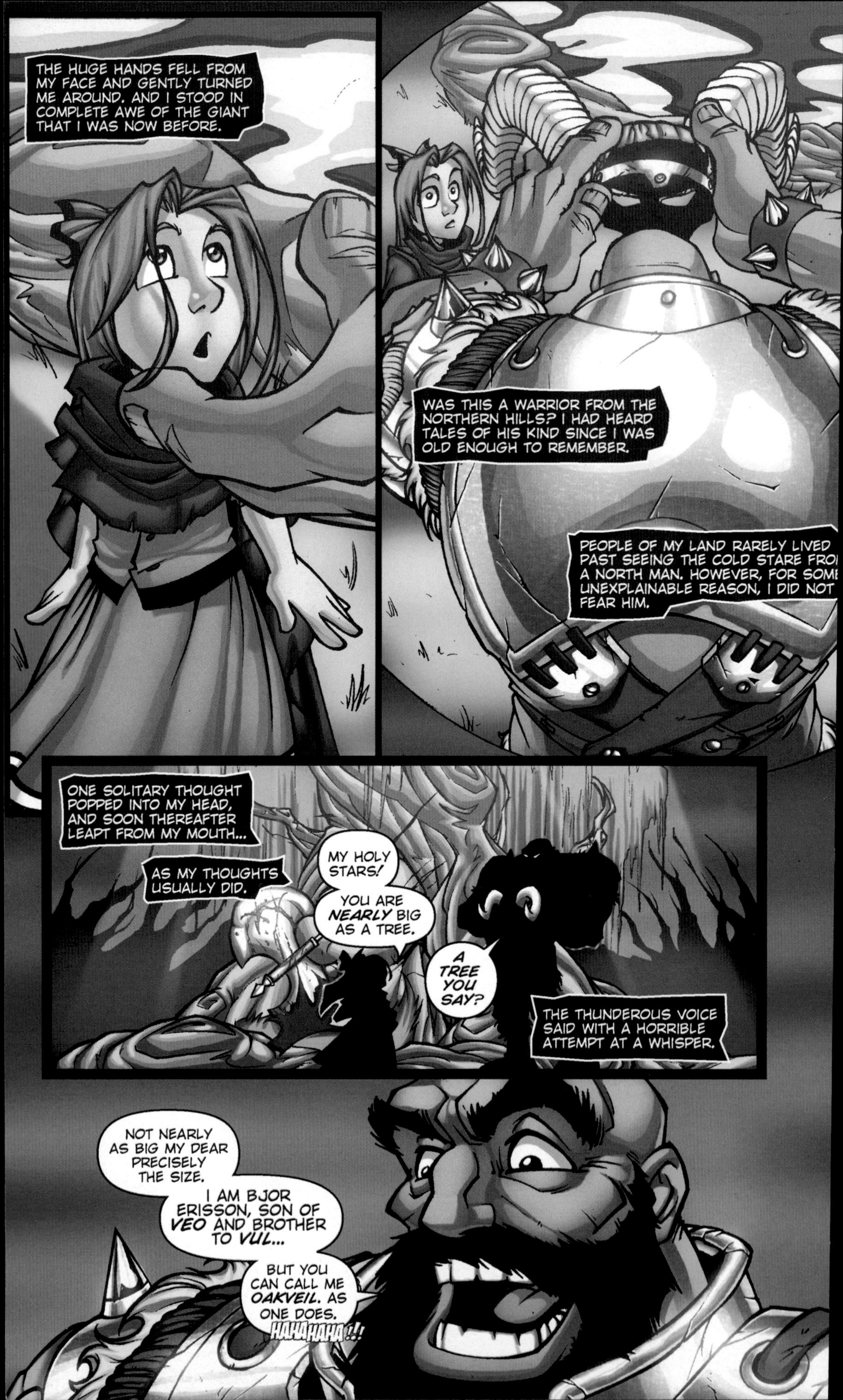
THE HUGE HANDS FELL FROM MY FACE AND GENTLY TURNED ME AROUND. AND I STOOD IN COMPLETE AWE OF THE GIANT THAT I WAS NOW BEFORE.
WAS THIS A WARRIOR FROM THE NORTHERN HILLS? I HAD HEARD TALES OF HIS KIND SINCE I WAS OLD ENOUGH TO REMEMBER.
PEOPLE OF MY LAND RARELY LIVED PAST SEEING THE COLD STARE FROM A NORTH MAN. HOWEVER, FOR SOME UNEXPLAINABLE REASON, I DID NOT FEAR HIM.
ONE SOLITARY THOUGHT POPPED INTO MY HEAD, AND SOON THEREAFTER LEAPT FROM MY MOUTH...
AS MY THOUGHTS USUALLY DID.
MY HOLY STARS!
YOU ARE *NEARLY* BIG AS A TREE.
A TREE YOU SAY?
THE THUNDEROUS VOICE SAID WITH A HORRIBLE ATTEMPT AT A WHISPER.
NOT NEARLY AS BIG MY DEAR PRECISELY THE SIZE.
I AM BJOR ERISSON, SON OF *VEO* AND BROTHER TO *VUL*...
BUT YOU CAN CALL ME *OAKVEIL*. AS ONE DOES.
HAHAHAHA!!!

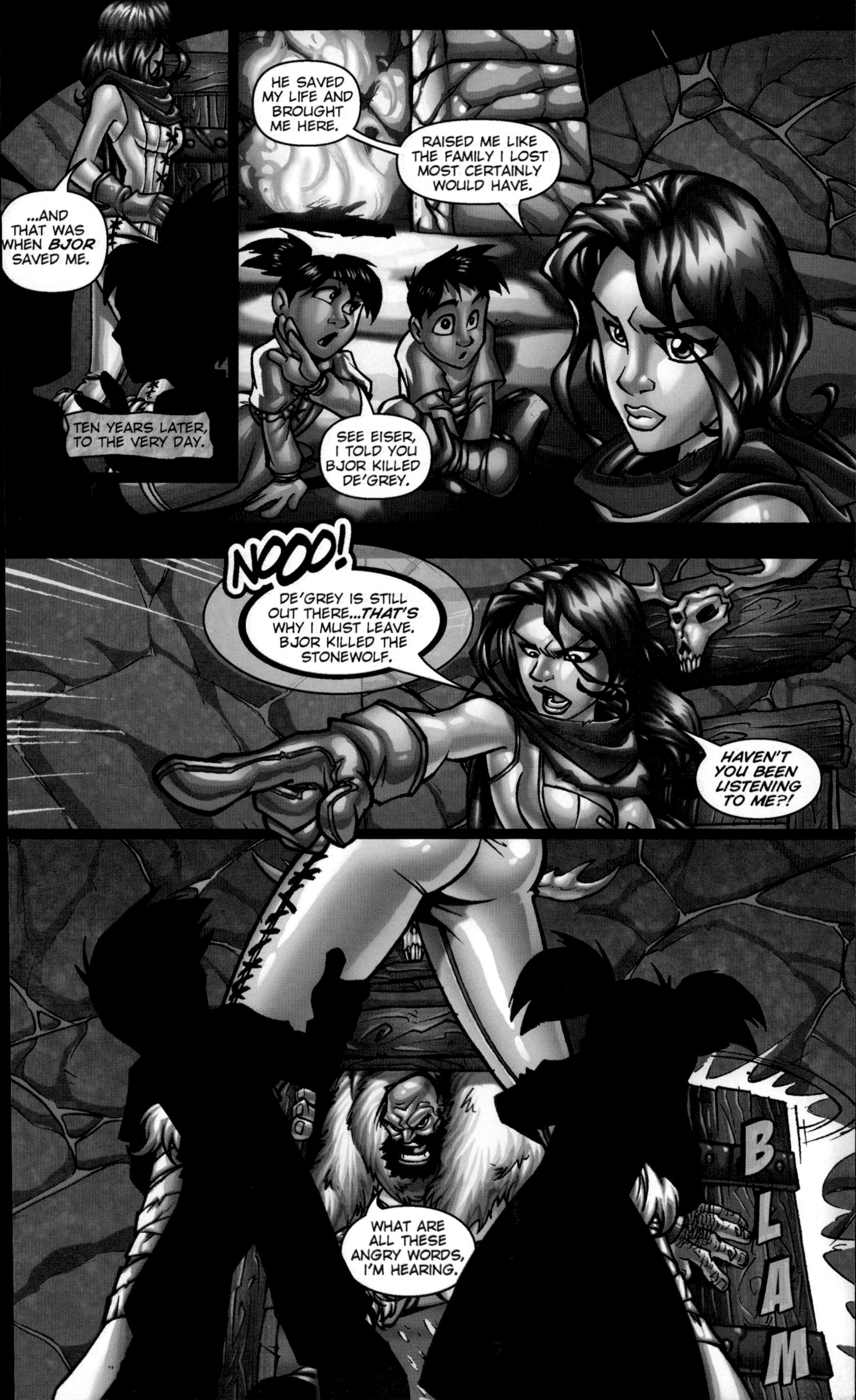
...AND THAT WAS WHEN BJOR SAVED ME.
TEN YEARS LATER, TO THE VERY DAY.
HE SAVED MY LIFE AND BROUGHT ME HERE.
RAISED ME LIKE THE FAMILY I LOST MOST CERTAINLY WOULD HAVE.
SEE EISER, I TOLD YOU BJOR KILLED DE'GREY.
NOOO!
DE'GREY IS STILL OUT THERE...THAT'S WHY I MUST LEAVE. BJOR KILLED THE STONEWOLF.
HAVEN'T YOU BEEN LISTENING TO ME?!
BLAM
WHAT ARE ALL THESE ANGRY WORDS, I'M HEARING.

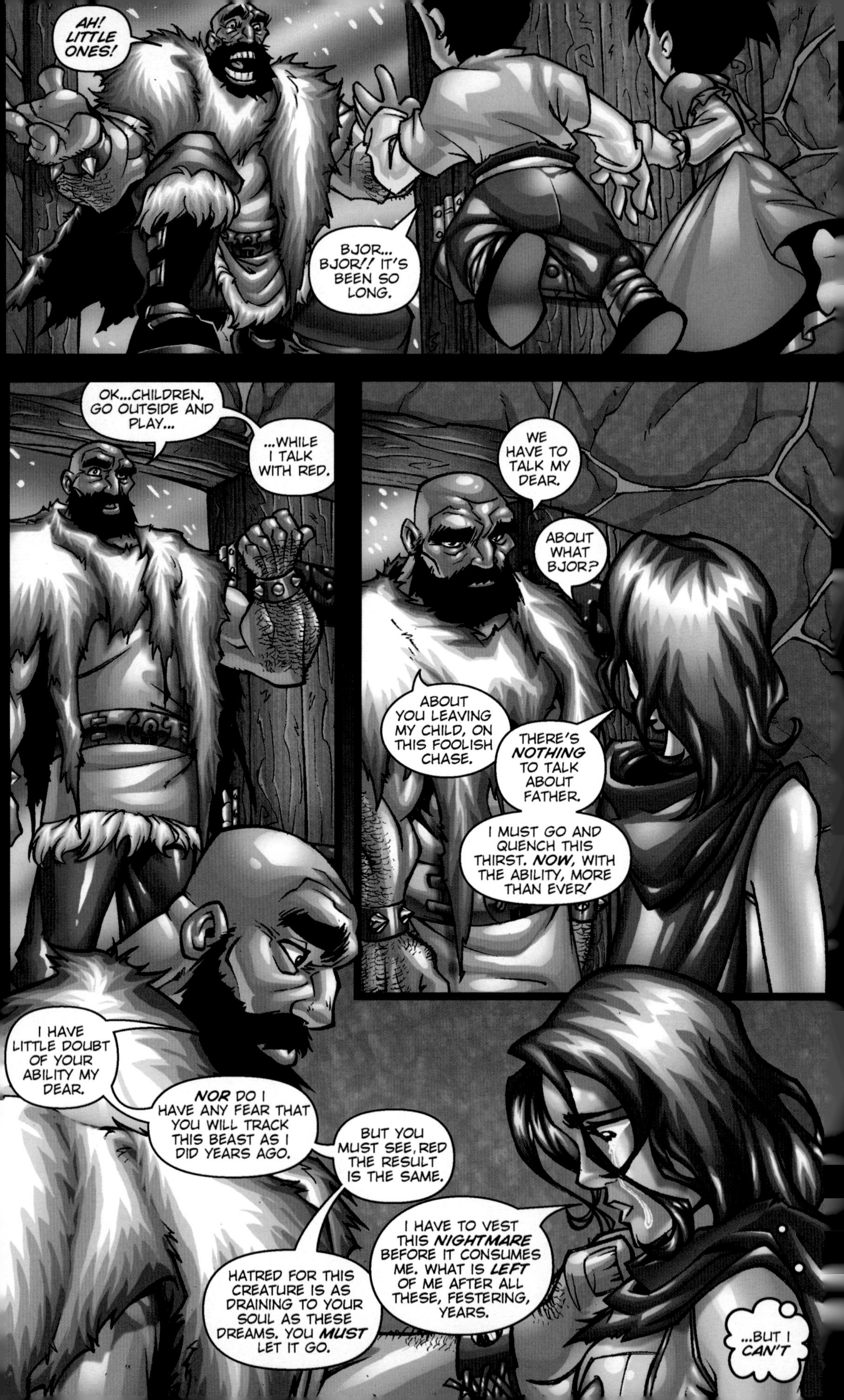
AH! LITTLE ONES!
BJOR... BJOR!! IT'S BEEN SO LONG.
OK...CHILDREN. GO OUTSIDE AND PLAY...
...WHILE I TALK WITH RED.
WE HAVE TO TALK MY DEAR.
ABOUT WHAT BJOR?
ABOUT YOU LEAVING MY CHILD, ON THIS FOOLISH CHASE.
THERE'S NOTHING TO TALK ABOUT FATHER.
I MUST GO AND QUENCH THIS THIRST. NOW, WITH THE ABILITY, MORE THAN EVER!
I HAVE LITTLE DOUBT OF YOUR ABILITY MY DEAR.
NOR DO I HAVE ANY FEAR THAT YOU WILL TRACK THIS BEAST AS I DID YEARS AGO.
BUT YOU MUST SEE, RED THE RESULT IS THE SAME.
HATRED FOR THIS CREATURE IS AS DRAINING TO YOUR SOUL AS THESE DREAMS. YOU MUST LET IT GO.
I HAVE TO VEST THIS NIGHTMARE BEFORE IT CONSUMES ME. WHAT IS LEFT OF ME AFTER ALL THESE, FESTERING, YEARS.
...BUT I CAN'T

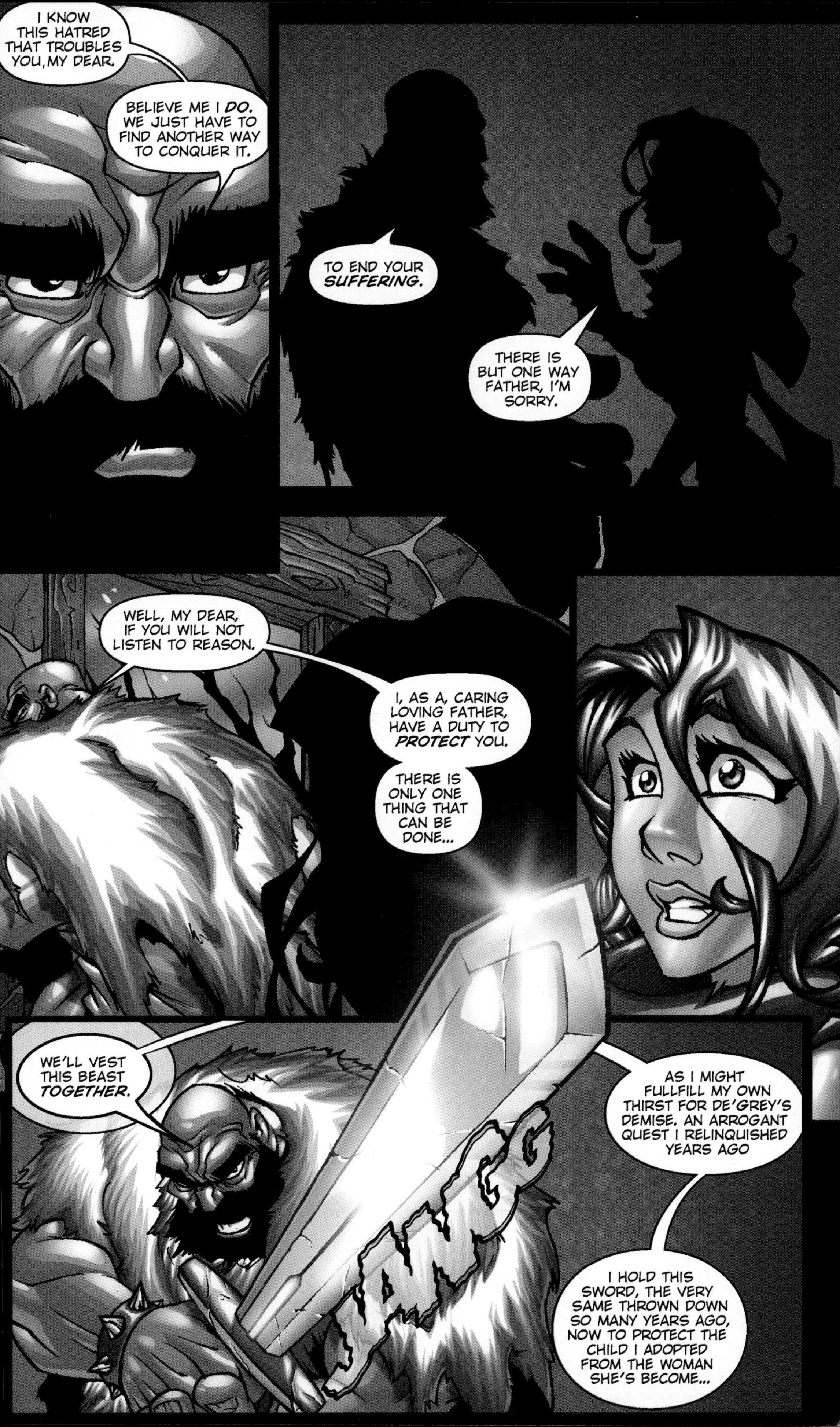
I KNOW THIS HATRED THAT TROUBLES YOU, MY DEAR.
BELIEVE ME I *DO*. WE JUST HAVE TO FIND ANOTHER WAY TO CONQUER IT.
TO END YOUR *SUFFERING*.
THERE IS BUT ONE WAY FATHER, I'M SORRY.
WELL, MY DEAR, IF YOU WILL NOT LISTEN TO REASON.
I, AS A, CARING LOVING FATHER, HAVE A DUTY TO *PROTECT* YOU.
THERE IS ONLY ONE THING THAT CAN BE DONE...
WE'LL VEST THIS BEAST *TOGETHER*.
AS I MIGHT FULLFILL MY OWN THIRST FOR DE'GREY'S DEMISE. AN ARROGANT QUEST I RELINQUISHED YEARS AGO
I HOLD THIS SWORD, THE VERY SAME THROWN DOWN SO MANY YEARS AGO, NOW TO PROTECT THE CHILD I ADOPTED FROM THE WOMAN SHE'S BECOME...

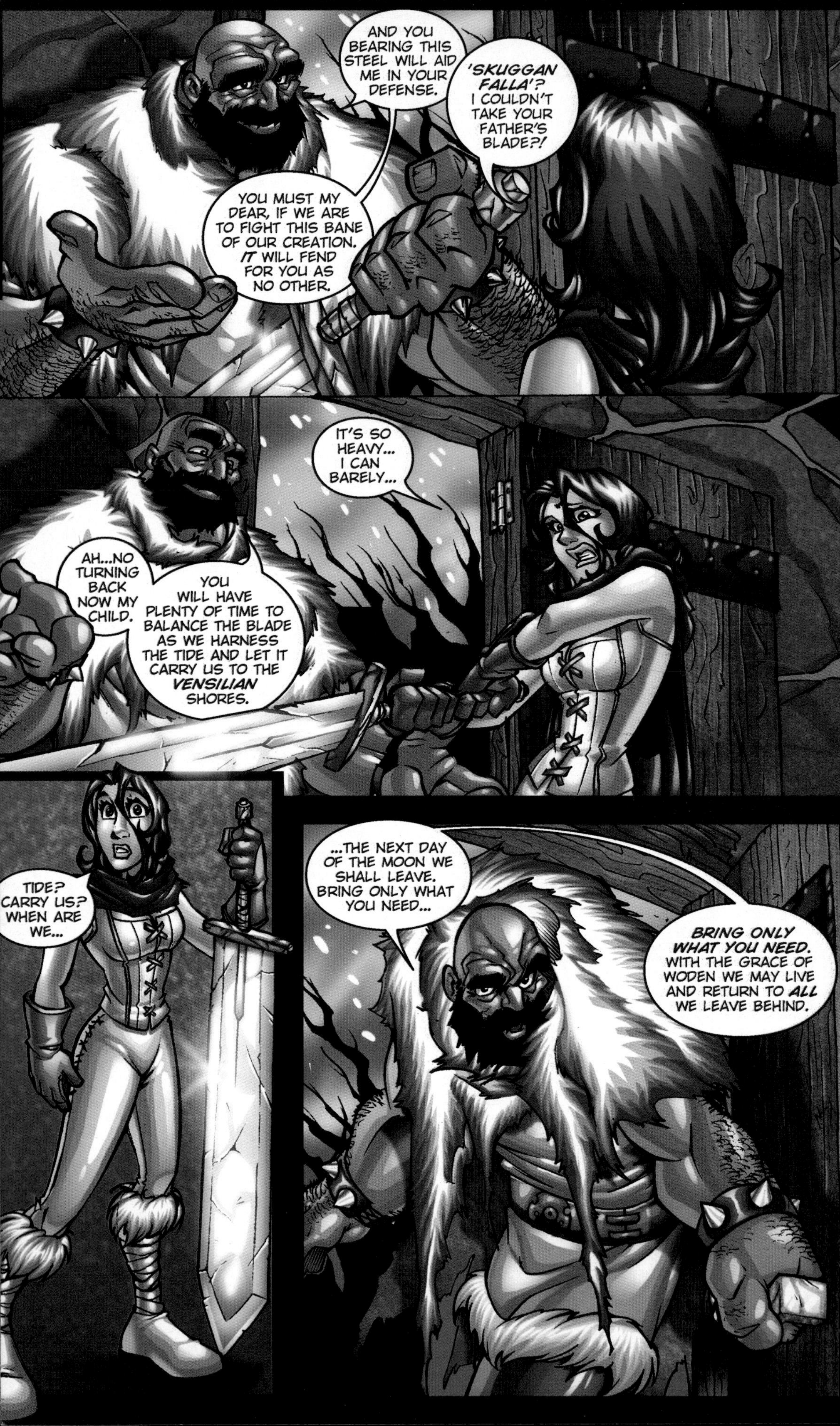
AND YOU BEARING THIS STEEL WILL AID ME IN YOUR DEFENSE.
'SKUGGAN FALLA'? I COULDN'T TAKE YOUR FATHER'S BLADE?!
YOU MUST MY DEAR, IF WE ARE TO FIGHT THIS BANE OF OUR CREATION. IT WILL FEND FOR YOU AS NO OTHER.
IT'S SO HEAVY... I CAN BARELY...
AH...NO TURNING BACK NOW MY CHILD.
YOU WILL HAVE PLENTY OF TIME TO BALANCE THE BLADE AS WE HARNESS THE TIDE AND LET IT CARRY US TO THE VENSILIAN SHORES.
TIDE? CARRY US? WHEN ARE WE...
...THE NEXT DAY OF THE MOON WE SHALL LEAVE. BRING ONLY WHAT YOU NEED...
BRING ONLY WHAT YOU NEED. WITH THE GRACE OF WODEN WE MAY LIVE AND RETURN TO ALL WE LEAVE BEHIND.

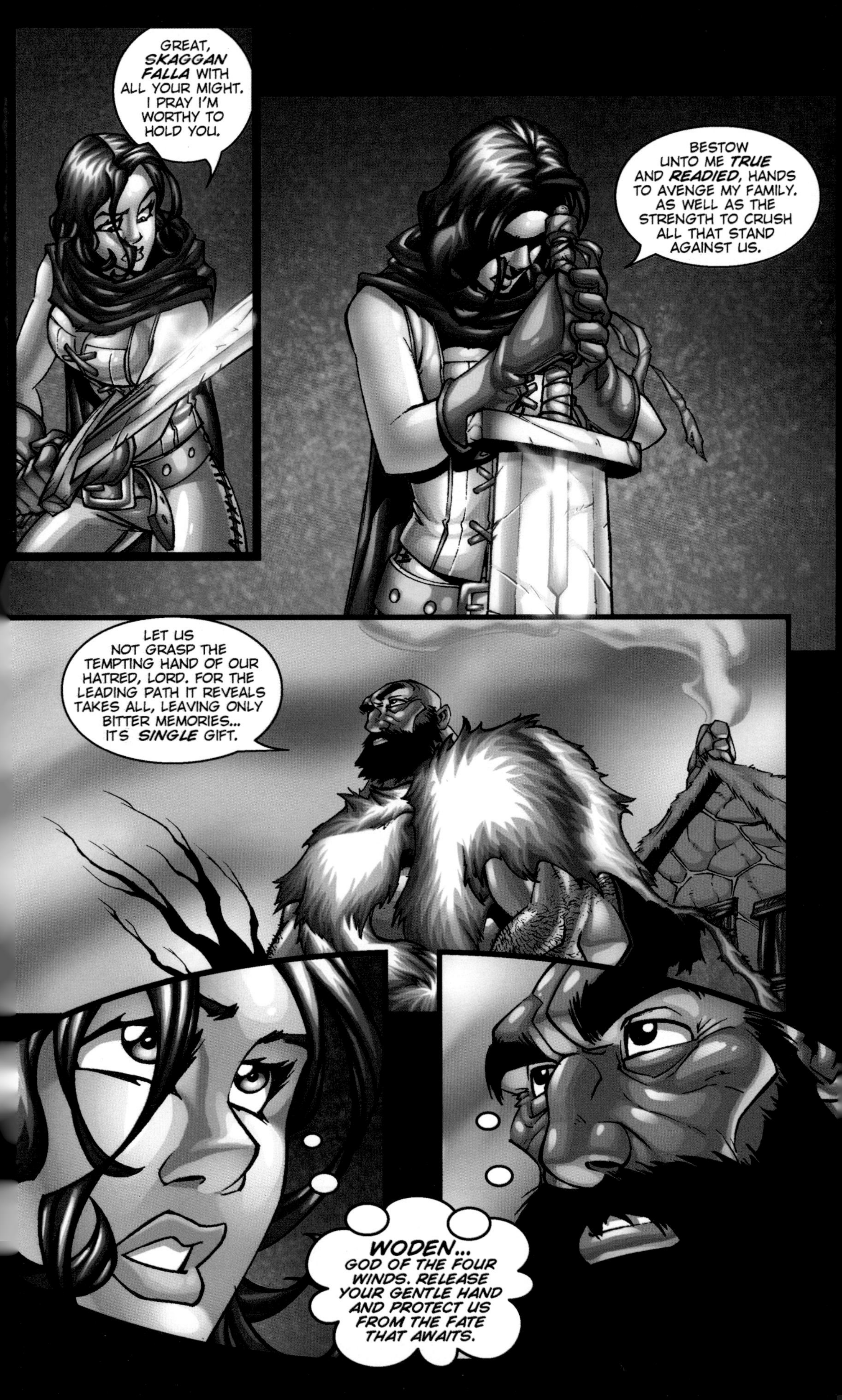
GREAT, SKAGGAN FALLA WITH ALL YOUR MIGHT. I PRAY I'M WORTHY TO HOLD YOU.
BESTOW UNTO ME TRUE AND READIED, HANDS TO AVENGE MY FAMILY. AS WELL AS THE STRENGTH TO CRUSH ALL THAT STAND AGAINST US.
LET US NOT GRASP THE TEMPTING HAND OF OUR HATRED, LORD. FOR THE LEADING PATH IT REVEALS TAKES ALL, LEAVING ONLY BITTER MEMORIES... IT'S SINGLE GIFT.
WODEN... GOD OF THE FOUR WINDS. RELEASE YOUR GENTLE HAND AND PROTECT US FROM THE FATE THAT AWAITS.

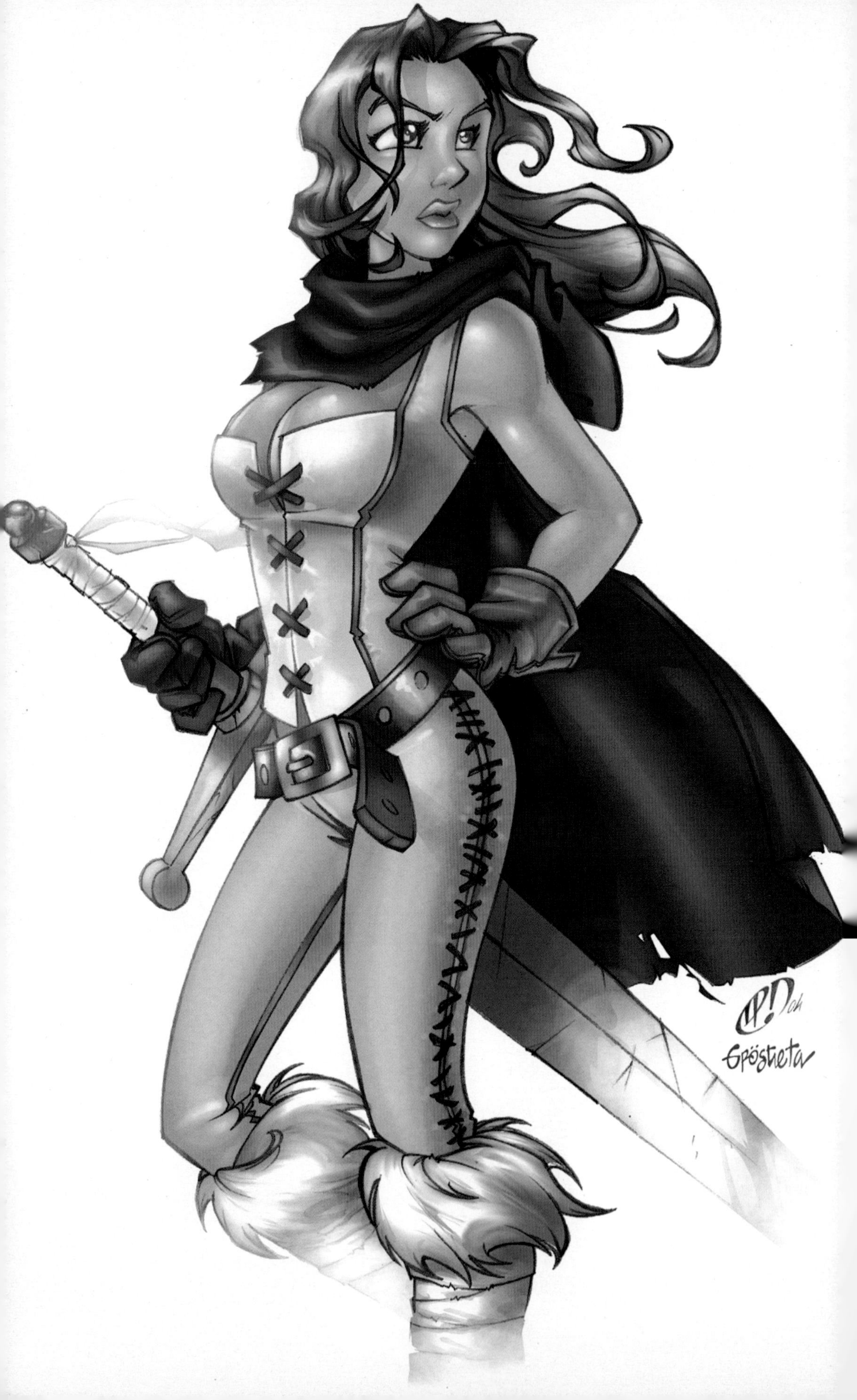

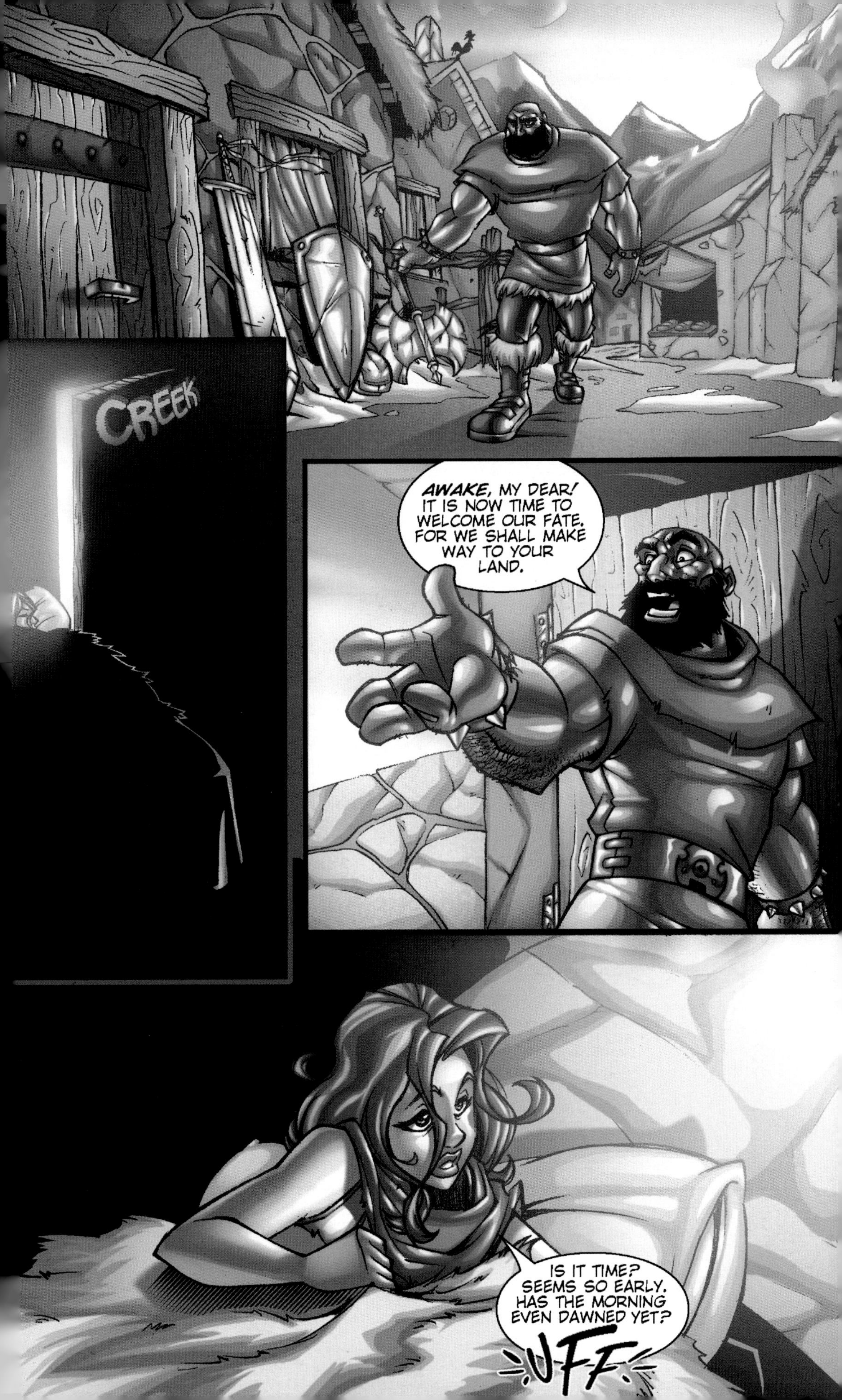
CREEK
AWAKE, MY DEAR! IT IS NOW TIME TO WELCOME OUR FATE. FOR WE SHALL MAKE WAY TO YOUR LAND.
IS IT TIME? SEEMS SO EARLY. HAS THE MORNING EVEN DAWNED YET?
UFF

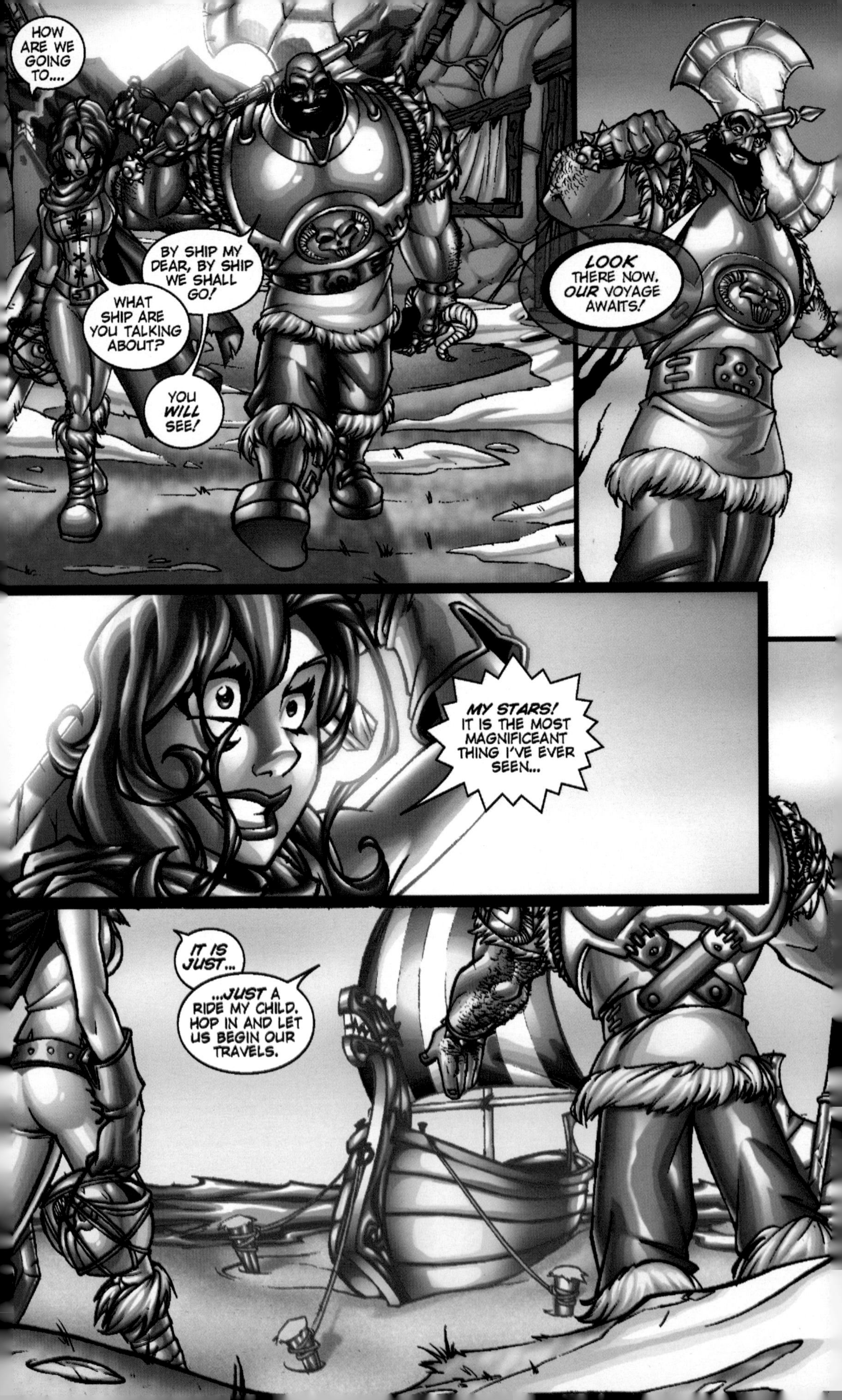
HOW ARE WE GOING TO....
BY SHIP MY DEAR, BY SHIP WE SHALL GO!
WHAT SHIP ARE YOU TALKING ABOUT?
YOU WILL SEE!
LOOK THERE NOW. OUR VOYAGE AWAITS!
MY STARS! IT IS THE MOST MAGNIFICEANT THING I'VE EVER SEEN...
IT IS JUST...
...JUST A RIDE MY CHILD. HOP IN AND LET US BEGIN OUR TRAVELS.

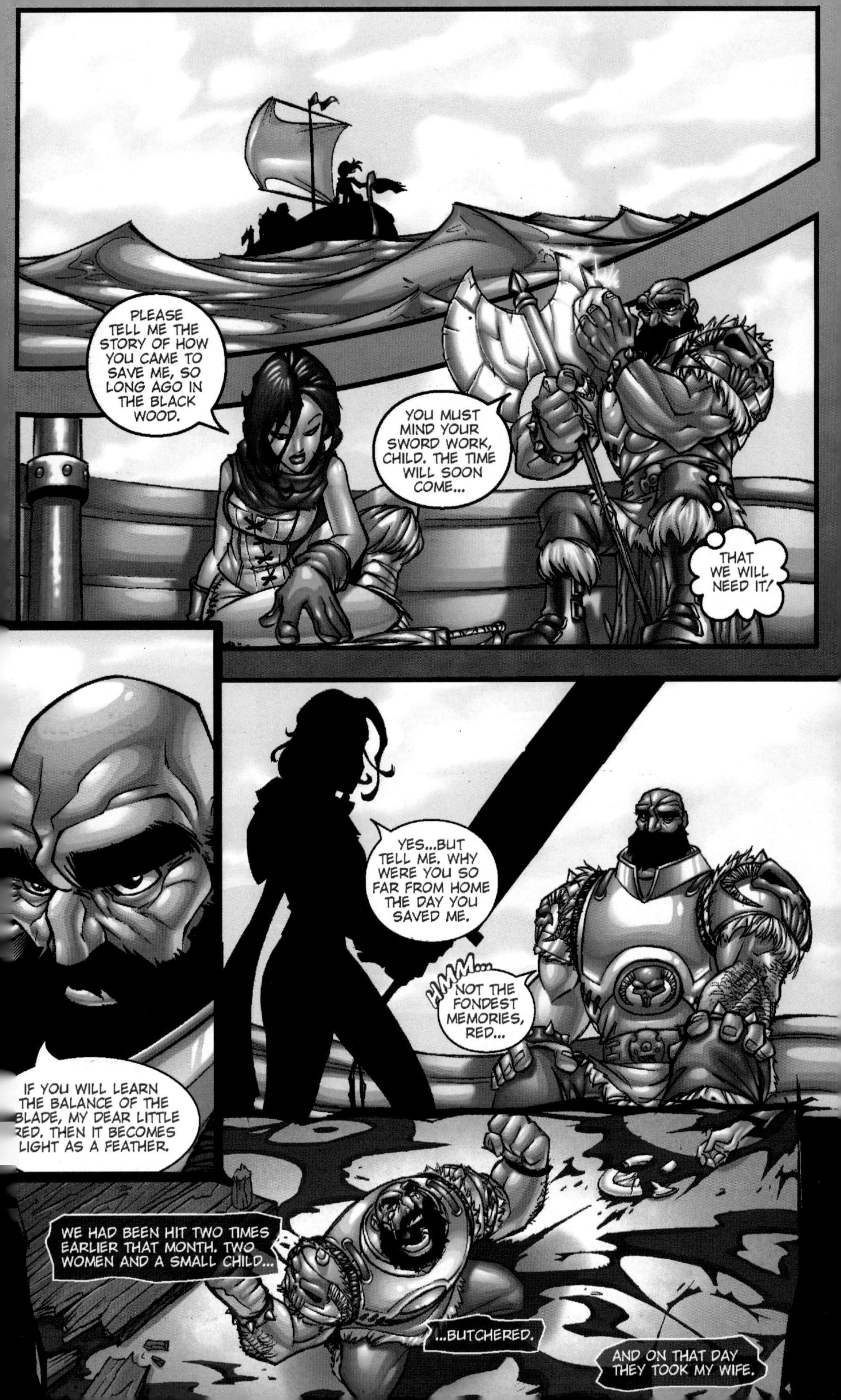
PLEASE TELL ME THE STORY OF HOW YOU CAME TO SAVE ME, SO LONG AGO IN THE BLACK WOOD.
YOU MUST MIND YOUR SWORD WORK, CHILD. THE TIME WILL SOON COME...
THAT WE WILL NEED IT!
IF YOU WILL LEARN THE BALANCE OF THE BLADE, MY DEAR LITTLE RED. THEN IT BECOMES LIGHT AS A FEATHER.
YES...BUT TELL ME. WHY WERE YOU SO FAR FROM HOME THE DAY YOU SAVED ME.
HMM...
NOT THE FONDEST MEMORIES, RED...
WE HAD BEEN HIT TWO TIMES EARLIER THAT MONTH. TWO WOMEN AND A SMALL CHILD...
...BUTCHERED.
AND ON THAT DAY THEY TOOK MY WIFE.

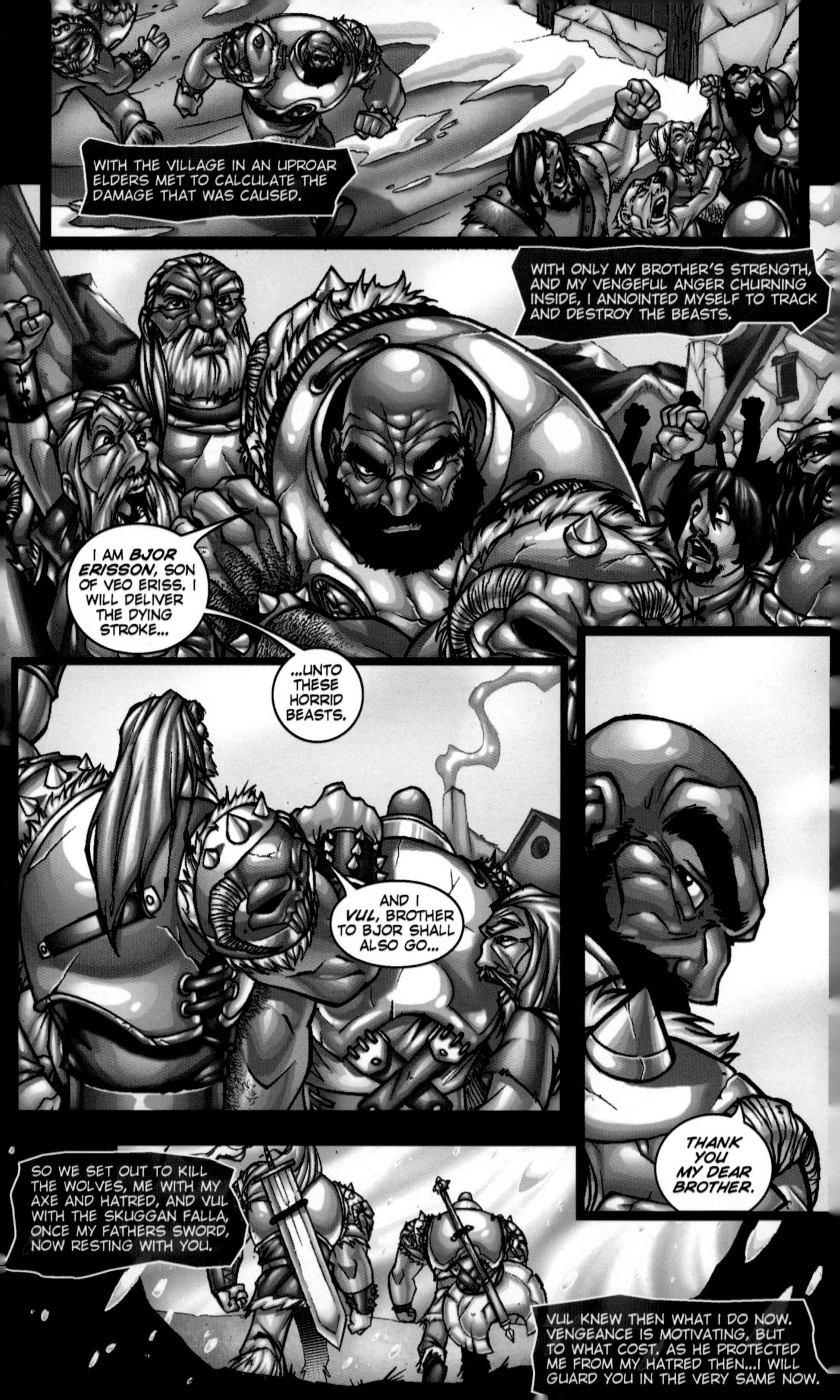
WITH THE VILLAGE IN AN UPROAR ELDERS MET TO CALCULATE THE DAMAGE THAT WAS CAUSED.
WITH ONLY MY BROTHER'S STRENGTH, AND MY VENGEFUL ANGER CHURNING INSIDE, I ANNOINTED MYSELF TO TRACK AND DESTROY THE BEASTS.
I AM BJOR ERISSON, SON OF VEO ERISS. I WILL DELIVER THE DYING STROKE...
...UNTO THESE HORRID BEASTS.
AND I VUL, BROTHER TO BJOR SHALL ALSO GO...
THANK YOU MY DEAR BROTHER.
SO WE SET OUT TO KILL THE WOLVES, ME WITH MY AXE AND HATRED, AND VUL WITH THE SKUGGAN FALLA, ONCE MY FATHERS SWORD, NOW RESTING WITH YOU.
VUL KNEW THEN WHAT I DO NOW. VENGEANCE IS MOTIVATING, BUT TO WHAT COST. AS HE PROTECTED ME FROM MY HATRED THEN...I WILL GUARD YOU IN THE VERY SAME NOW.

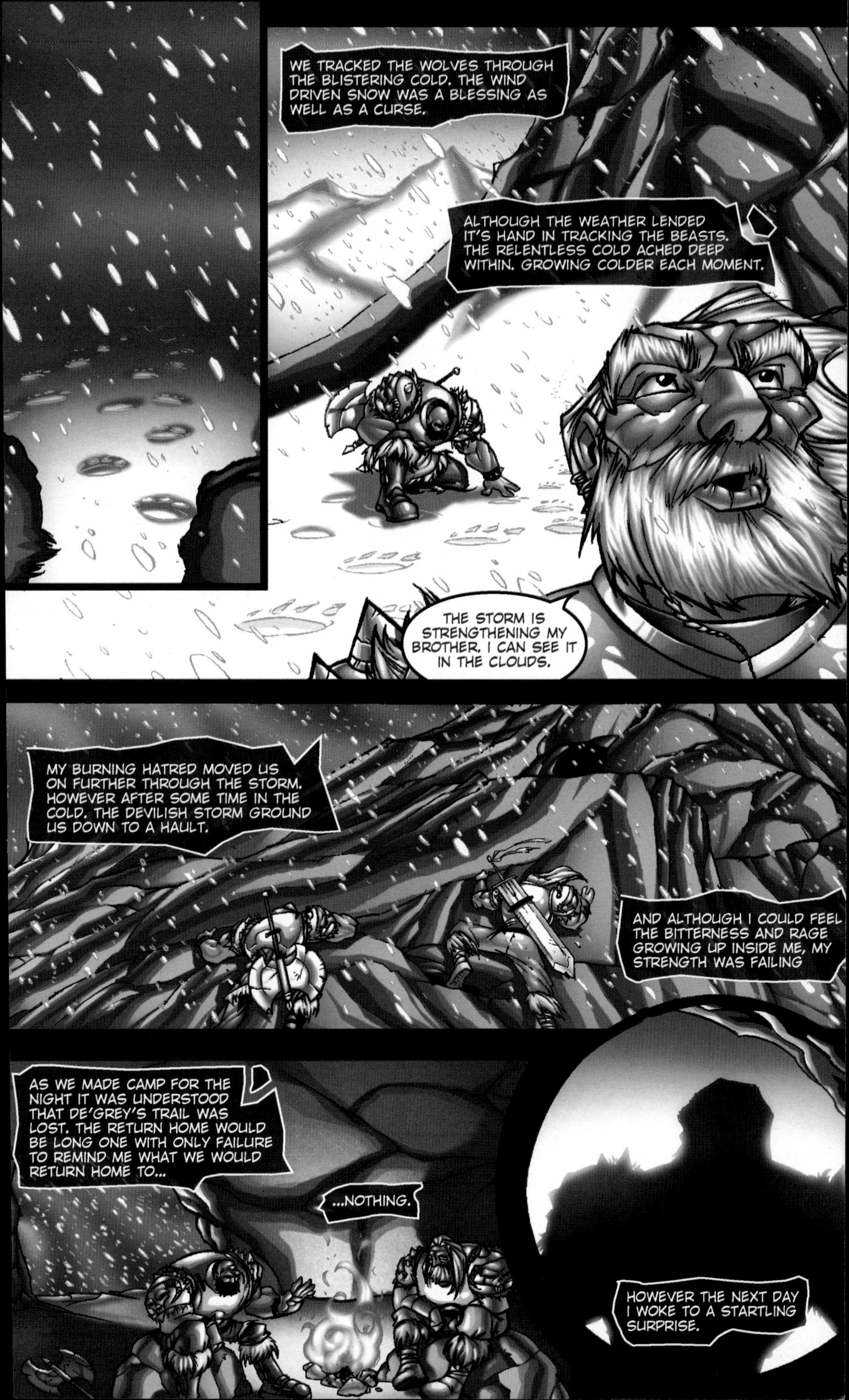
WE TRACKED THE WOLVES THROUGH THE BLISTERING COLD. THE WIND DRIVEN SNOW WAS A BLESSING AS WELL AS A CURSE.
ALTHOUGH THE WEATHER LENDED IT'S HAND IN TRACKING THE BEASTS. THE RELENTLESS COLD ACHED DEEP WITHIN. GROWING COLDER EACH MOMENT.
THE STORM IS STRENGTHENING MY BROTHER. I CAN SEE IT IN THE CLOUDS.
MY BURNING HATRED MOVED US ON FURTHER THROUGH THE STORM. HOWEVER AFTER SOME TIME IN THE COLD. THE DEVILISH STORM GROUND US DOWN TO A HAULT.
AND ALTHOUGH I COULD FEEL THE BITTERNESS AND RAGE GROWING UP INSIDE ME, MY STRENGTH WAS FAILING
AS WE MADE CAMP FOR THE NIGHT IT WAS UNDERSTOOD THAT DE'GREY'S TRAIL WAS LOST. THE RETURN HOME WOULD BE LONG ONE WITH ONLY FAILURE TO REMIND ME WHAT WE WOULD RETURN HOME TO...
...NOTHING.
HOWEVER THE NEXT DAY I WOKE TO A STARTLING SURPRISE.

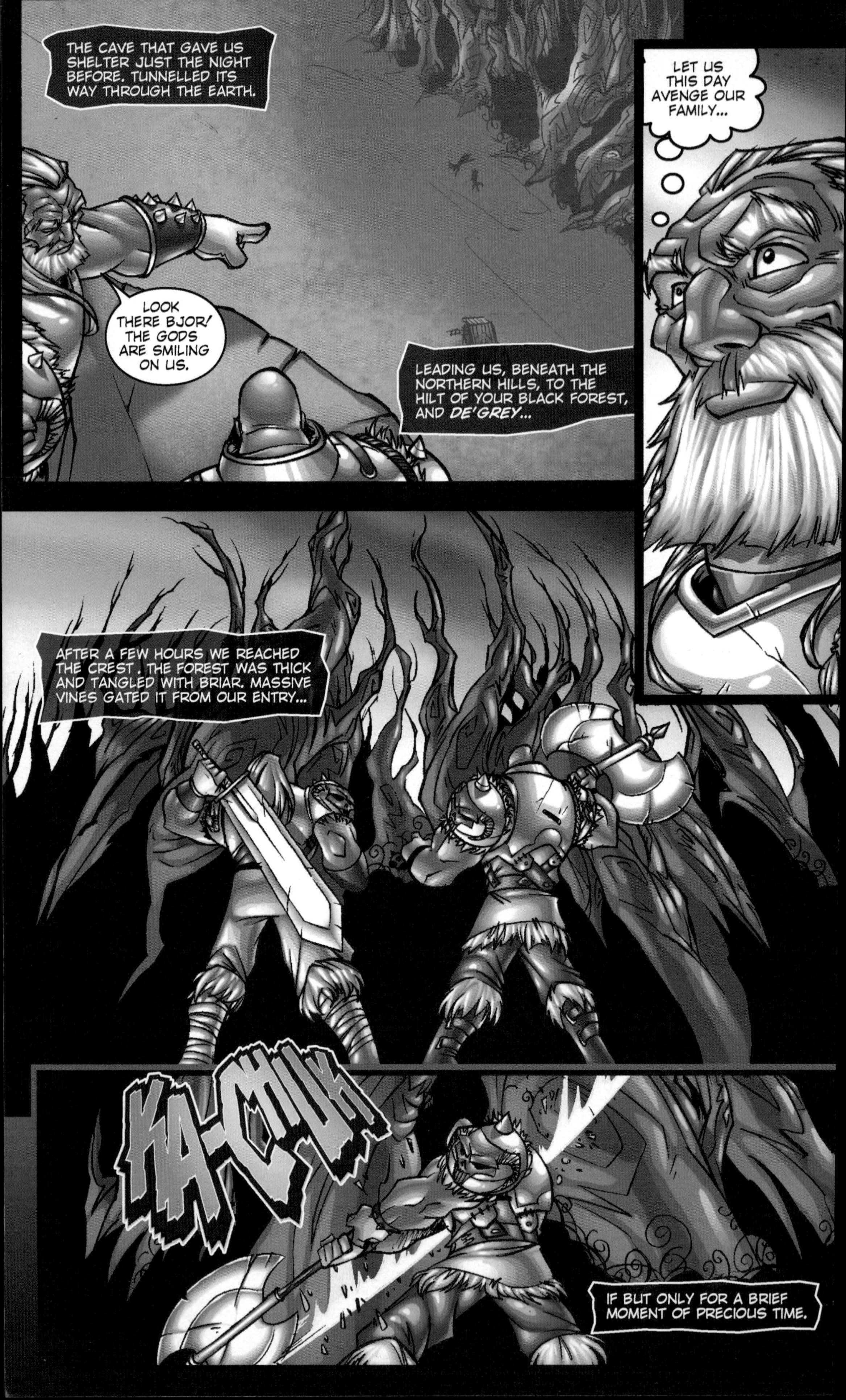
THE CAVE THAT GAVE US SHELTER JUST THE NIGHT BEFORE. TUNNELLED ITS WAY THROUGH THE EARTH.
LOOK THERE BJOR! THE GODS ARE SMILING ON US.
LEADING US, BENEATH THE NORTHERN HILLS, TO THE HILT OF YOUR BLACK FOREST, AND DE'GREY...
LET US THIS DAY AVENGE OUR FAMILY...
AFTER A FEW HOURS WE REACHED THE CREST. THE FOREST WAS THICK AND TANGLED WITH BRIAR. MASSIVE VINES GATED IT FROM OUR ENTRY...
KA-CHUK
IF BUT ONLY FOR A BRIEF MOMENT OF PRECIOUS TIME.

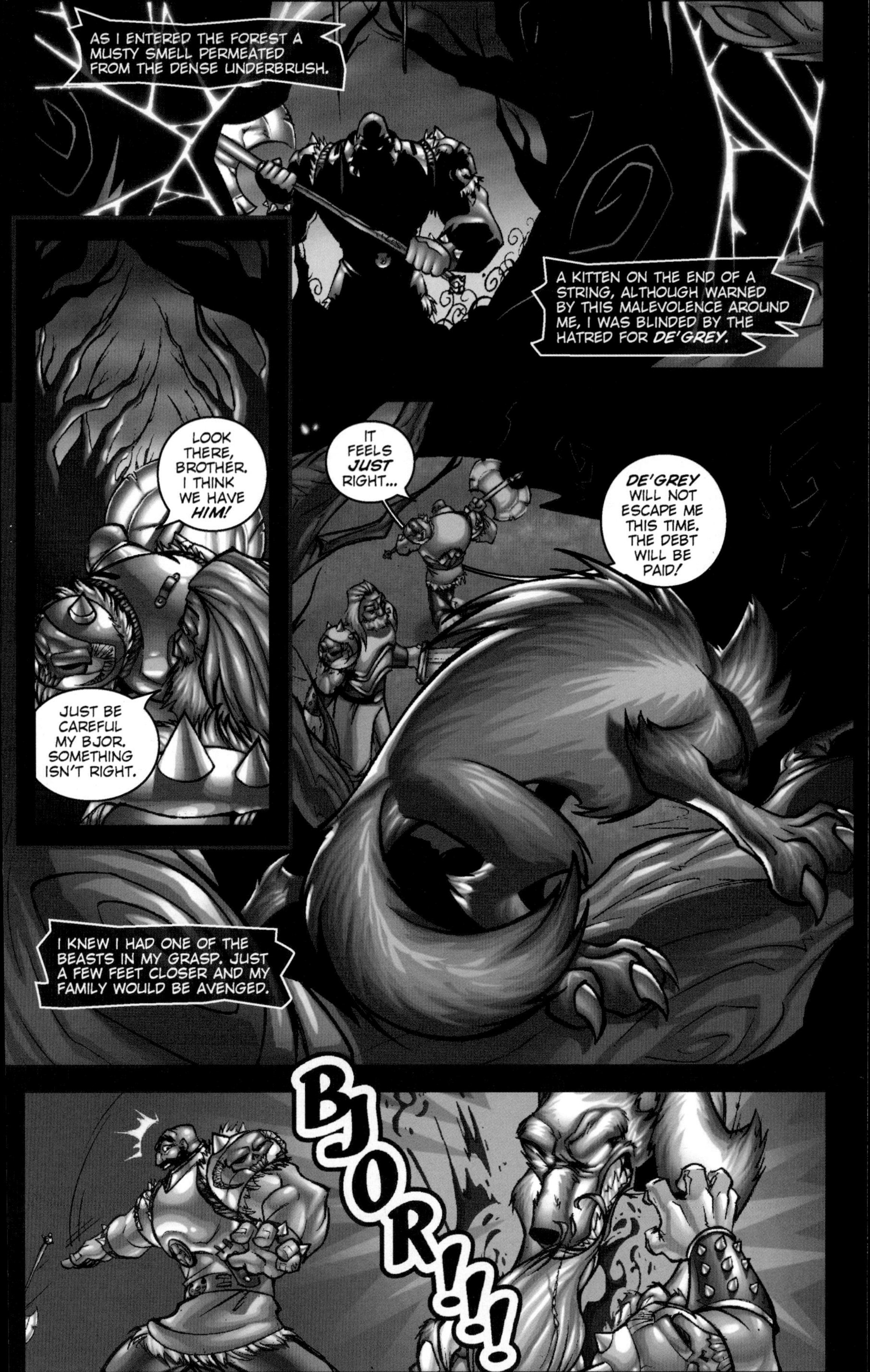
AS I ENTERED THE FOREST A MUSTY SMELL PERMEATED FROM THE DENSE UNDERBRUSH.
A KITTEN ON THE END OF A STRING, ALTHOUGH WARNED BY THIS MALEVOLENCE AROUND ME, I WAS BLINDED BY THE HATRED FOR DE'GREY.
LOOK THERE, BROTHER. I THINK WE HAVE HIM!
JUST BE CAREFUL MY BJOR. SOMETHING ISN'T RIGHT.
IT FEELS JUST RIGHT...
DE'GREY WILL NOT ESCAPE ME THIS TIME. THE DEBT WILL BE PAID!
I KNEW I HAD ONE OF THE BEASTS IN MY GRASP. JUST A FEW FEET CLOSER AND MY FAMILY WOULD BE AVENGED.
BJOR!!!

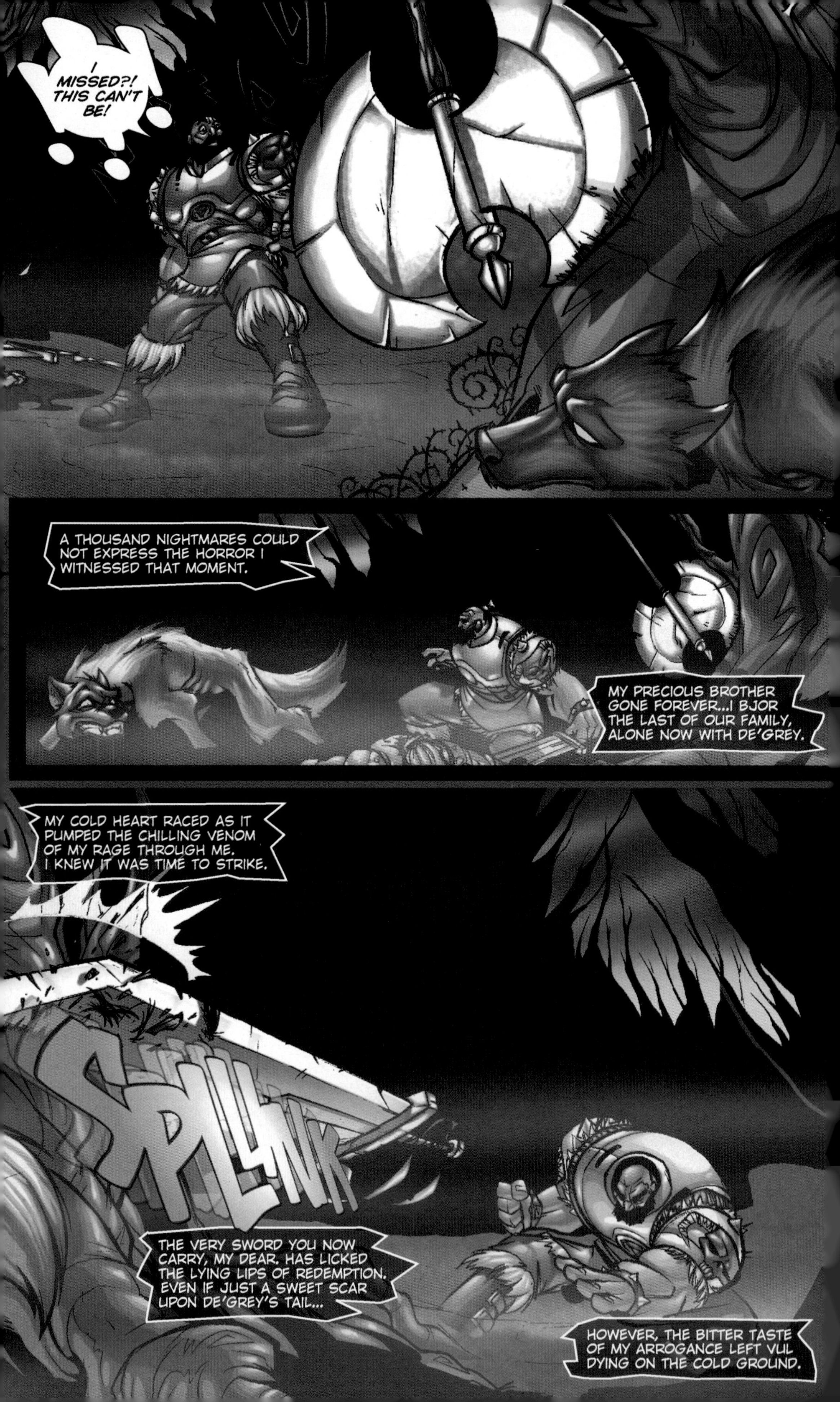
I MISSED?! THIS CAN'T BE!
A THOUSAND NIGHTMARES COULD NOT EXPRESS THE HORROR I WITNESSED THAT MOMENT.
MY PRECIOUS BROTHER GONE FOREVER...I BJOR THE LAST OF OUR FAMILY, ALONE NOW WITH DE'GREY.
MY COLD HEART RACED AS IT PUMPED THE CHILLING VENOM OF MY RAGE THROUGH ME. I KNEW IT WAS TIME TO STRIKE.
SPLUNK
THE VERY SWORD YOU NOW CARRY, MY DEAR, HAS LICKED THE LYING LIPS OF REDEMPTION. EVEN IF JUST A SWEET SCAR UPON DE'GREY'S TAIL...
HOWEVER, THE BITTER TASTE OF MY ARROGANCE LEFT VUL DYING ON THE COLD GROUND.

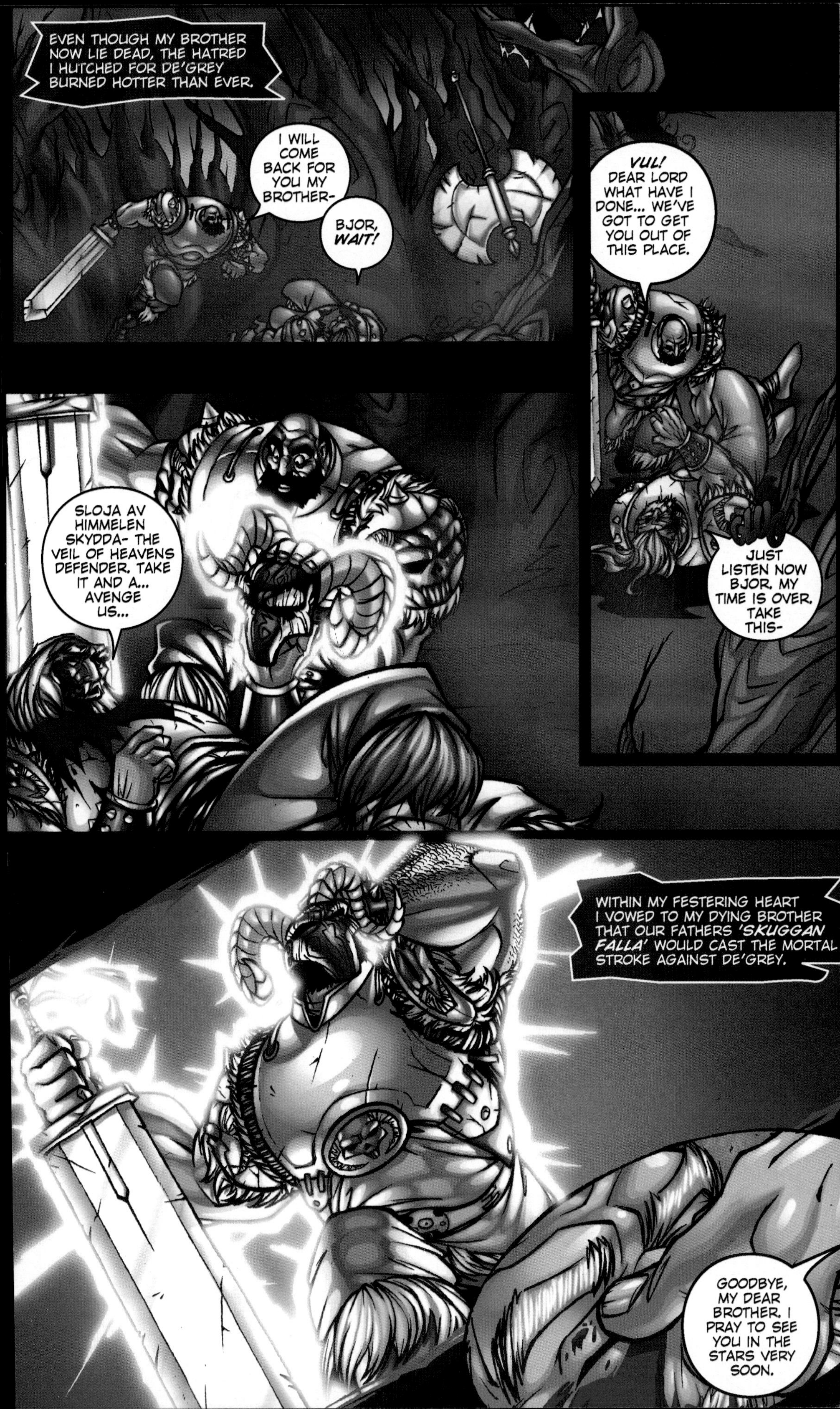
EVEN THOUGH MY BROTHER NOW LIE DEAD, THE HATRED I HUTCHED FOR DE'GREY BURNED HOTTER THAN EVER.
I WILL COME BACK FOR YOU MY BROTHER-
BJOR, *WAIT!*
VUL! DEAR LORD WHAT HAVE I DONE... WE'VE GOT TO GET YOU OUT OF THIS PLACE.
JUST LISTEN NOW BJOR. MY TIME IS OVER. TAKE THIS-
SLOJA AV HIMMELEN SKYDDA- THE VEIL OF HEAVENS DEFENDER. TAKE IT AND A... AVENGE US...
WITHIN MY FESTERING HEART I VOWED TO MY DYING BROTHER THAT OUR FATHERS *'SKUGGAN FALLA'* WOULD CAST THE MORTAL STROKE AGAINST DE'GREY.
GOODBYE, MY DEAR BROTHER. I PRAY TO SEE YOU IN THE STARS VERY SOON.

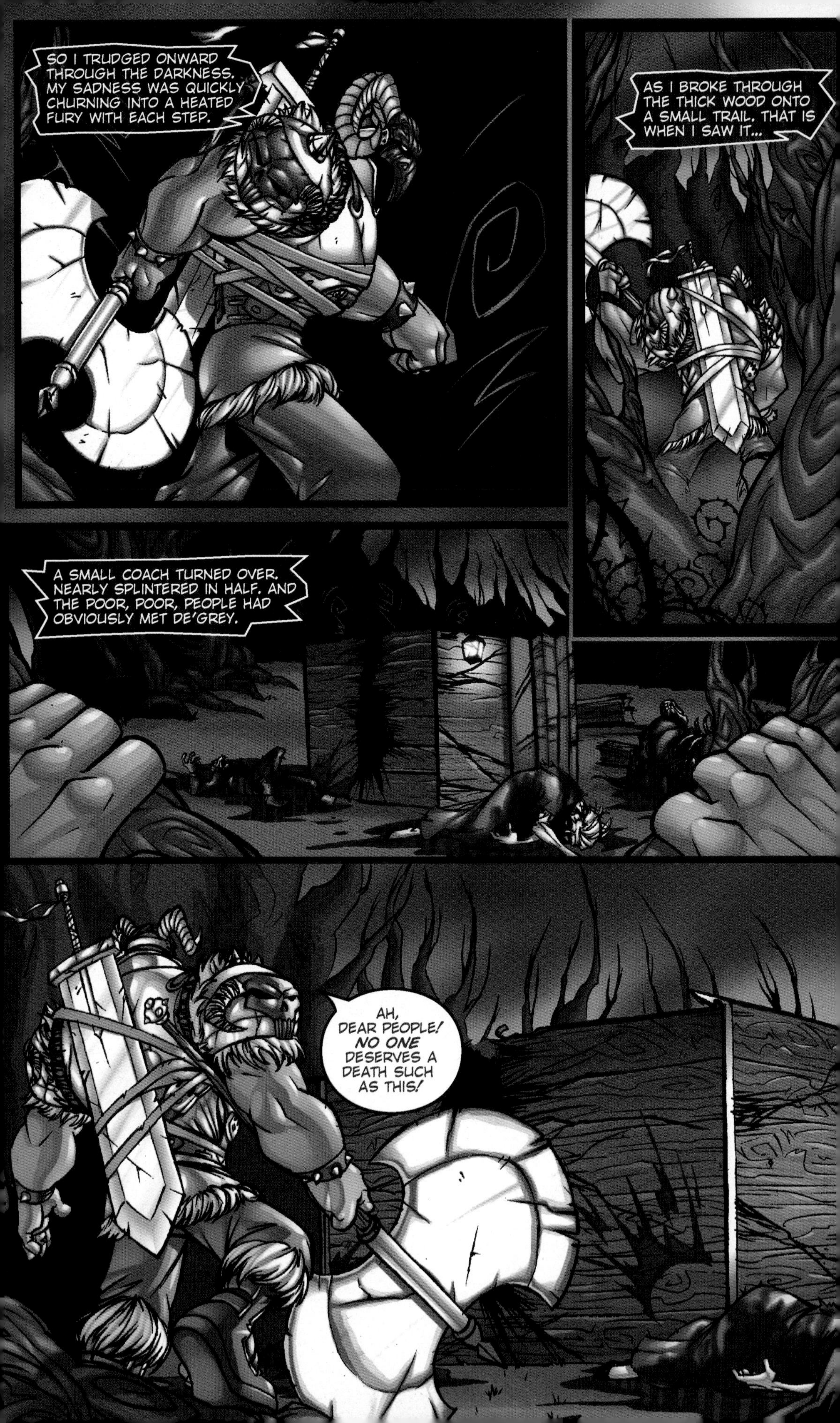
SO I TRUDGED ONWARD THROUGH THE DARKNESS. MY SADNESS WAS QUICKLY CHURNING INTO A HEATED FURY WITH EACH STEP.
AS I BROKE THROUGH THE THICK WOOD ONTO A SMALL TRAIL. THAT IS WHEN I SAW IT...
A SMALL COACH TURNED OVER. NEARLY SPLINTERED IN HALF. AND THE POOR, POOR, PEOPLE HAD OBVIOUSLY MET DE'GREY.
AH, DEAR PEOPLE! NO ONE DESERVES A DEATH SUCH AS THIS!

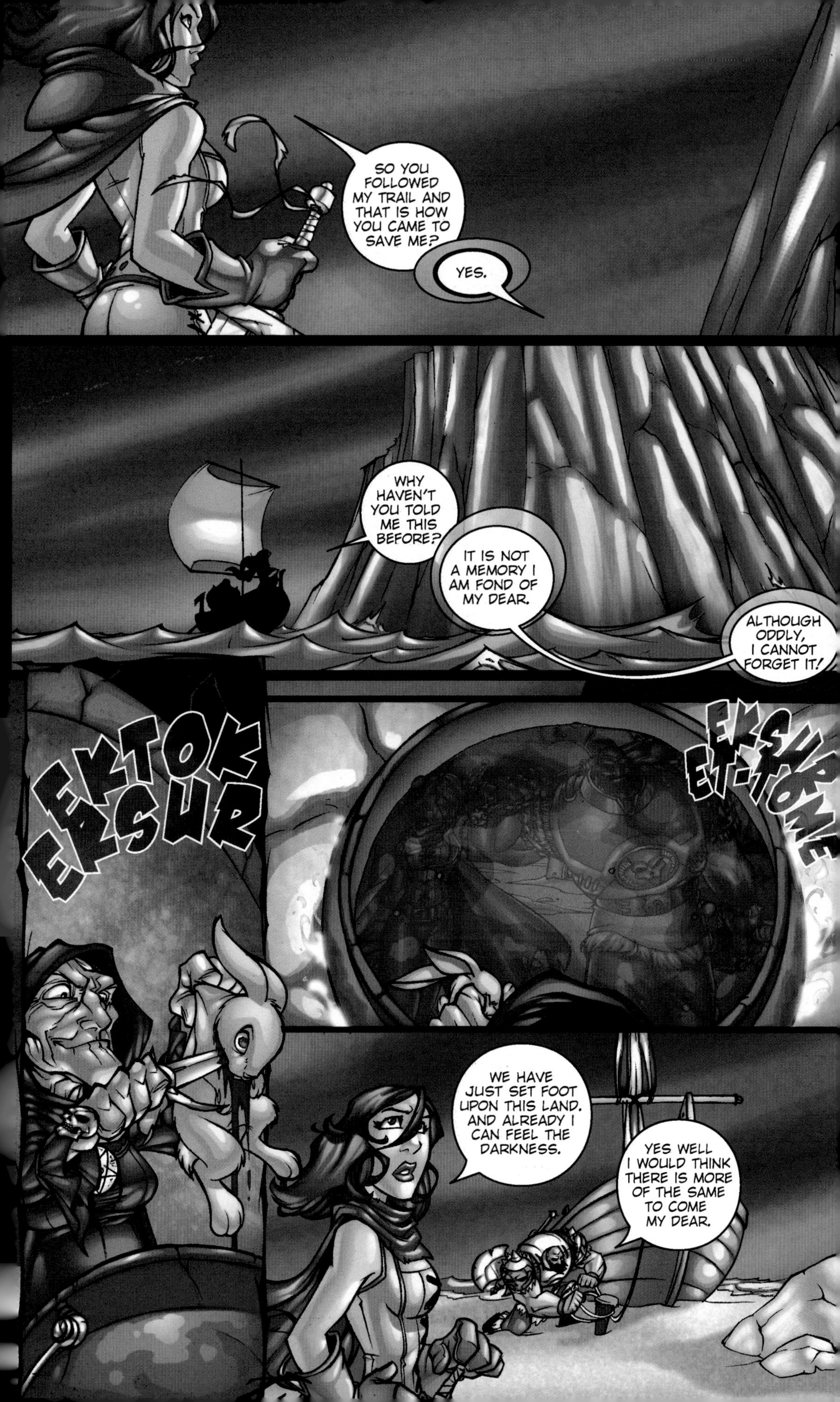
SO YOU FOLLOWED MY TRAIL AND THAT IS HOW YOU CAME TO SAVE ME?
YES.
WHY HAVEN'T YOU TOLD ME THIS BEFORE?
IT IS NOT A MEMORY I AM FOND OF MY DEAR.
ALTHOUGH ODDLY, I CANNOT FORGET IT!
EKTOK EKSUR
EKSUR ET-TOME
WE HAVE JUST SET FOOT UPON THIS LAND. AND ALREADY I CAN FEEL THE DARKNESS.
YES WELL I WOULD THINK THERE IS MORE OF THE SAME TO COME MY DEAR.

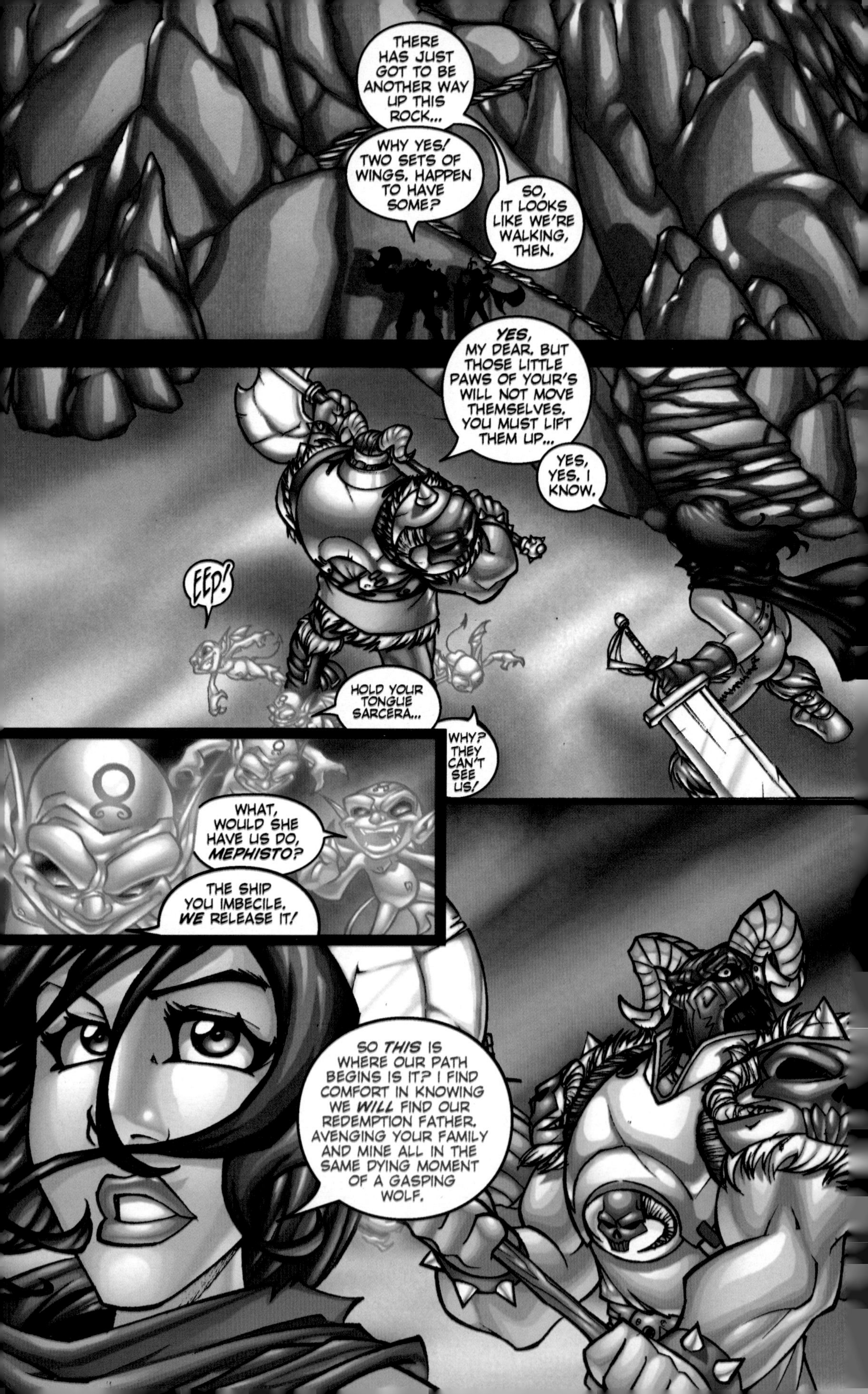
THERE HAS JUST GOT TO BE ANOTHER WAY UP THIS ROCK...
WHY YES! TWO SETS OF WINGS. HAPPEN TO HAVE SOME?
SO, IT LOOKS LIKE WE'RE WALKING, THEN.
YES, MY DEAR. BUT THOSE LITTLE PAWS OF YOUR'S WILL NOT MOVE THEMSELVES. YOU MUST LIFT THEM UP...
YES, YES. I KNOW.
EEP!
HOLD YOUR TONGUE SARCERA...
WHY? THEY CAN'T SEE US!
WHAT, WOULD SHE HAVE US DO, MEPHISTO?
THE SHIP YOU IMBECILE. WE RELEASE IT!
SO THIS IS WHERE OUR PATH BEGINS IS IT? I FIND COMFORT IN KNOWING WE WILL FIND OUR REDEMPTION FATHER. AVENGING YOUR FAMILY AND MINE ALL IN THE SAME DYING MOMENT OF A GASPING WOLF.

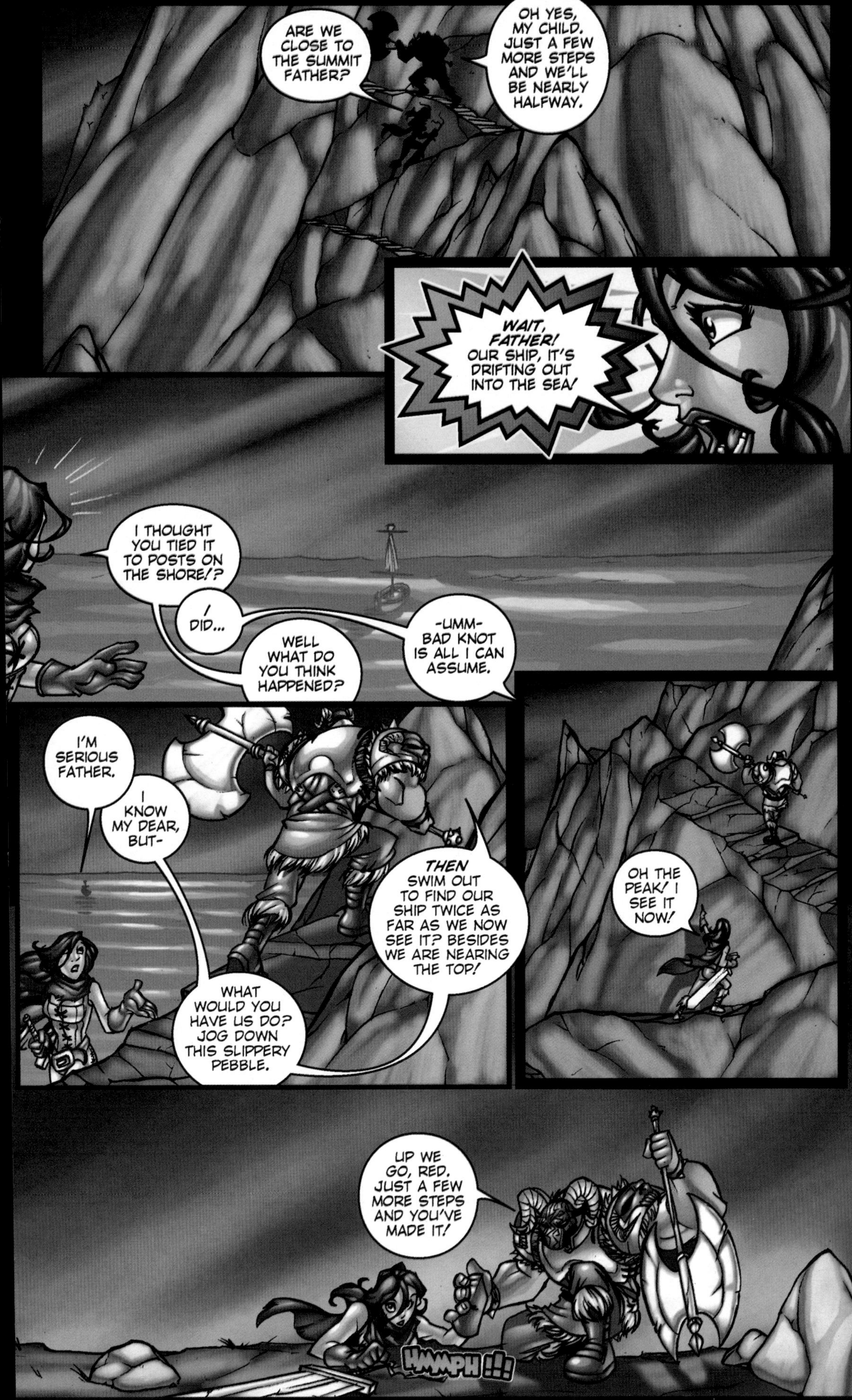

ARE WE CLOSE TO THE SUMMIT FATHER?
OH YES, MY CHILD. JUST A FEW MORE STEPS AND WE'LL BE NEARLY HALFWAY.
WAIT, FATHER! OUR SHIP, IT'S DRIFTING OUT INTO THE SEA!
I THOUGHT YOU TIED IT TO POSTS ON THE SHORE!?
I DID...
WELL WHAT DO YOU THINK HAPPENED?
-UMM- BAD KNOT IS ALL I CAN ASSUME.
I'M SERIOUS FATHER.
I KNOW MY DEAR, BUT-
WHAT WOULD YOU HAVE US DO? JOG DOWN THIS SLIPPERY PEBBLE.
THEN SWIM OUT TO FIND OUR SHIP TWICE AS FAR AS WE NOW SEE IT? BESIDES WE ARE NEARING THE TOP!
OH THE PEAK! I SEE IT NOW!
UP WE GO, RED. JUST A FEW MORE STEPS AND YOU'VE MADE IT!
HMMPH !!!

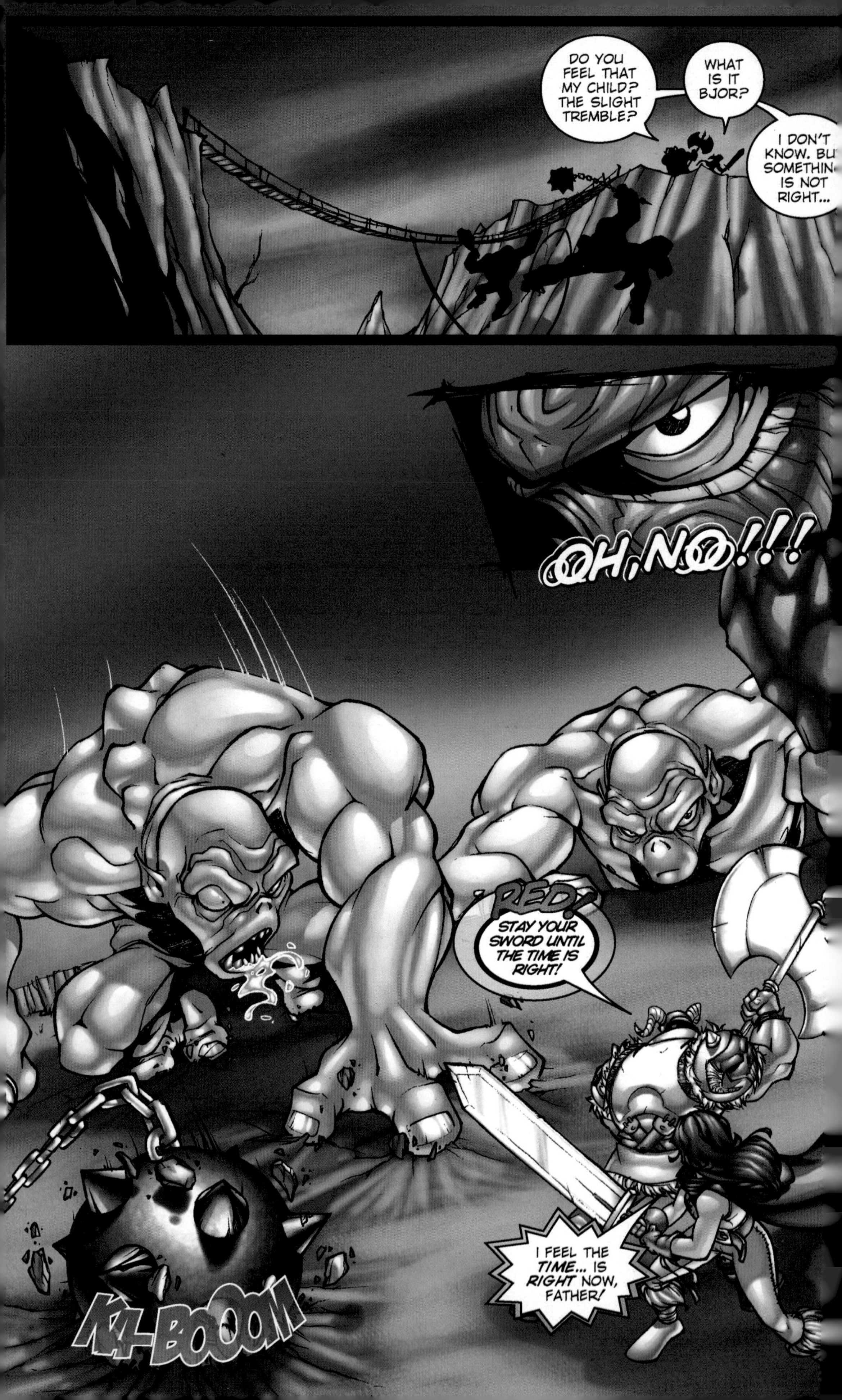
DO YOU FEEL THAT MY CHILD? THE SLIGHT TREMBLE?
WHAT IS IT BJOR?
I DON'T KNOW. BU SOMETHIN IS NOT RIGHT...
OH, NO!!!
RED!
STAY YOUR SWORD UNTIL THE TIME IS RIGHT!
I FEEL THE TIME... IS RIGHT NOW, FATHER!
KA-BOOOM

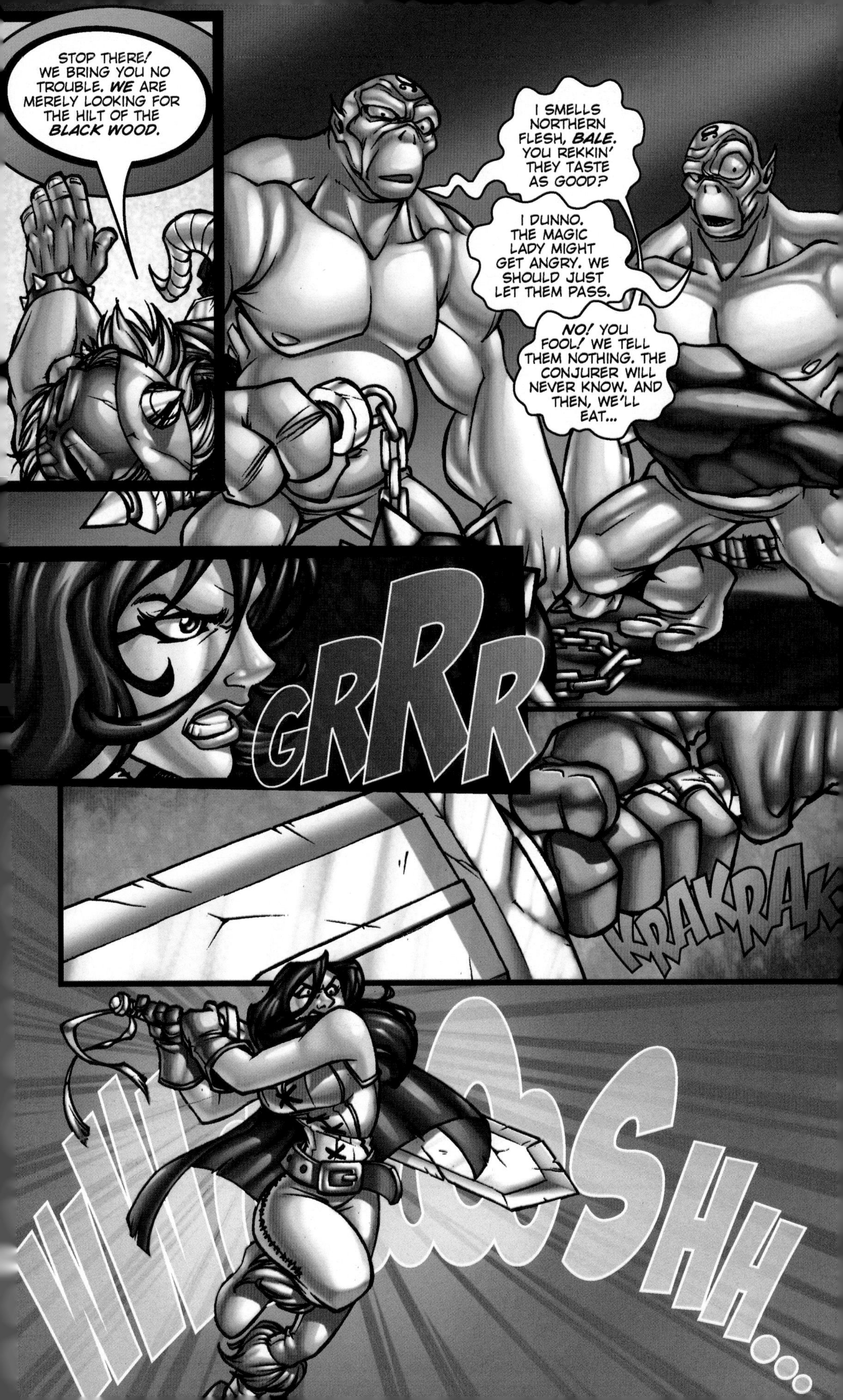
STOP THERE! WE BRING YOU NO TROUBLE. WE ARE MERELY LOOKING FOR THE HILT OF THE BLACK WOOD.
I SMELLS NORTHERN FLESH, BALE. YOU REKKIN' THEY TASTE AS GOOD?
I DUNNO. THE MAGIC LADY MIGHT GET ANGRY. WE SHOULD JUST LET THEM PASS.
NO! YOU FOOL! WE TELL THEM NOTHING. THE CONJURER WILL NEVER KNOW. AND THEN, WE'LL EAT...
GRRR
KRAKRAK
WHOOOSHH...

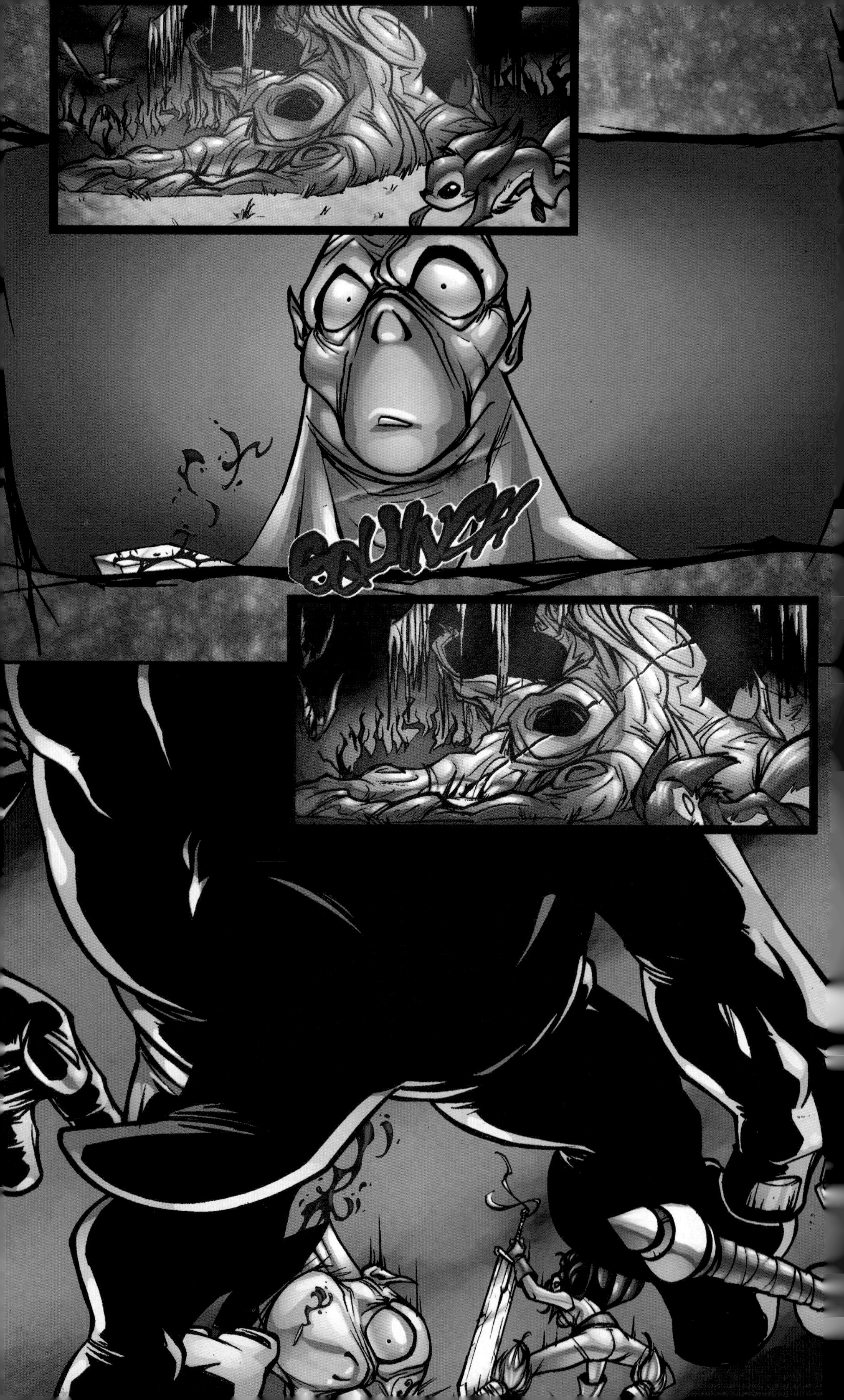
SQUINCH

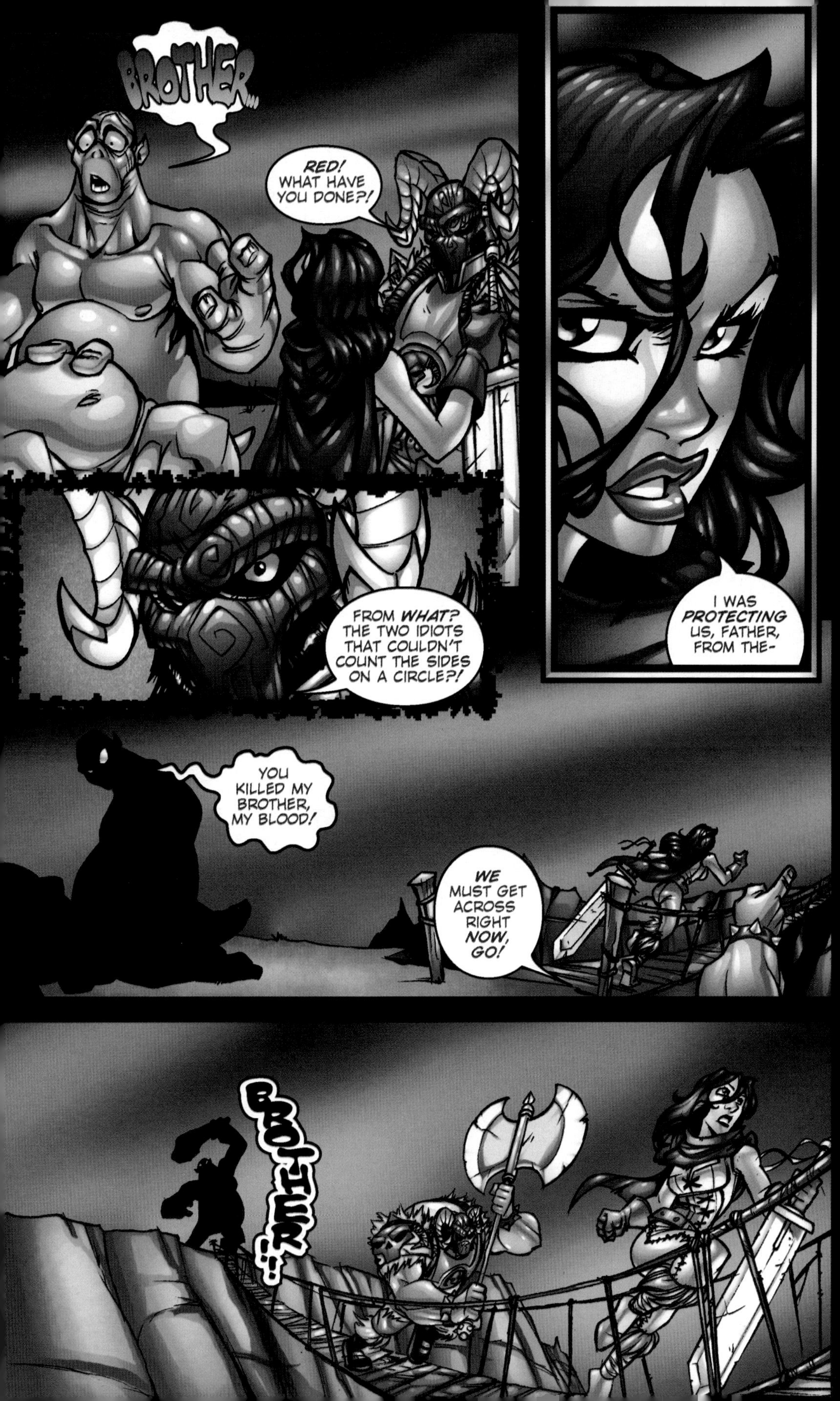
BROTHER...
RED! WHAT HAVE YOU DONE?!
I WAS PROTECTING US, FATHER, FROM THE-
FROM WHAT? THE TWO IDIOTS THAT COULDN'T COUNT THE SIDES ON A CIRCLE?!
YOU KILLED MY BROTHER, MY BLOOD!
WE MUST GET ACROSS RIGHT NOW, GO!
BROTHER!!!

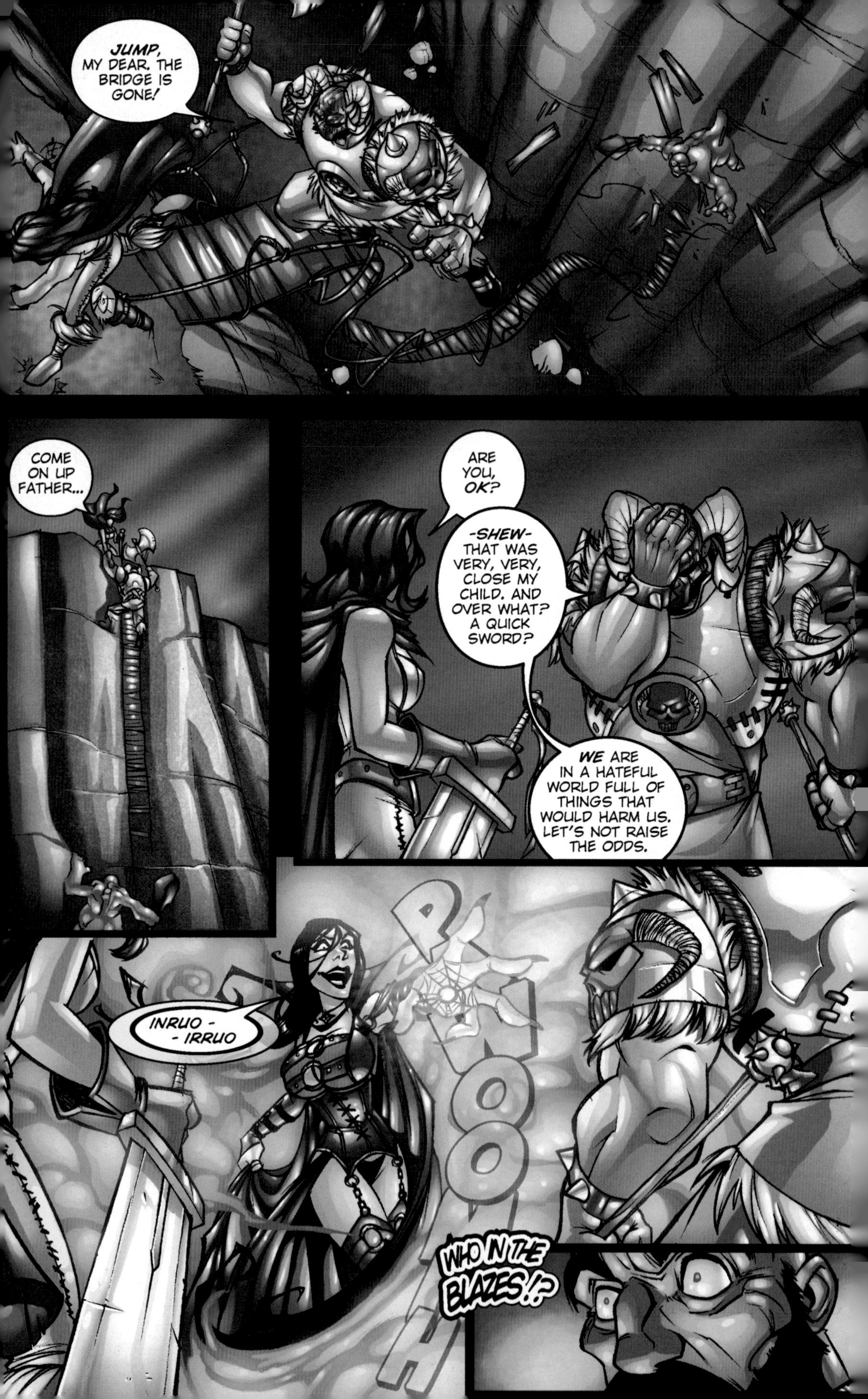
JUMP, MY DEAR. THE BRIDGE IS GONE!
COME ON UP FATHER...
ARE YOU, OK?
-SHEW- THAT WAS VERY, VERY, CLOSE MY CHILD. AND OVER WHAT? A QUICK SWORD?
WE ARE IN A HATEFUL WORLD FULL OF THINGS THAT WOULD HARM US. LET'S NOT RAISE THE ODDS.
INRUO - - IRRUO
WHO IN THE BLAZES!?

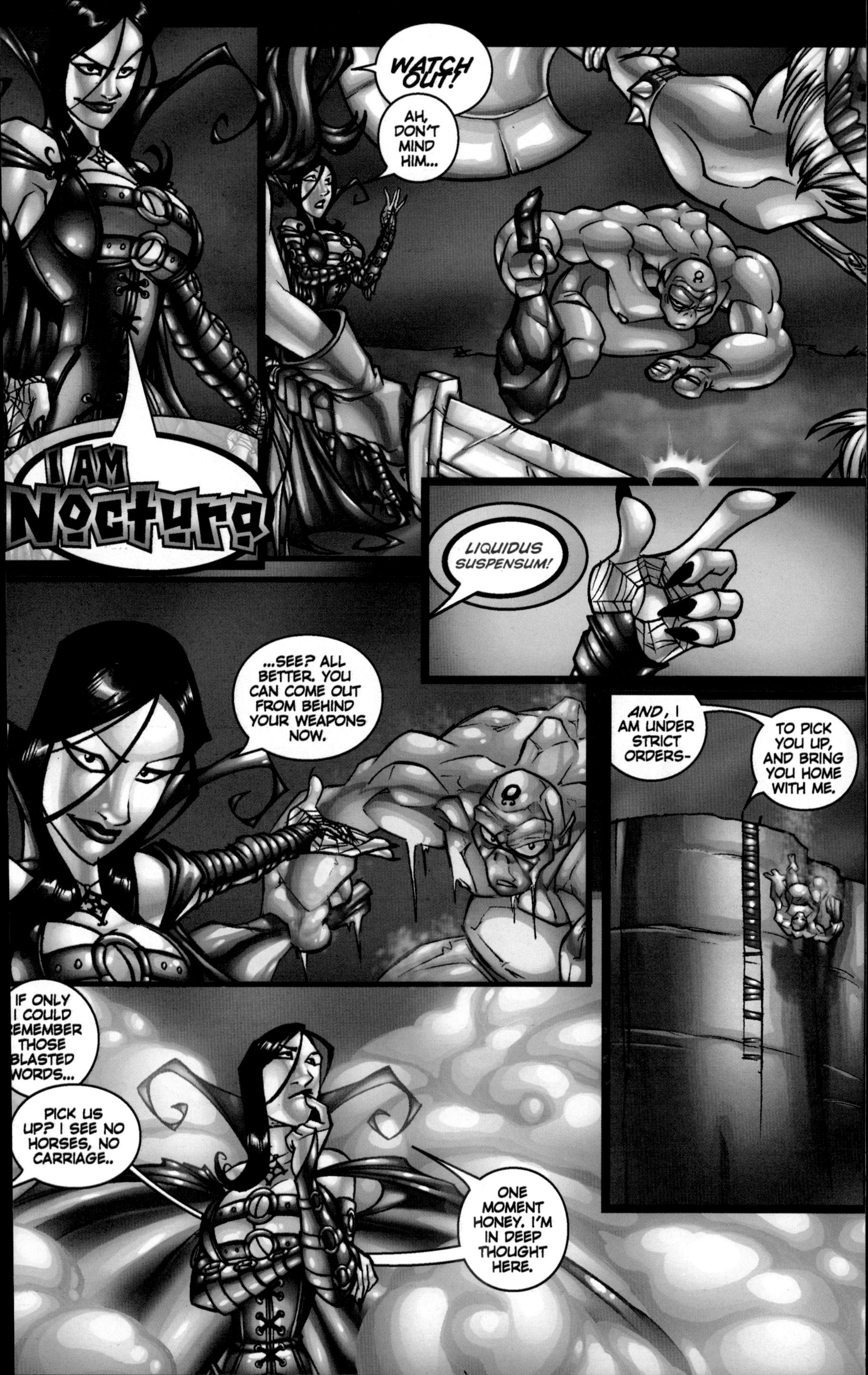
I AM Nocturo
WATCH OUT!
AH, DON'T MIND HIM...
LIQUIDUS SUSPENSUM!
...SEE? ALL BETTER. YOU CAN COME OUT FROM BEHIND YOUR WEAPONS NOW.
AND, I AM UNDER STRICT ORDERS-
TO PICK YOU UP, AND BRING YOU HOME WITH ME.
IF ONLY I COULD REMEMBER THOSE BLASTED WORDS...
PICK US UP? I SEE NO HORSES, NO CARRIAGE..
ONE MOMENT HONEY. I'M IN DEEP THOUGHT HERE.

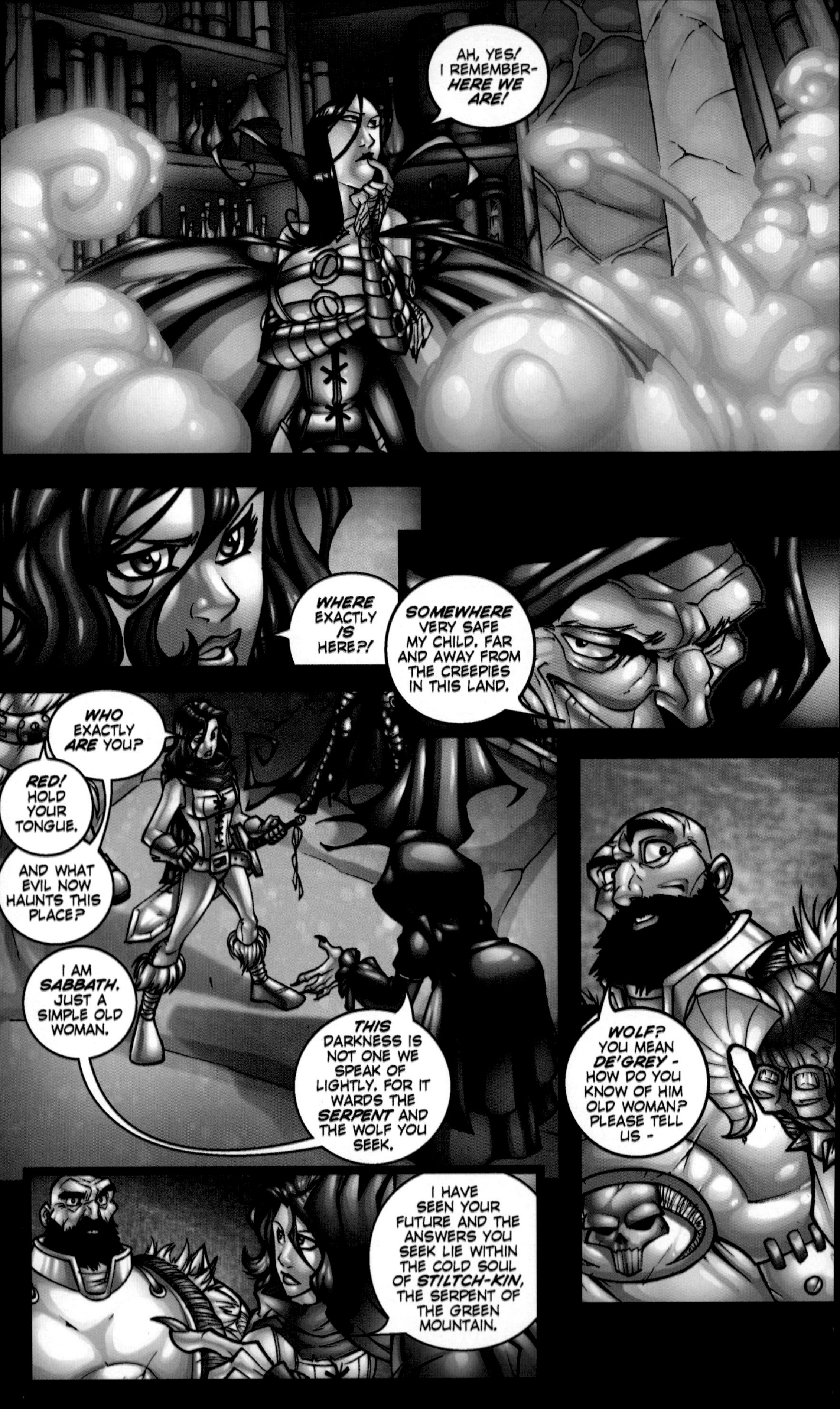

AH, YES! I REMEMBER- HERE WE ARE!
WHERE EXACTLY IS HERE?!
SOMEWHERE VERY SAFE MY CHILD. FAR AND AWAY FROM THE CREEPIES IN THIS LAND.
WHO EXACTLY ARE YOU?
RED! HOLD YOUR TONGUE.
AND WHAT EVIL NOW HAUNTS THIS PLACE?
I AM SABBATH. JUST A SIMPLE OLD WOMAN.
THIS DARKNESS IS NOT ONE WE SPEAK OF LIGHTLY. FOR IT WARDS THE SERPENT AND THE WOLF YOU SEEK.
WOLF? YOU MEAN DE'GREY - HOW DO YOU KNOW OF HIM OLD WOMAN? PLEASE TELL US -
I HAVE SEEN YOUR FUTURE AND THE ANSWERS YOU SEEK LIE WITHIN THE COLD SOUL OF STILTCH-KIN, THE SERPENT OF THE GREEN MOUNTAIN.

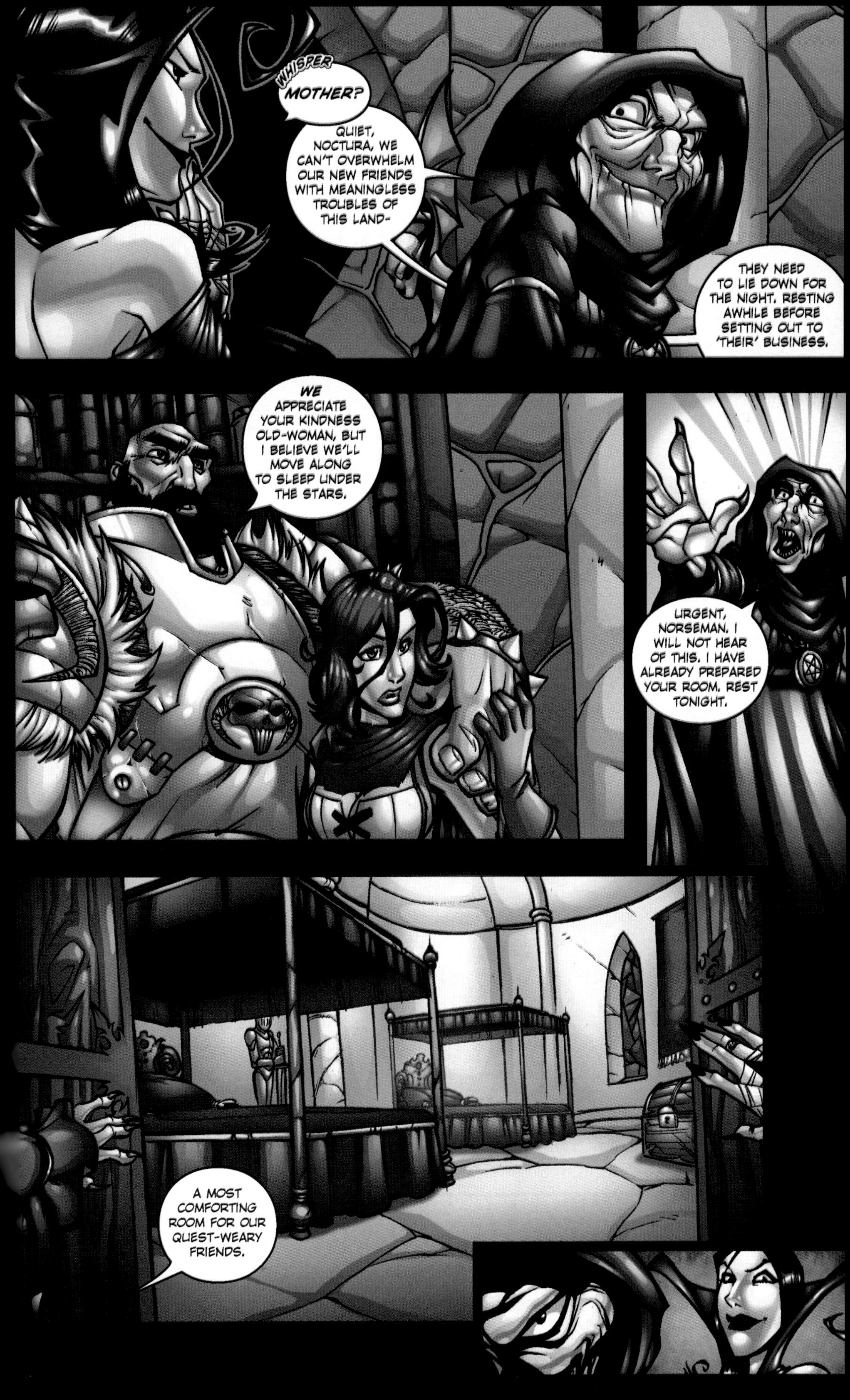
WHISPER
MOTHER?
QUIET, NOCTURA, WE CAN'T OVERWHELM OUR NEW FRIENDS WITH MEANINGLESS TROUBLES OF THIS LAND-
THEY NEED TO LIE DOWN FOR THE NIGHT. RESTING AWHILE BEFORE SETTING OUT TO 'THEIR' BUSINESS.
WE APPRECIATE YOUR KINDNESS OLD-WOMAN, BUT I BELIEVE WE'LL MOVE ALONG TO SLEEP UNDER THE STARS.
URGENT, NORSEMAN. I WILL NOT HEAR OF THIS. I HAVE ALREADY PREPARED YOUR ROOM. REST TONIGHT.
A MOST COMFORTING ROOM FOR OUR QUEST-WEARY FRIENDS.

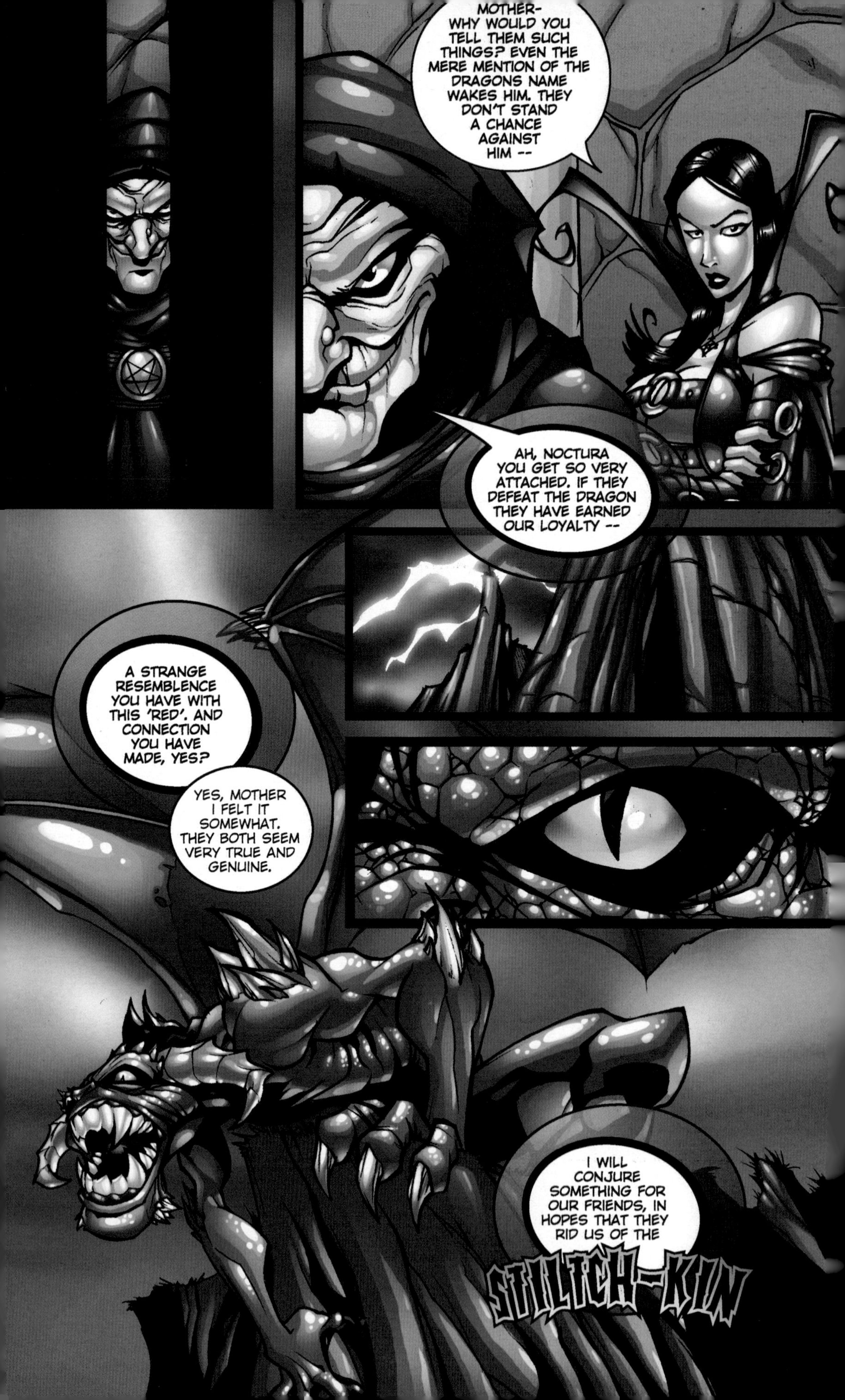
MOTHER- WHY WOULD YOU TELL THEM SUCH THINGS? EVEN THE MERE MENTION OF THE DRAGONS NAME WAKES HIM. THEY DON'T STAND A CHANCE AGAINST HIM --
AH, NOCTURA YOU GET SO VERY ATTACHED. IF THEY DEFEAT THE DRAGON THEY HAVE EARNED OUR LOYALTY --
A STRANGE RESEMBLENCE YOU HAVE WITH THIS 'RED'. AND CONNECTION YOU HAVE MADE, YES?
YES, MOTHER I FELT IT SOMEWHAT. THEY BOTH SEEM VERY TRUE AND GENUINE.
I WILL CONJURE SOMETHING FOR OUR FRIENDS, IN HOPES THAT THEY RID US OF THE
STILTCH-KIN

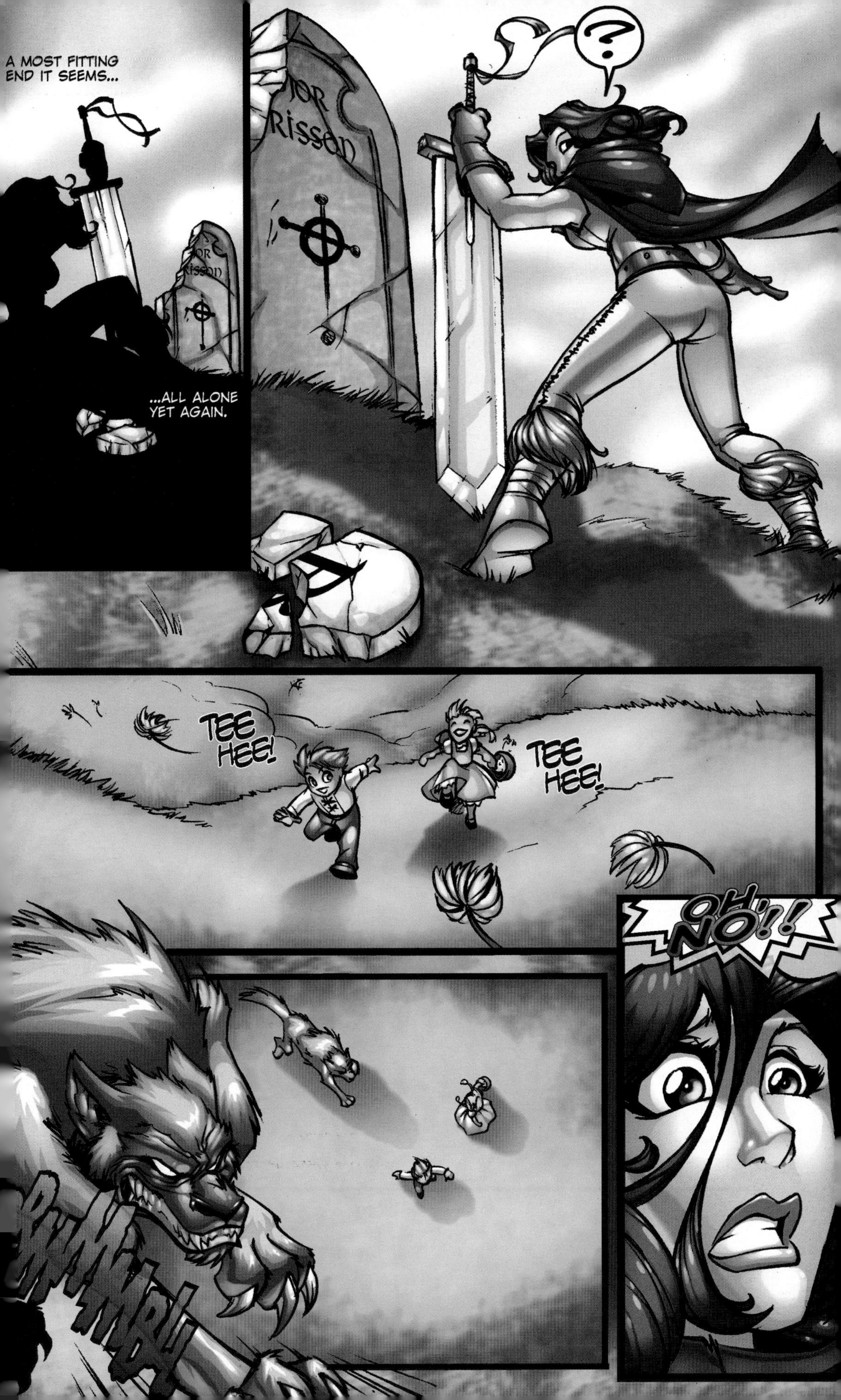

A MOST FITTING END IT SEEMS...
...ALL ALONE YET AGAIN.
?
TEE HEE!
TEE HEE!
OH NO!!

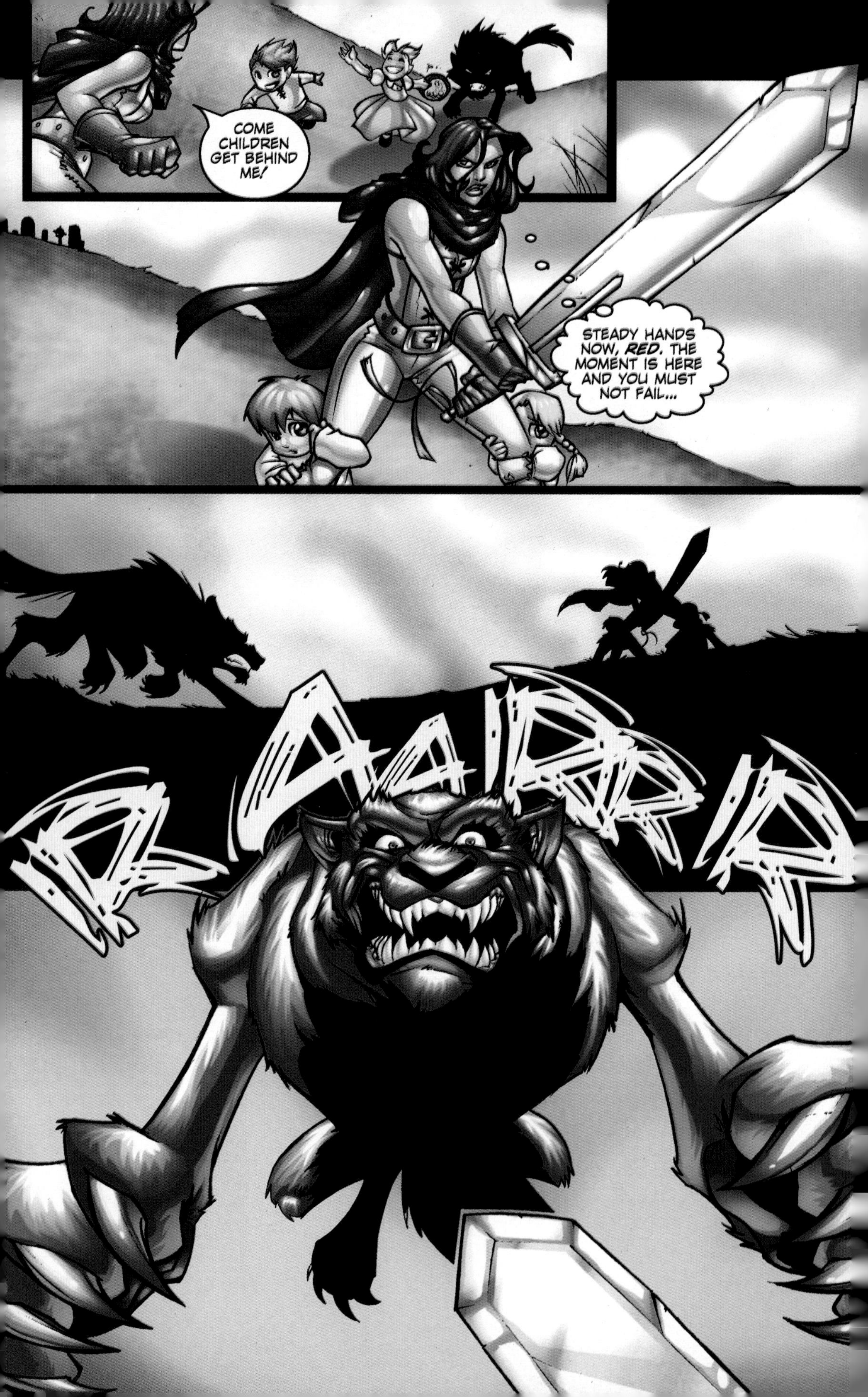
COME CHILDREN GET BEHIND ME!
STEADY HANDS NOW, RED. THE MOMENT IS HERE AND YOU MUST NOT FAIL...
RAARRR

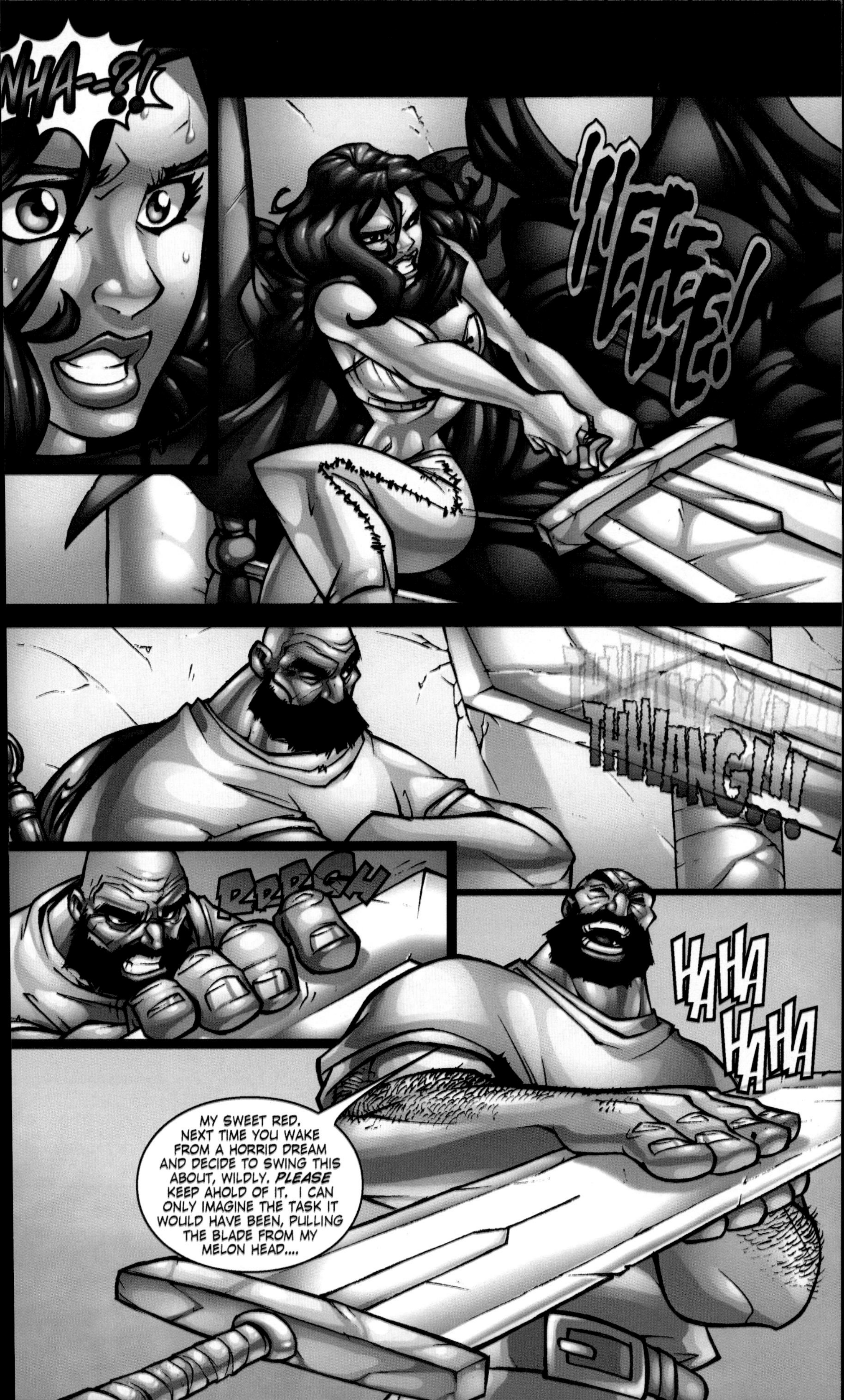
WHA--?!
YEEEE!
THWANG!!!
RRRGH
HAHA HAHA
MY SWEET RED. NEXT TIME YOU WAKE FROM A HORRID DREAM AND DECIDE TO SWING THIS ABOUT, WILDLY. *PLEASE* KEEP AHOLD OF IT. I CAN ONLY IMAGINE THE TASK IT WOULD HAVE BEEN, PULLING THE BLADE FROM MY MELON HEAD....

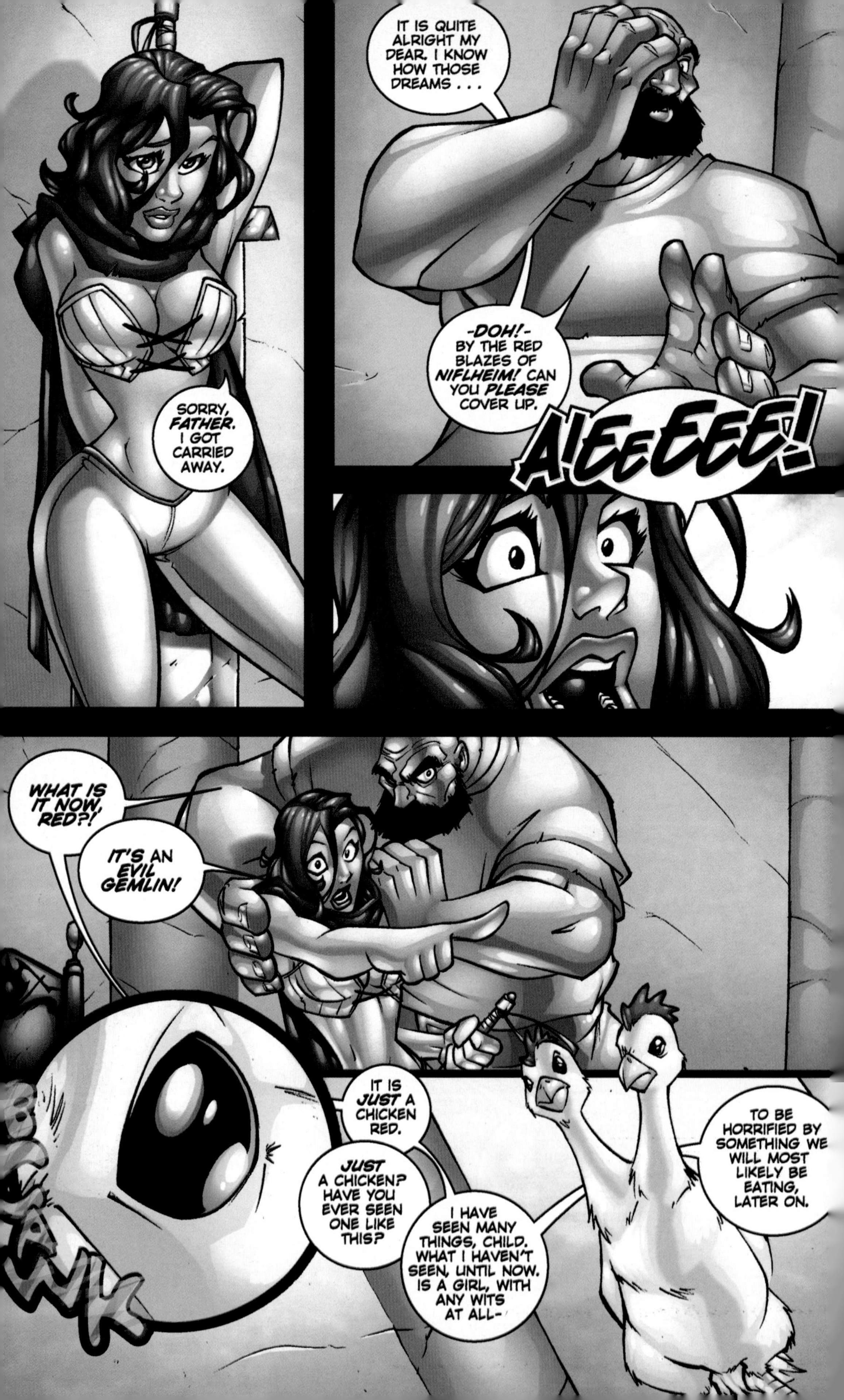
SORRY, FATHER. I GOT CARRIED AWAY.
IT IS QUITE ALRIGHT MY DEAR. I KNOW HOW THOSE DREAMS . . .
-DOH!- BY THE RED BLAZES OF NIFLHEIM! CAN YOU PLEASE COVER UP.
AIEEEEE!
WHAT IS IT NOW, RED?!
IT'S AN EVIL GEMLIN!
IT IS JUST A CHICKEN RED.
JUST A CHICKEN? HAVE YOU EVER SEEN ONE LIKE THIS?
I HAVE SEEN MANY THINGS, CHILD. WHAT I HAVEN'T SEEN, UNTIL NOW. IS A GIRL, WITH ANY WITS AT ALL-
TO BE HORRIFIED BY SOMETHING WE WILL MOST LIKELY BE EATING, LATER ON.

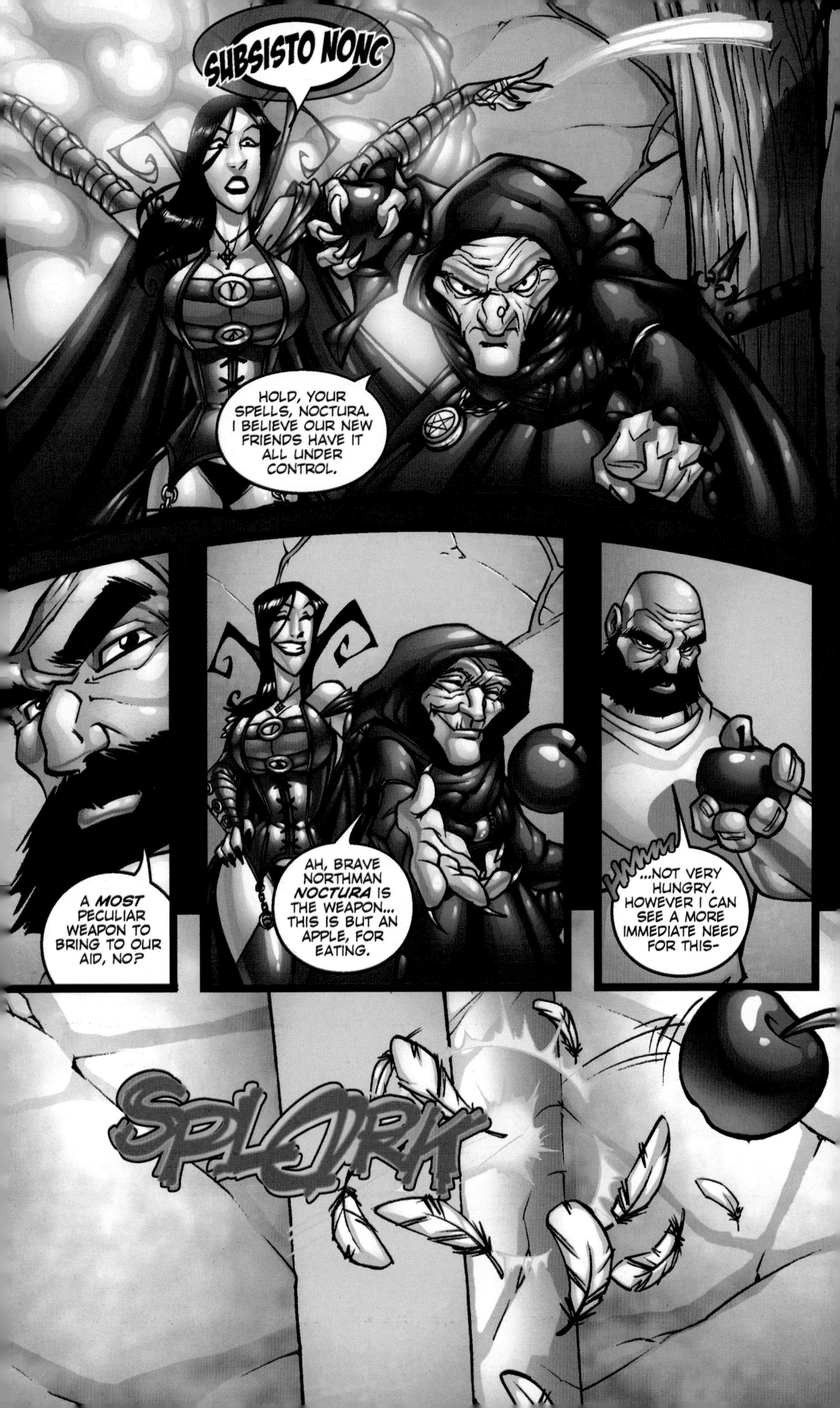
SUBSISTO NONC
HOLD, YOUR SPELLS, NOCTURA. I BELIEVE OUR NEW FRIENDS HAVE IT ALL UNDER CONTROL.
A MOST PECULIAR WEAPON TO BRING TO OUR AID, NO?
AH, BRAVE NORTHMAN NOCTURA IS THE WEAPON... THIS IS BUT AN APPLE, FOR EATING.
HMMM
...NOT VERY HUNGRY. HOWEVER I CAN SEE A MORE IMMEDIATE NEED FOR THIS-
SPLORK

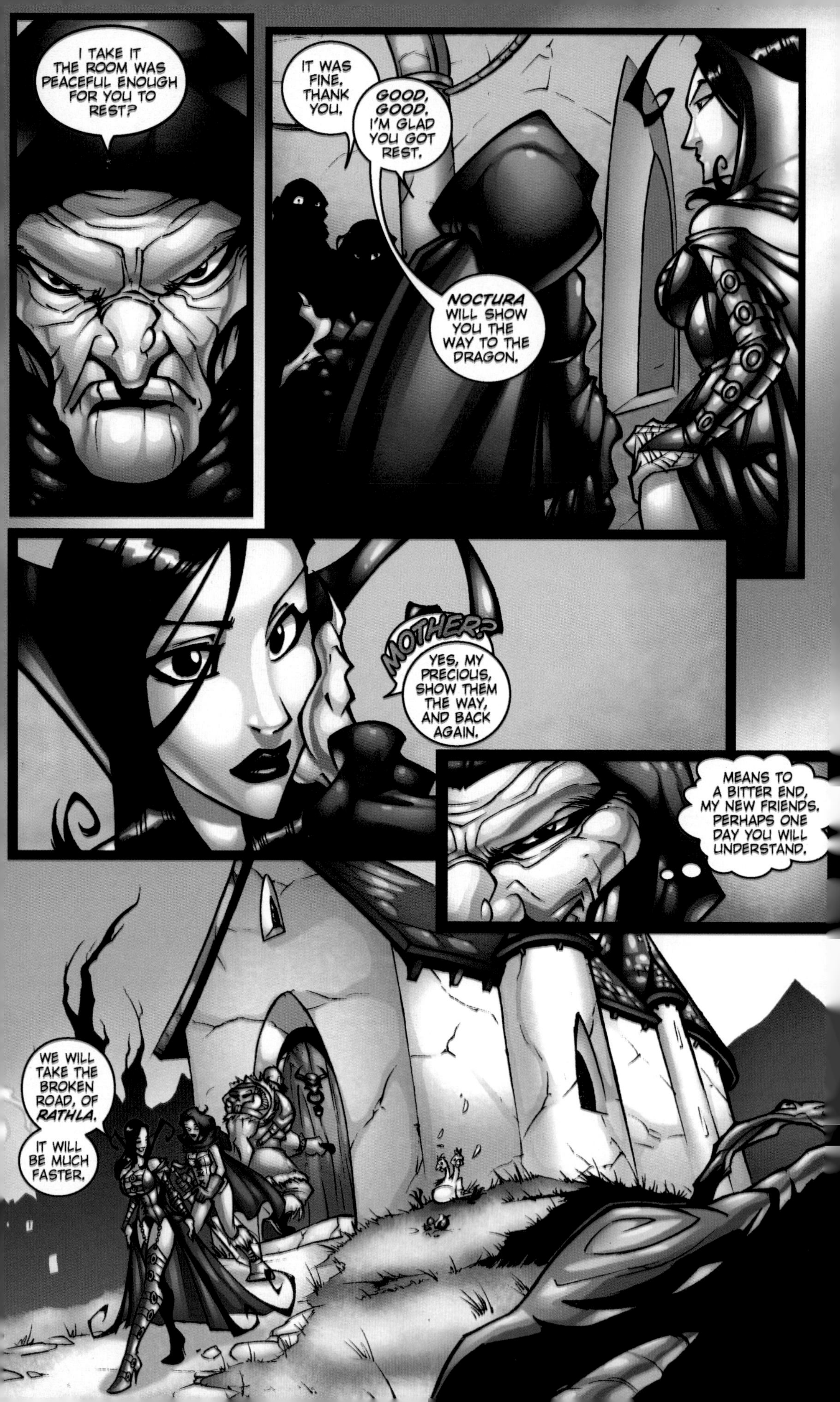
I TAKE IT THE ROOM WAS PEACEFUL ENOUGH FOR YOU TO REST?
IT WAS FINE. THANK YOU.
GOOD, GOOD. I'M GLAD YOU GOT REST.
NOCTURA WILL SHOW YOU THE WAY TO THE DRAGON.
MOTHER?
YES, MY PRECIOUS, SHOW THEM THE WAY, AND BACK AGAIN.
MEANS TO A BITTER END, MY NEW FRIENDS. PERHAPS ONE DAY YOU WILL UNDERSTAND.
WE WILL TAKE THE BROKEN ROAD, OF RATHLA.
IT WILL BE MUCH FASTER.

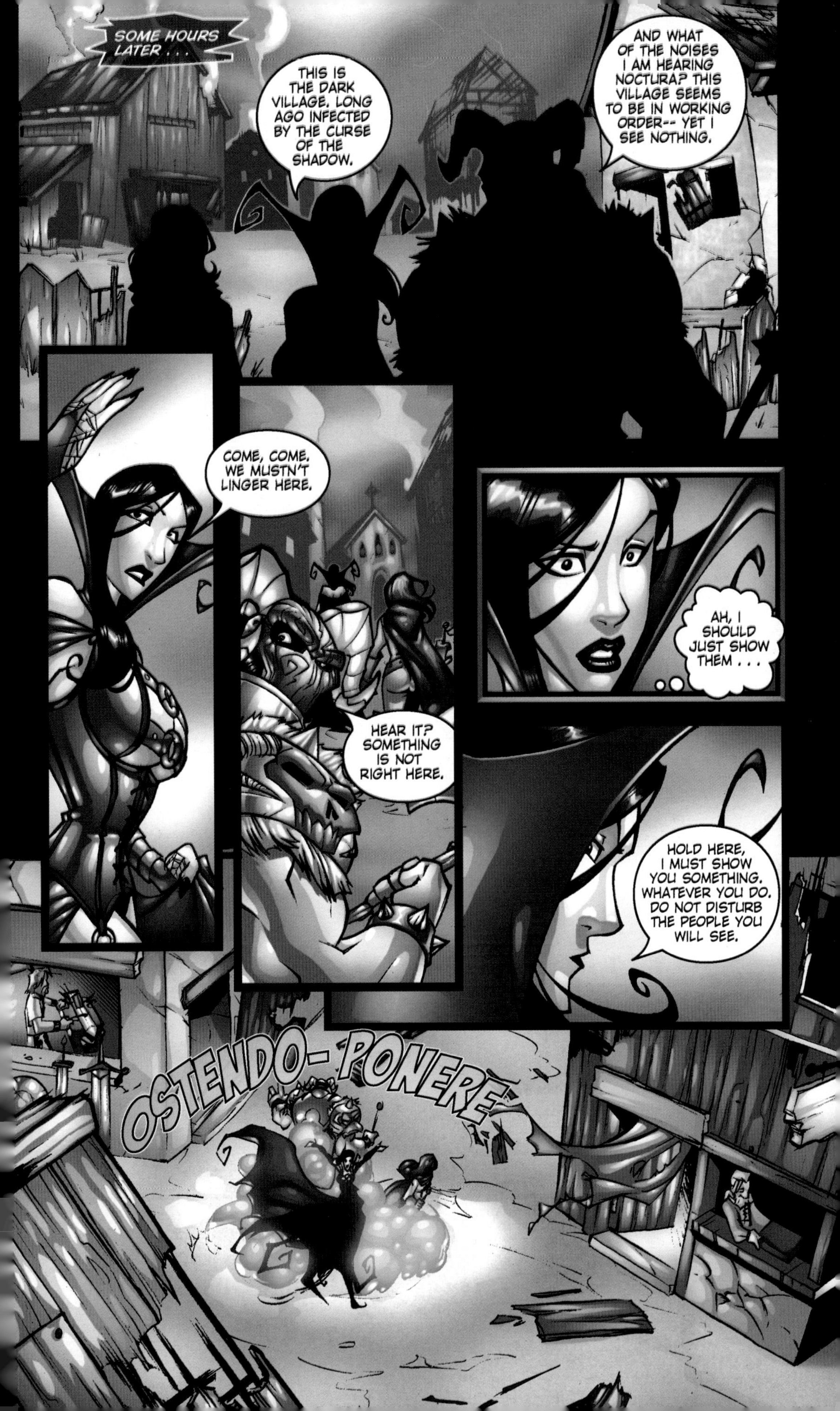
SOME HOURS LATER . . .
THIS IS THE DARK VILLAGE. LONG AGO INFECTED BY THE CURSE OF THE SHADOW.
AND WHAT OF THE NOISES I AM HEARING NOCTURA? THIS VILLAGE SEEMS TO BE IN WORKING ORDER-- YET I SEE NOTHING.
COME, COME. WE MUSTN'T LINGER HERE.
HEAR IT? SOMETHING IS NOT RIGHT HERE.
AH, I SHOULD JUST SHOW THEM . . .
HOLD HERE, I MUST SHOW YOU SOMETHING. WHATEVER YOU DO. DO NOT DISTURB THE PEOPLE YOU WILL SEE.
OSTENDO- PONERE

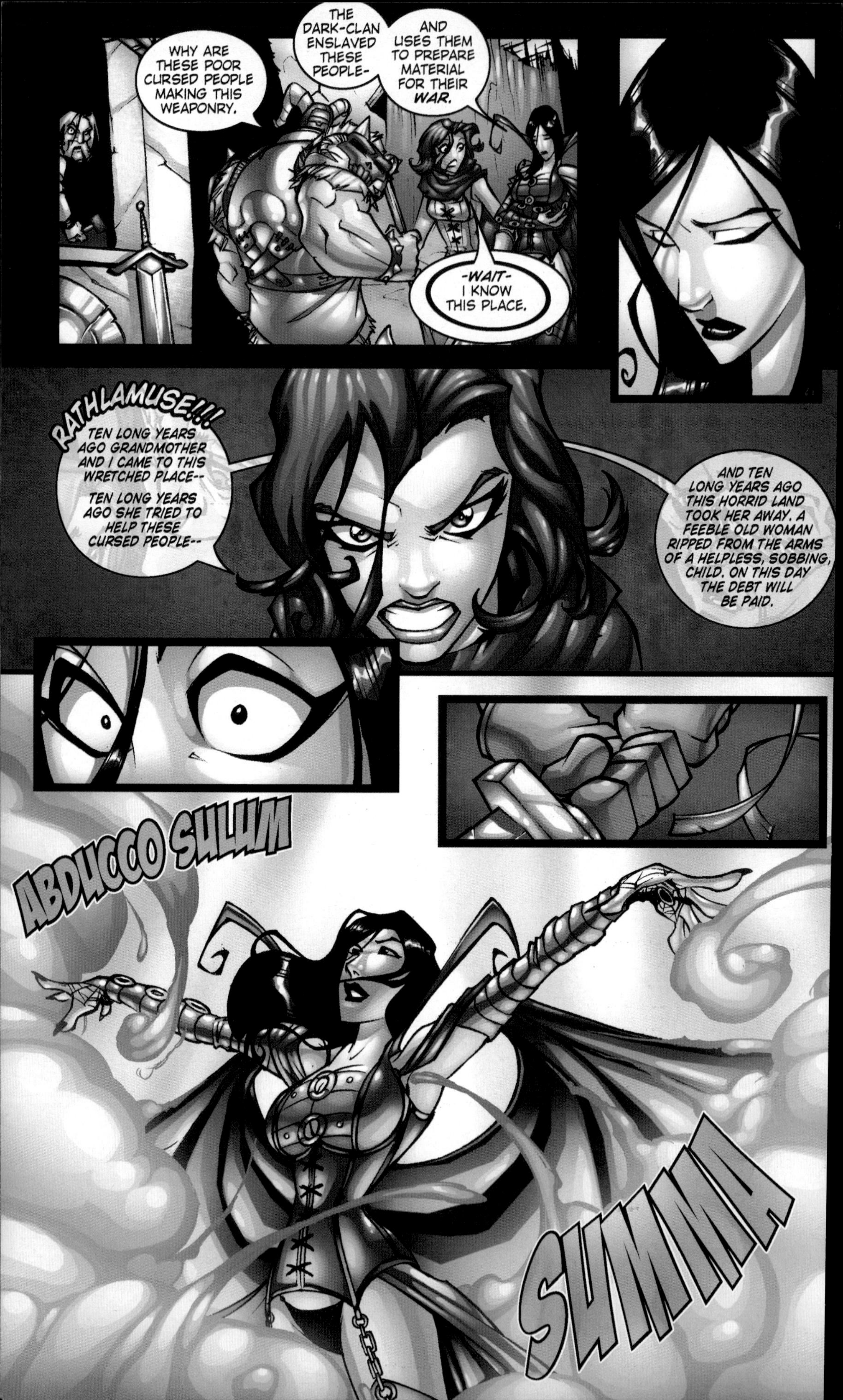
WHY ARE THESE POOR CURSED PEOPLE MAKING THIS WEAPONRY.
THE DARK-CLAN ENSLAVED THESE PEOPLE-
AND USES THEM TO PREPARE MATERIAL FOR THEIR WAR.
-WAIT- I KNOW THIS PLACE.
RATHLAMUSE!!!
TEN LONG YEARS AGO GRANDMOTHER AND I CAME TO THIS WRETCHED PLACE--
TEN LONG YEARS AGO SHE TRIED TO HELP THESE CURSED PEOPLE--
AND TEN LONG YEARS AGO THIS HORRID LAND TOOK HER AWAY. A FEEBLE OLD WOMAN RIPPED FROM THE ARMS OF A HELPLESS, SOBBING, CHILD. ON THIS DAY THE DEBT WILL BE PAID.
ABDUCCO SULUM
SUMMA

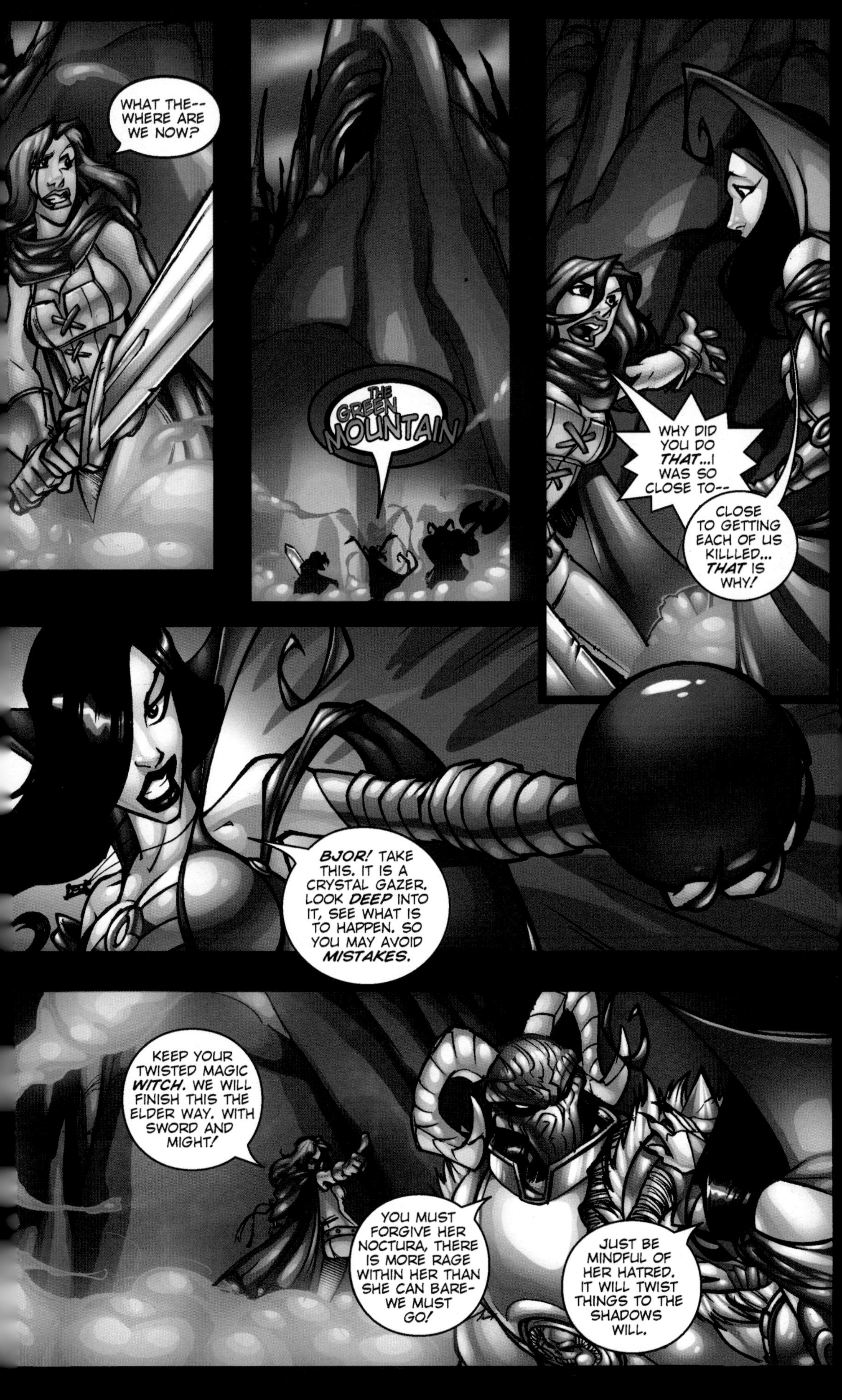
WHAT THE-- WHERE ARE WE NOW?
THE GREEN MOUNTAIN
WHY DID YOU DO THAT...I WAS SO CLOSE TO--
CLOSE TO GETTING EACH OF US KILLLED... THAT IS WHY!
BJOR! TAKE THIS. IT IS A CRYSTAL GAZER. LOOK DEEP INTO IT, SEE WHAT IS TO HAPPEN. SO YOU MAY AVOID MISTAKES.
KEEP YOUR TWISTED MAGIC WITCH. WE WILL FINISH THIS THE ELDER WAY. WITH SWORD AND MIGHT!
YOU MUST FORGIVE HER NOCTURA, THERE IS MORE RAGE WITHIN HER THAN SHE CAN BARE- WE MUST GO!
JUST BE MINDFUL OF HER HATRED. IT WILL TWIST THINGS TO THE SHADOWS WILL.

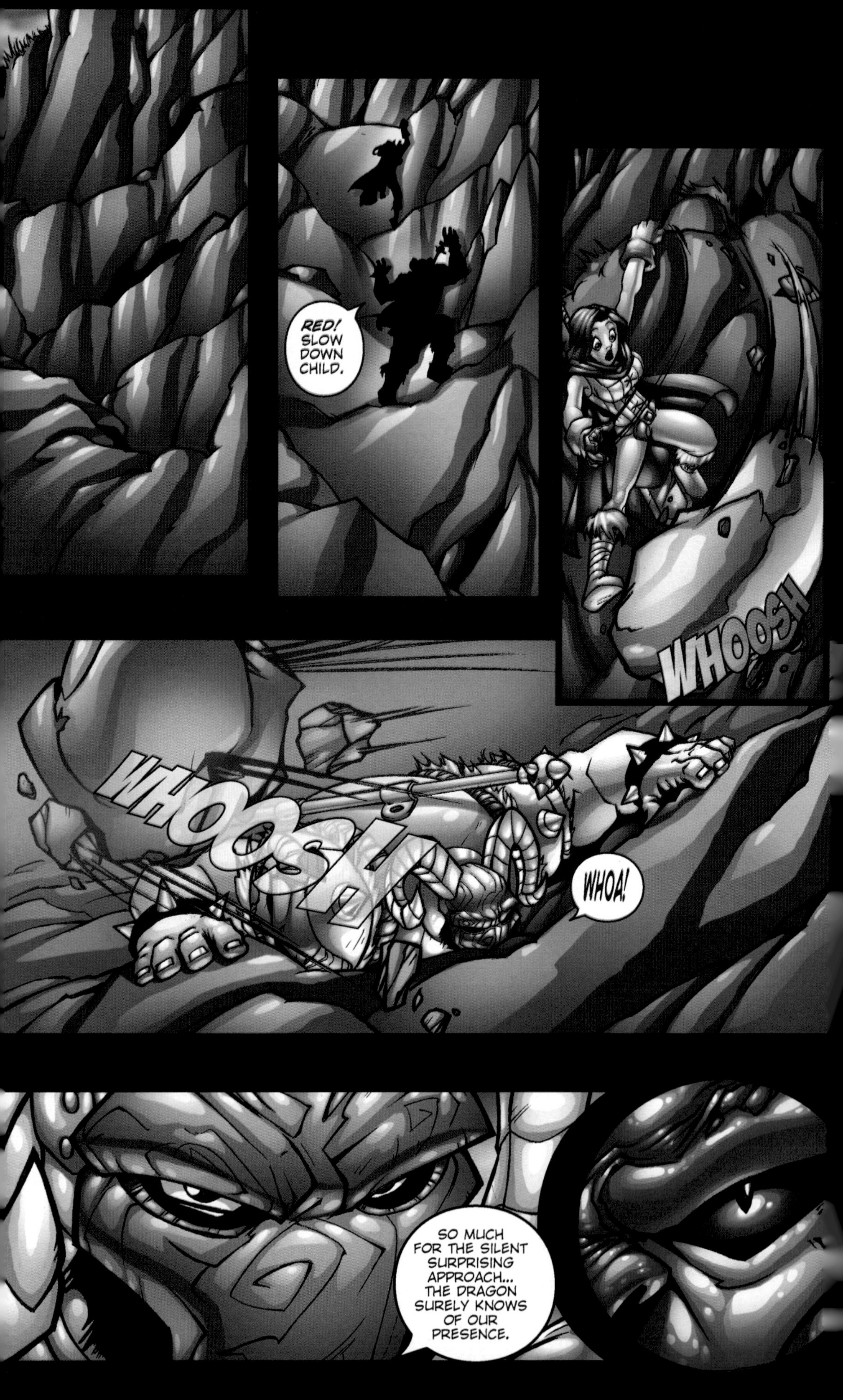
RED! SLOW DOWN CHILD.
WHOOSH
WHOOSH!
WHOA!
SO MUCH FOR THE SILENT SURPRISING APPROACH... THE DRAGON SURELY KNOWS OF OUR PRESENCE.

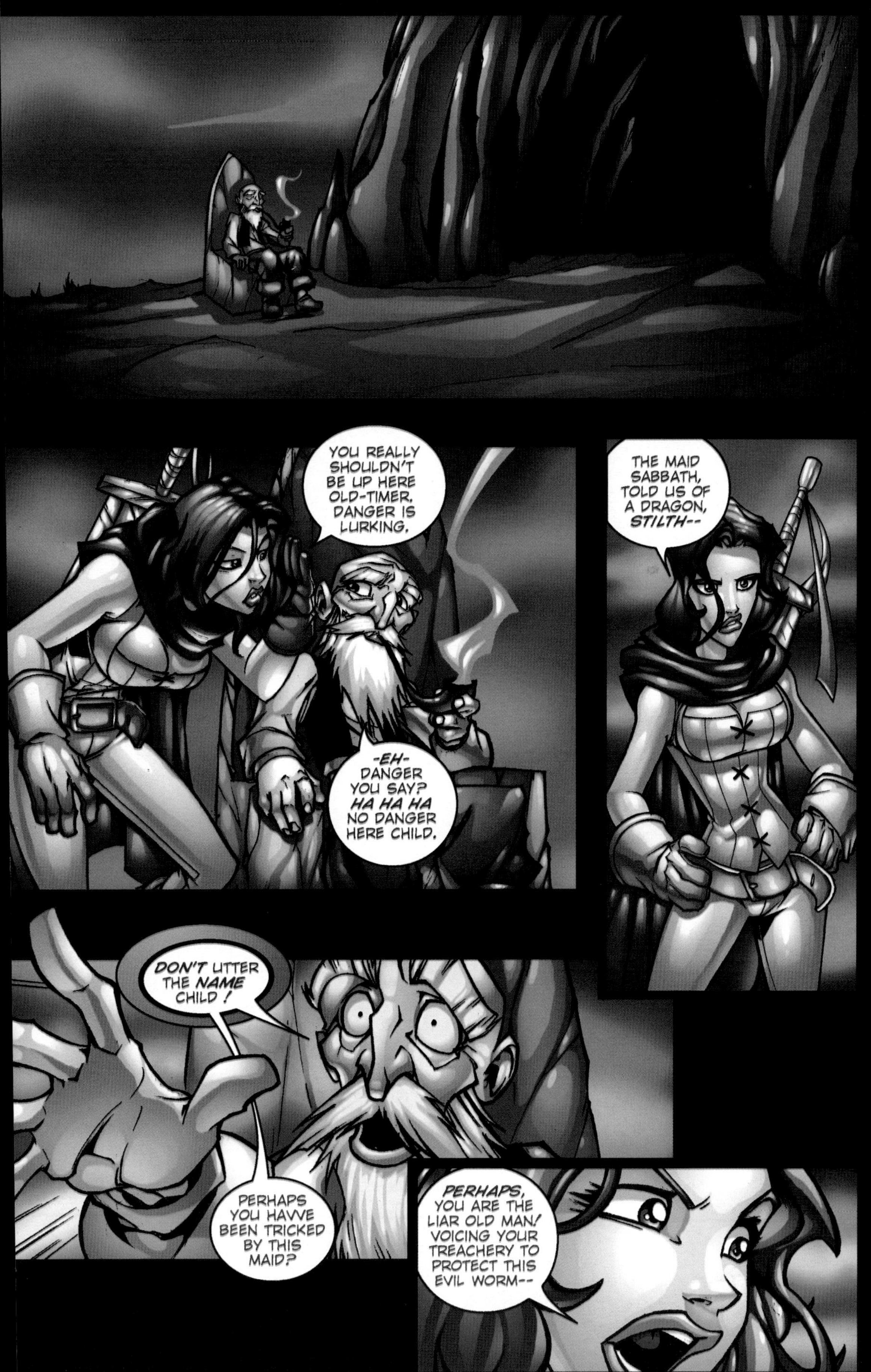
YOU REALLY SHOULDN'T BE UP HERE OLD-TIMER. DANGER IS LURKING.
-EH- DANGER YOU SAY? HA HA HA NO DANGER HERE CHILD.
THE MAID SABBATH, TOLD US OF A DRAGON, STILTH--
DON'T UTTER THE NAME CHILD!
PERHAPS YOU HAVVE BEEN TRICKED BY THIS MAID?
PERHAPS, YOU ARE THE LIAR OLD MAN! VOICING YOUR TREACHERY TO PROTECT THIS EVIL WORM--

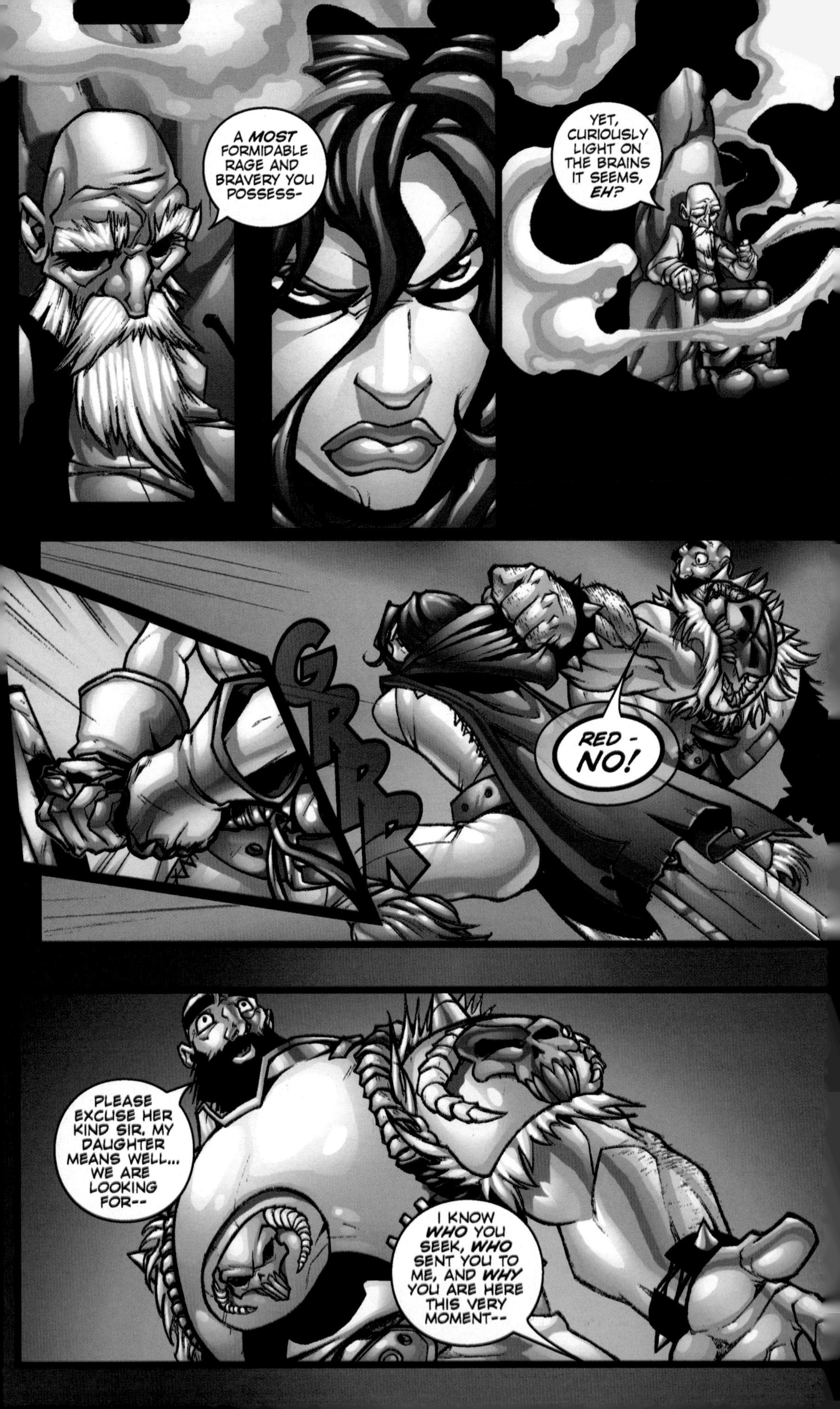

A MOST FORMIDABLE RAGE AND BRAVERY YOU POSSESS-
YET, CURIOUSLY LIGHT ON THE BRAINS IT SEEMS, EH?
GRRR
RED - NO!
PLEASE EXCUSE HER KIND SIR, MY DAUGHTER MEANS WELL... WE ARE LOOKING FOR--
I KNOW WHO YOU SEEK, WHO SENT YOU TO ME, AND WHY YOU ARE HERE THIS VERY MOMENT--

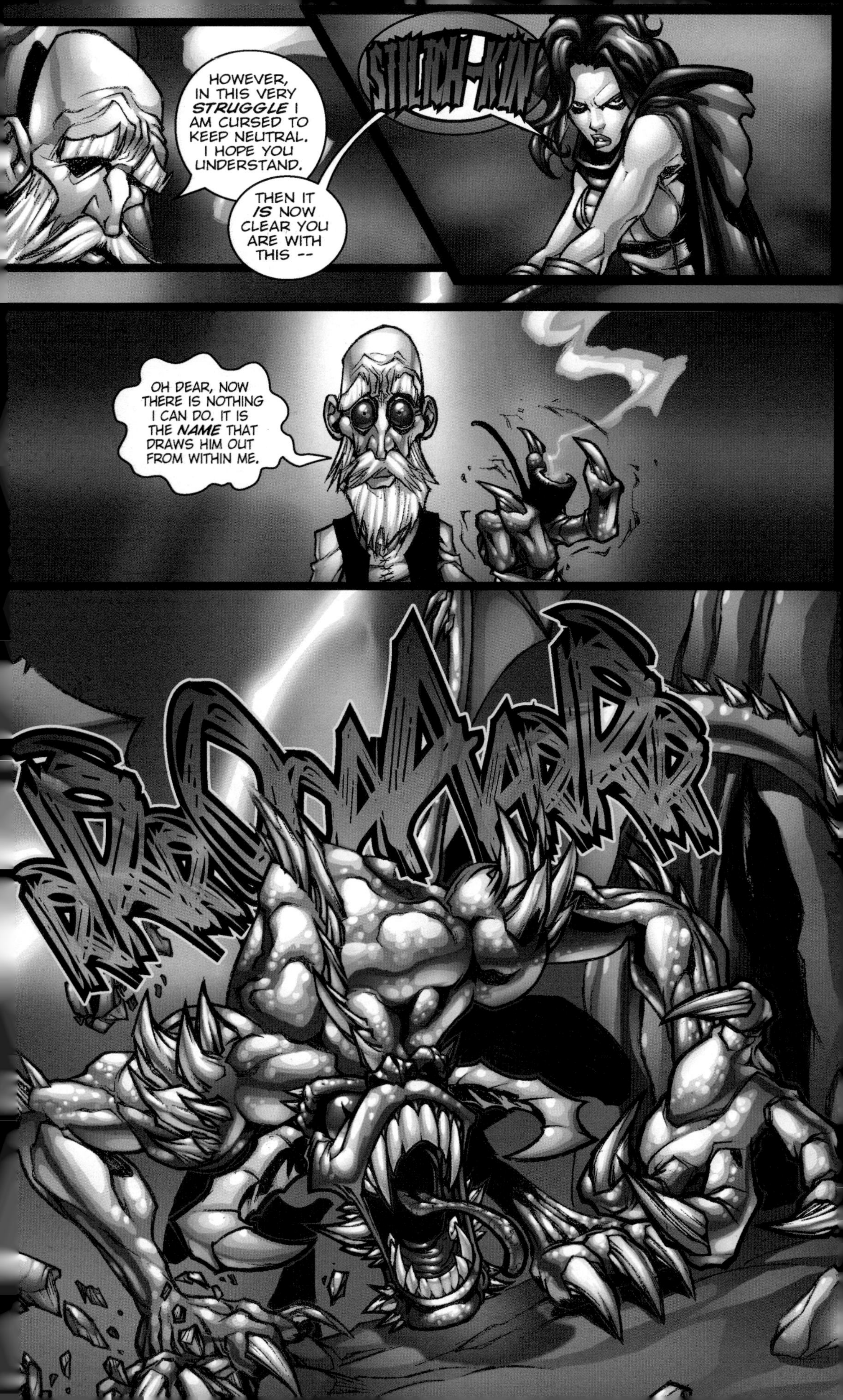
HOWEVER, IN THIS VERY STRUGGLE I AM CURSED TO KEEP NEUTRAL. I HOPE YOU UNDERSTAND.
STILCH-KIN
THEN IT IS NOW CLEAR YOU ARE WITH THIS --
OH DEAR, NOW THERE IS NOTHING I CAN DO. IT IS THE NAME THAT DRAWS HIM OUT FROM WITHIN ME.

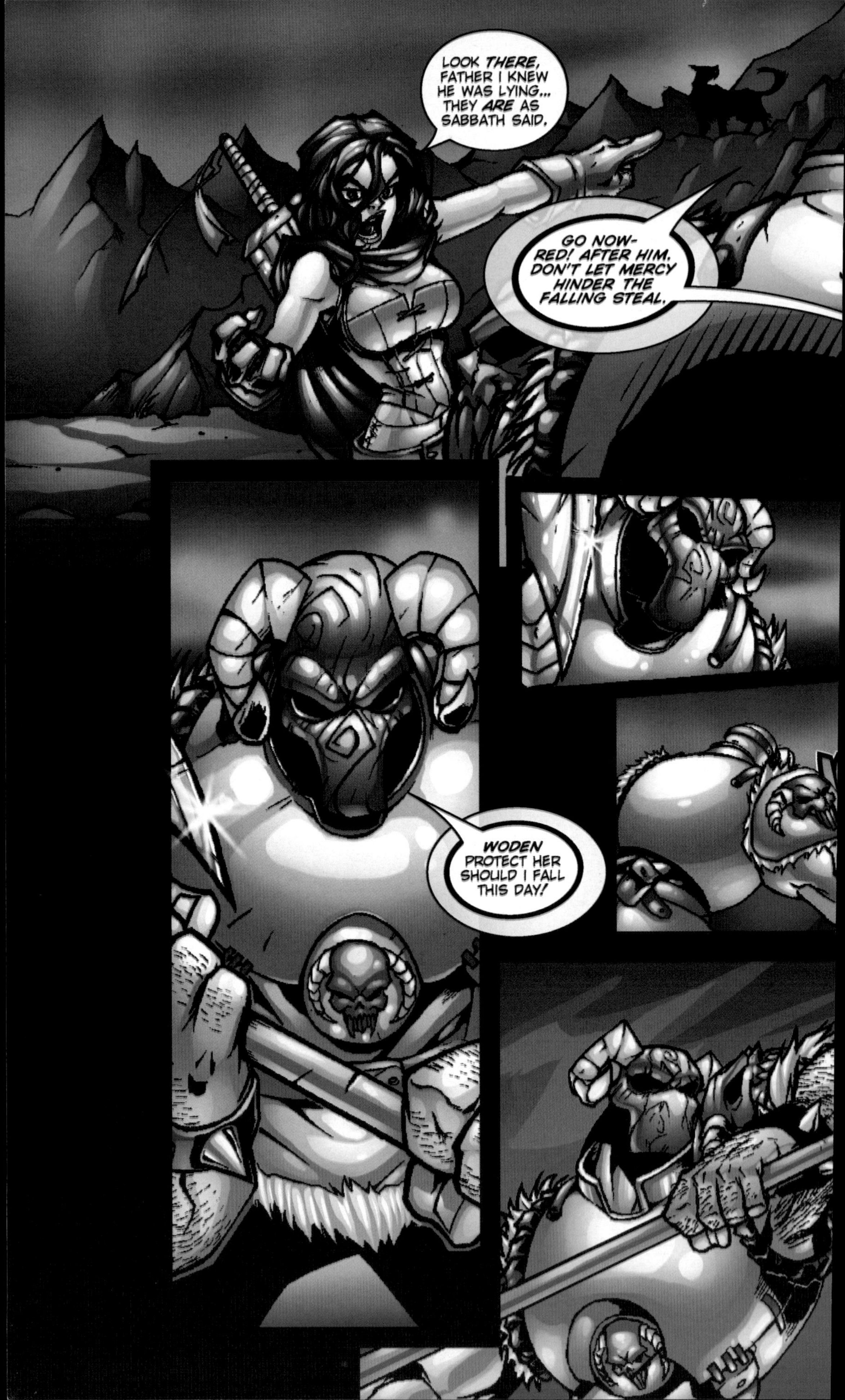
LOOK THERE, FATHER I KNEW HE WAS LYING... THEY ARE AS SABBATH SAID.
GO NOW-RED! AFTER HIM. DON'T LET MERCY HINDER THE FALLING STEAL.
WODEN PROTECT HER SHOULD I FALL THIS DAY!

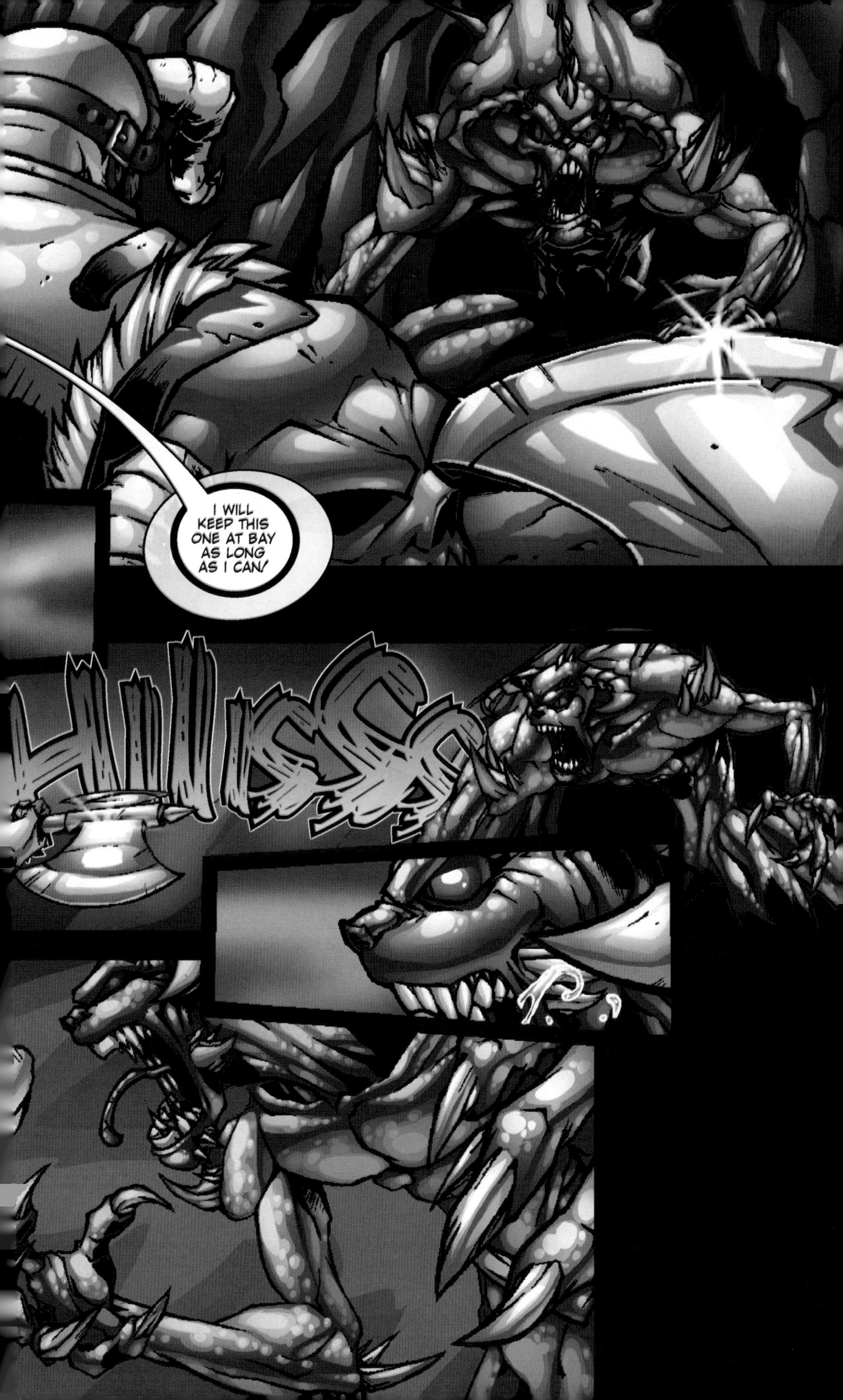
I WILL KEEP THIS ONE AT BAY AS LONG AS I CAN!
HHISSS

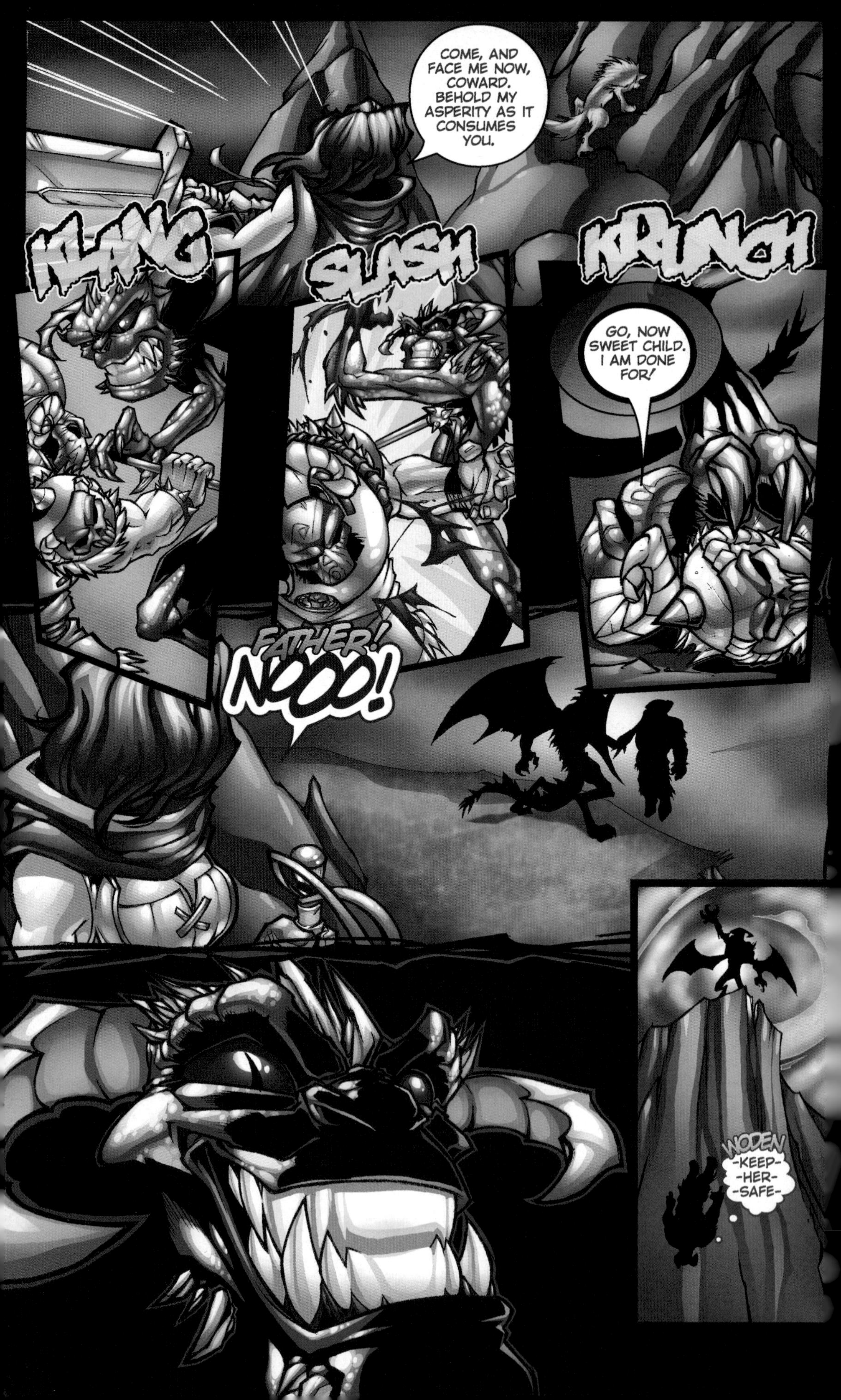
COME, AND FACE ME NOW, COWARD. BEHOLD MY ASPERITY AS IT CONSUMES YOU.
KLANG
SLASH
KRUNCH
GO, NOW SWEET CHILD. I AM DONE FOR!
FATHER! NOOO!
WODEN -KEEP- -HER- -SAFE-

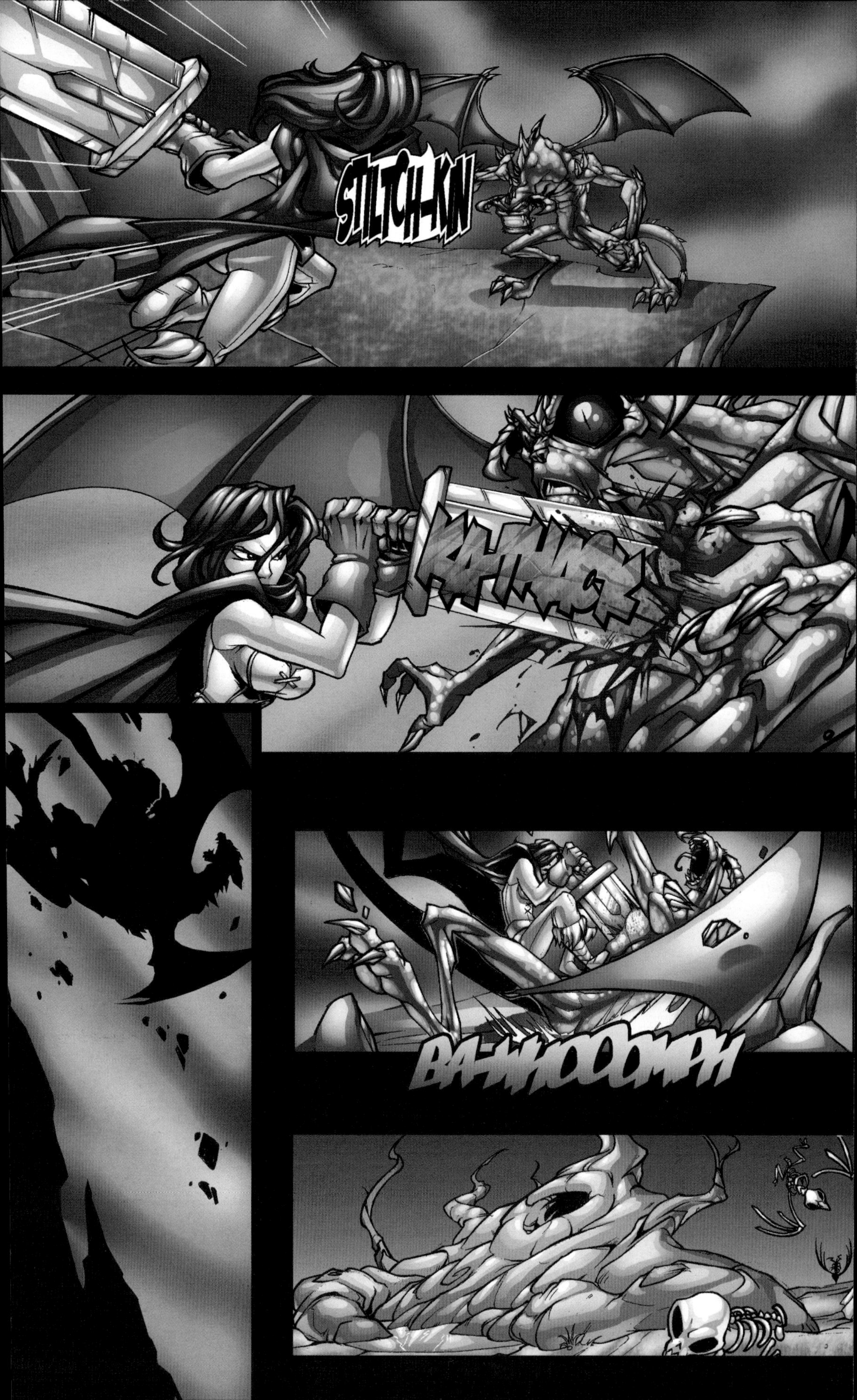
STILTCH-KIN
KA-THACK
BA-WHOOOMPH

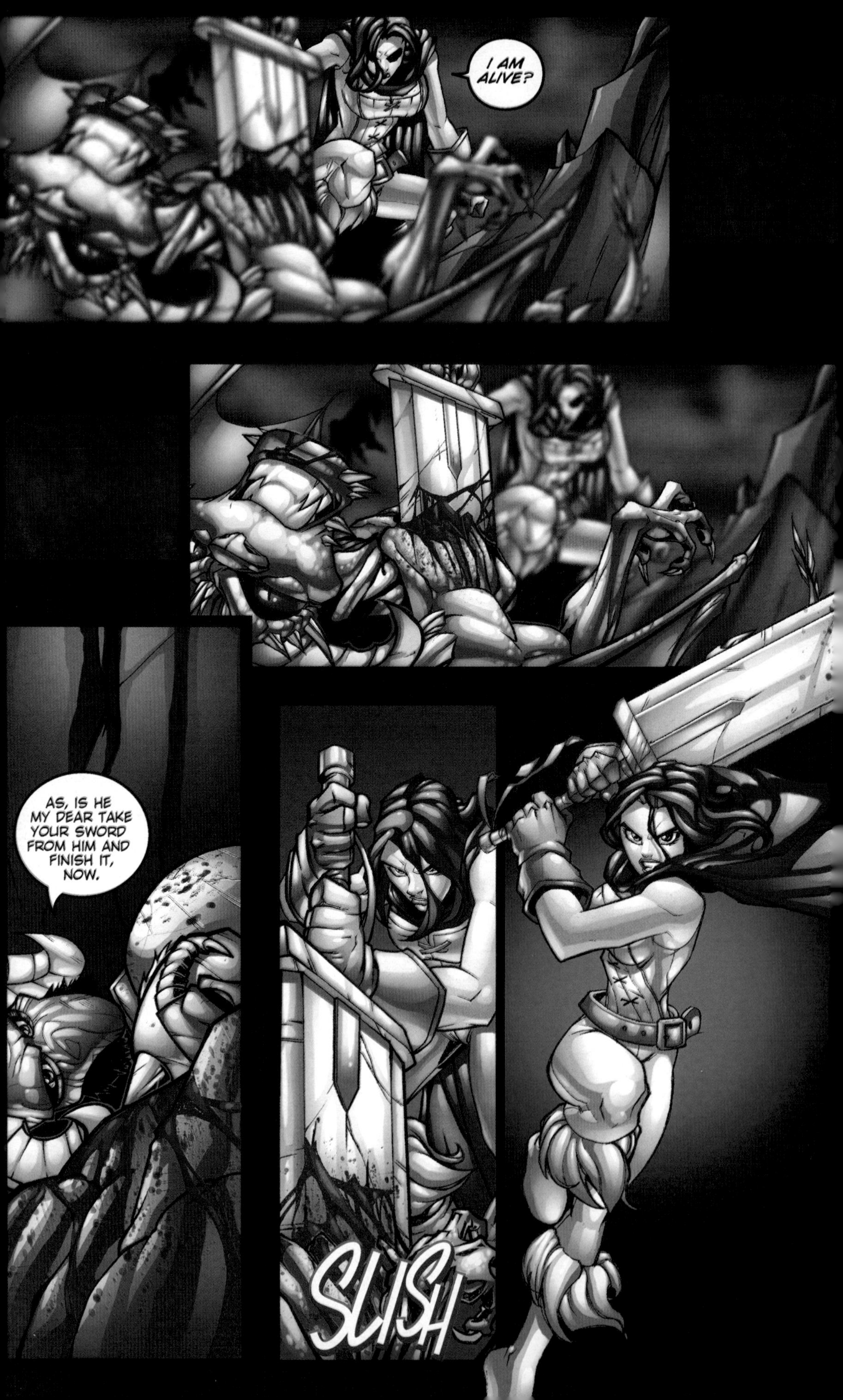
I AM ALIVE?
AS, IS HE MY DEAR TAKE YOUR SWORD FROM HIM AND FINISH IT, NOW.
SLISH

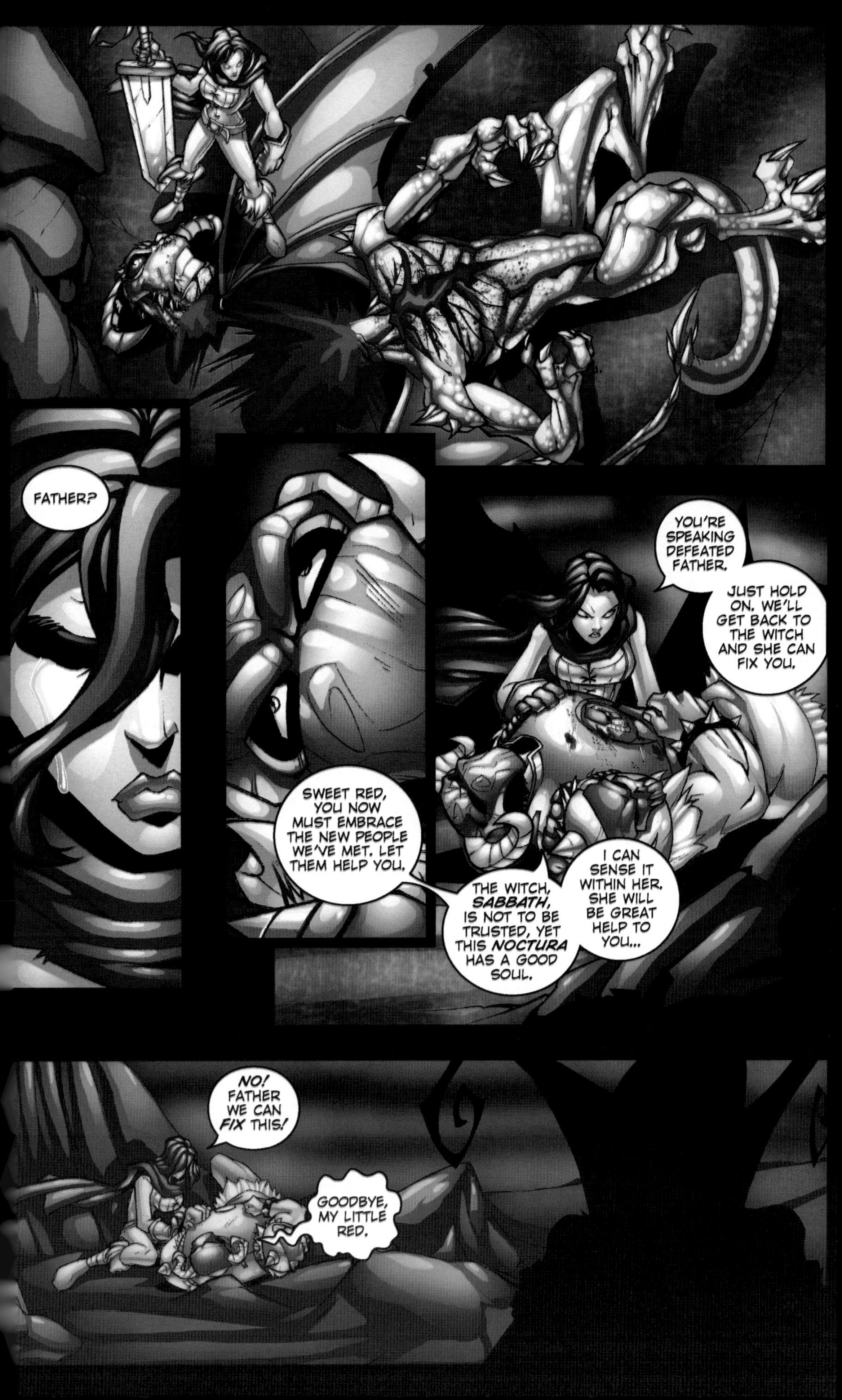
FATHER?
SWEET RED, YOU NOW MUST EMBRACE THE NEW PEOPLE WE'VE MET. LET THEM HELP YOU.
YOU'RE SPEAKING DEFEATED FATHER.
JUST HOLD ON. WE'LL GET BACK TO THE WITCH AND SHE CAN FIX YOU.
THE WITCH, SABBATH, IS NOT TO BE TRUSTED, YET THIS NOCTURA HAS A GOOD SOUL.
I CAN SENSE IT WITHIN HER. SHE WILL BE GREAT HELP TO YOU...
NO! FATHER WE CAN FIX THIS!
GOODBYE, MY LITTLE RED.

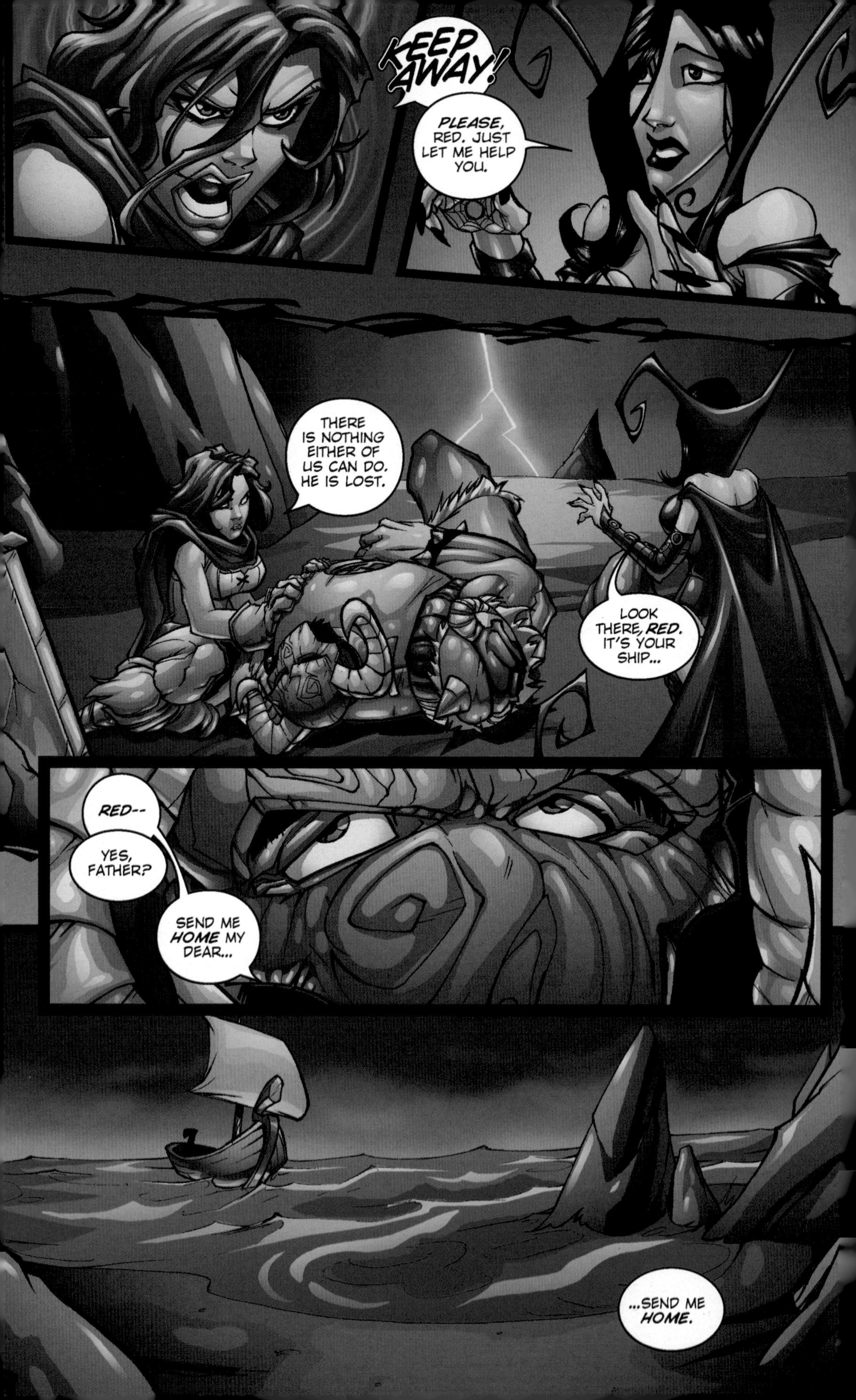
KEEP AWAY!
PLEASE, RED. JUST LET ME HELP YOU.
THERE IS NOTHING EITHER OF US CAN DO. HE IS LOST.
LOOK THERE, RED. IT'S YOUR SHIP...
RED--
YES, FATHER?
SEND ME HOME MY DEAR...
...SEND ME HOME.

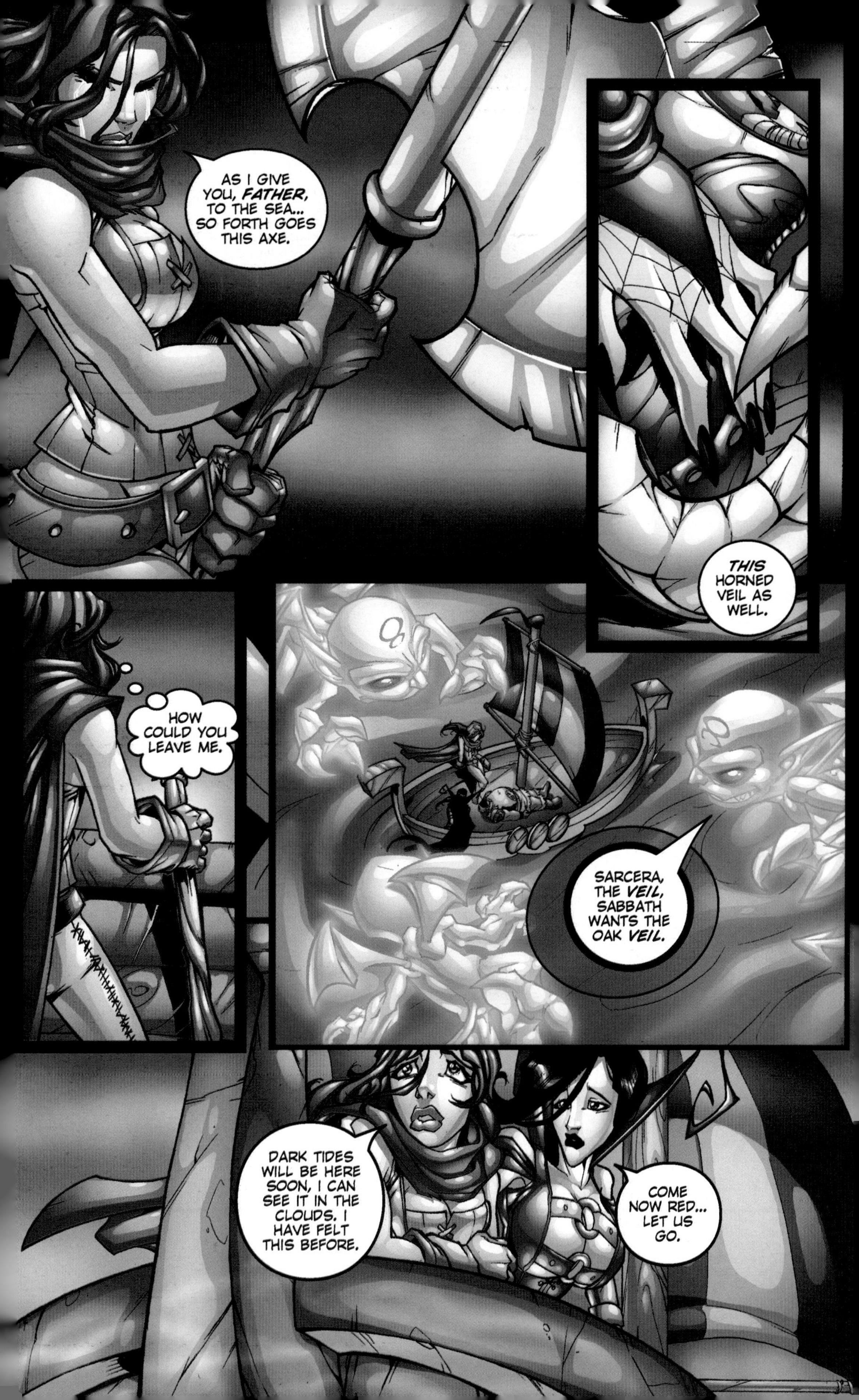
AS I GIVE YOU, FATHER, TO THE SEA... SO FORTH GOES THIS AXE.
THIS HORNED VEIL AS WELL.
HOW COULD YOU LEAVE ME.
SARCERA, THE VEIL, SABBATH WANTS THE OAK VEIL.
DARK TIDES WILL BE HERE SOON, I CAN SEE IT IN THE CLOUDS. I HAVE FELT THIS BEFORE.
COME NOW RED... LET US GO.

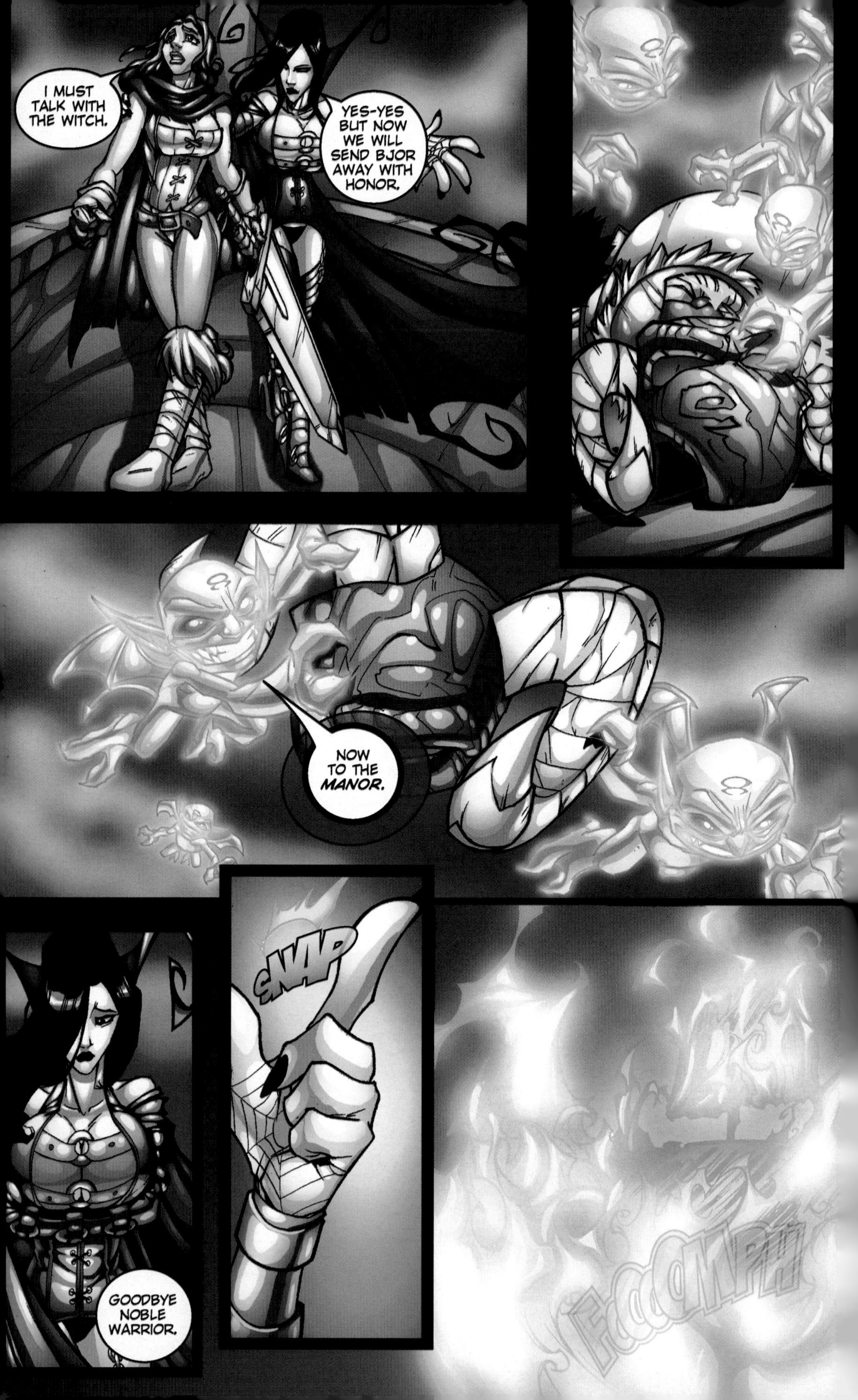
I MUST TALK WITH THE WITCH.
YES-YES BUT NOW WE WILL SEND BJOR AWAY WITH HONOR.
NOW TO THE MANOR.
GOODBYE NOBLE WARRIOR.
SNAP
FOOOMPH

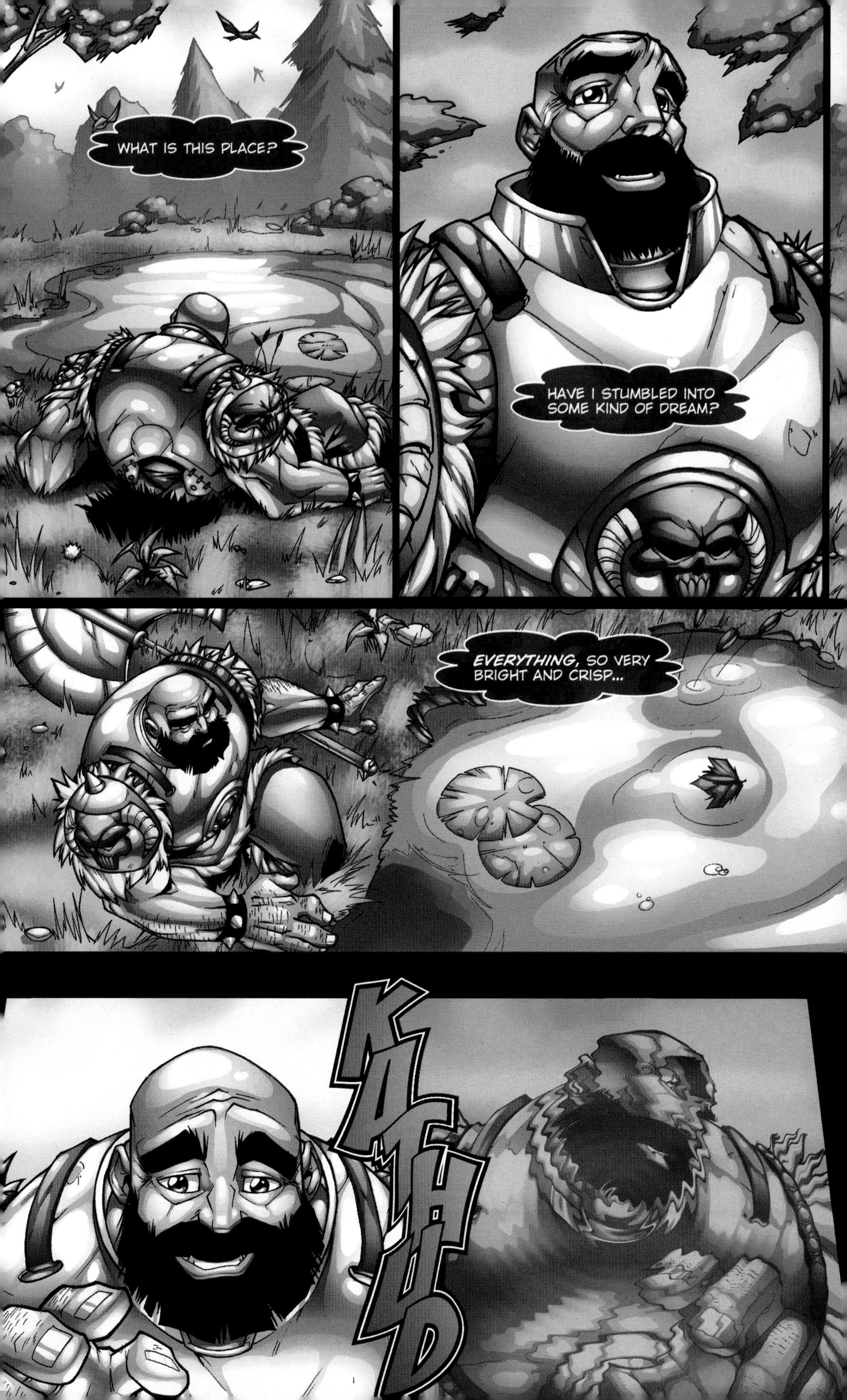
WHAT IS THIS PLACE?
HAVE I STUMBLED INTO SOME KIND OF DREAM?
EVERYTHING, SO VERY BRIGHT AND CRISP...
KUTHUD

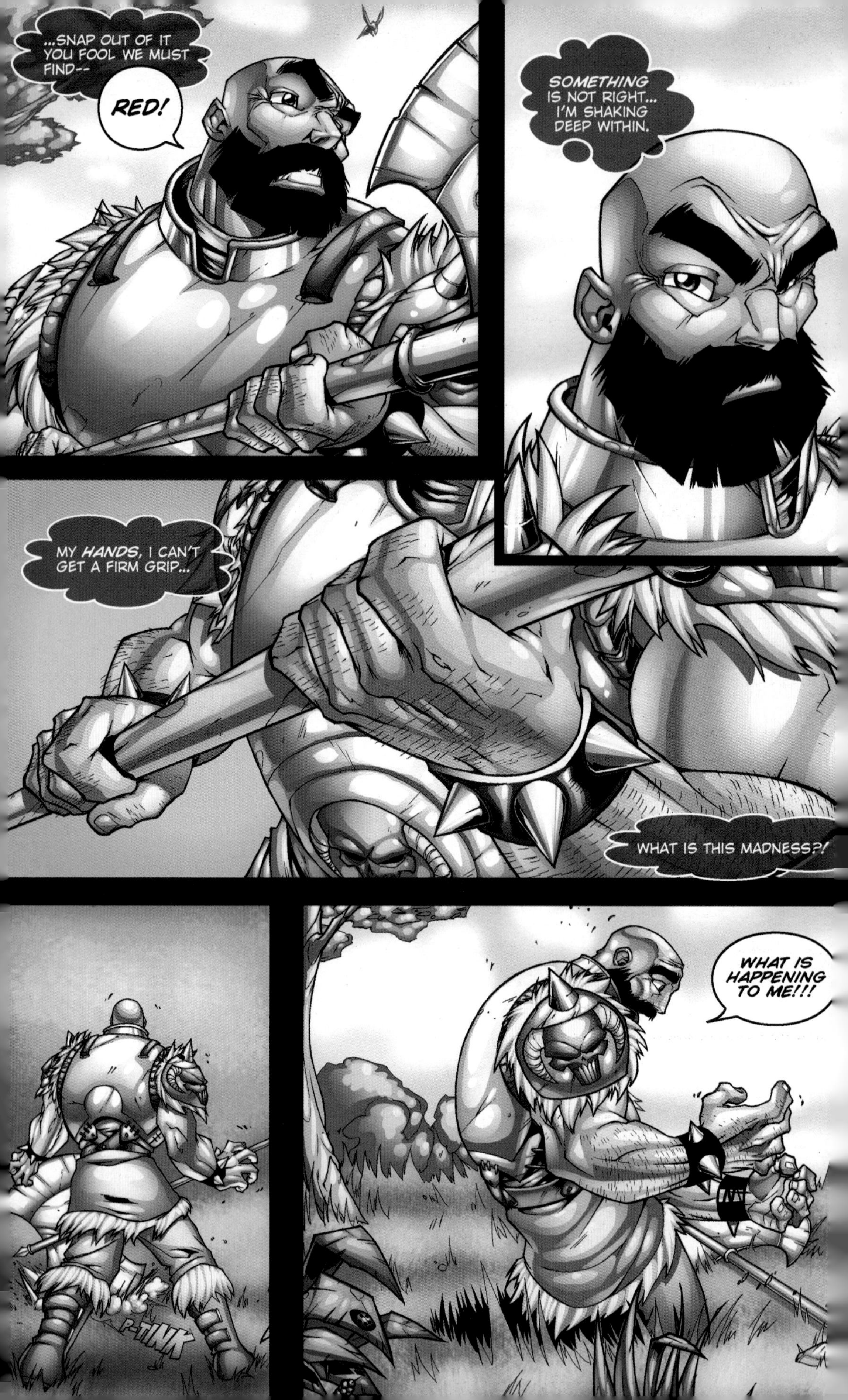
...SNAP OUT OF IT YOU FOOL WE MUST FIND--
RED!
SOMETHING IS NOT RIGHT... I'M SHAKING DEEP WITHIN.
MY HANDS, I CAN'T GET A FIRM GRIP...
WHAT IS THIS MADNESS?!
P-TINK
WHAT IS HAPPENING TO ME!!!

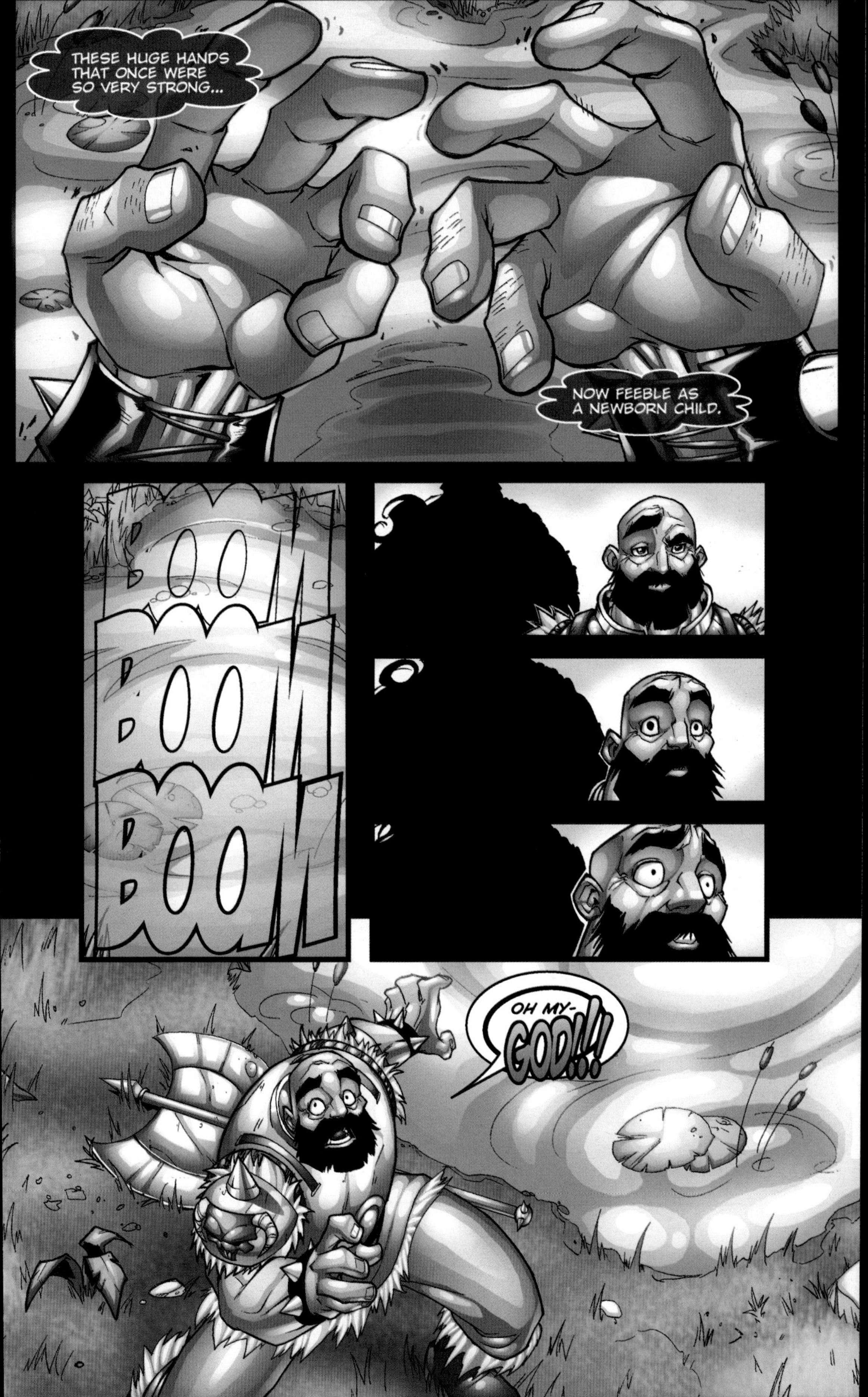
THESE HUGE HANDS THAT ONCE WERE SO VERY STRONG...
NOW FEEBLE AS A NEWBORN CHILD.
DOOM
DOOM
DOOM
OH MY-
GOD!!!

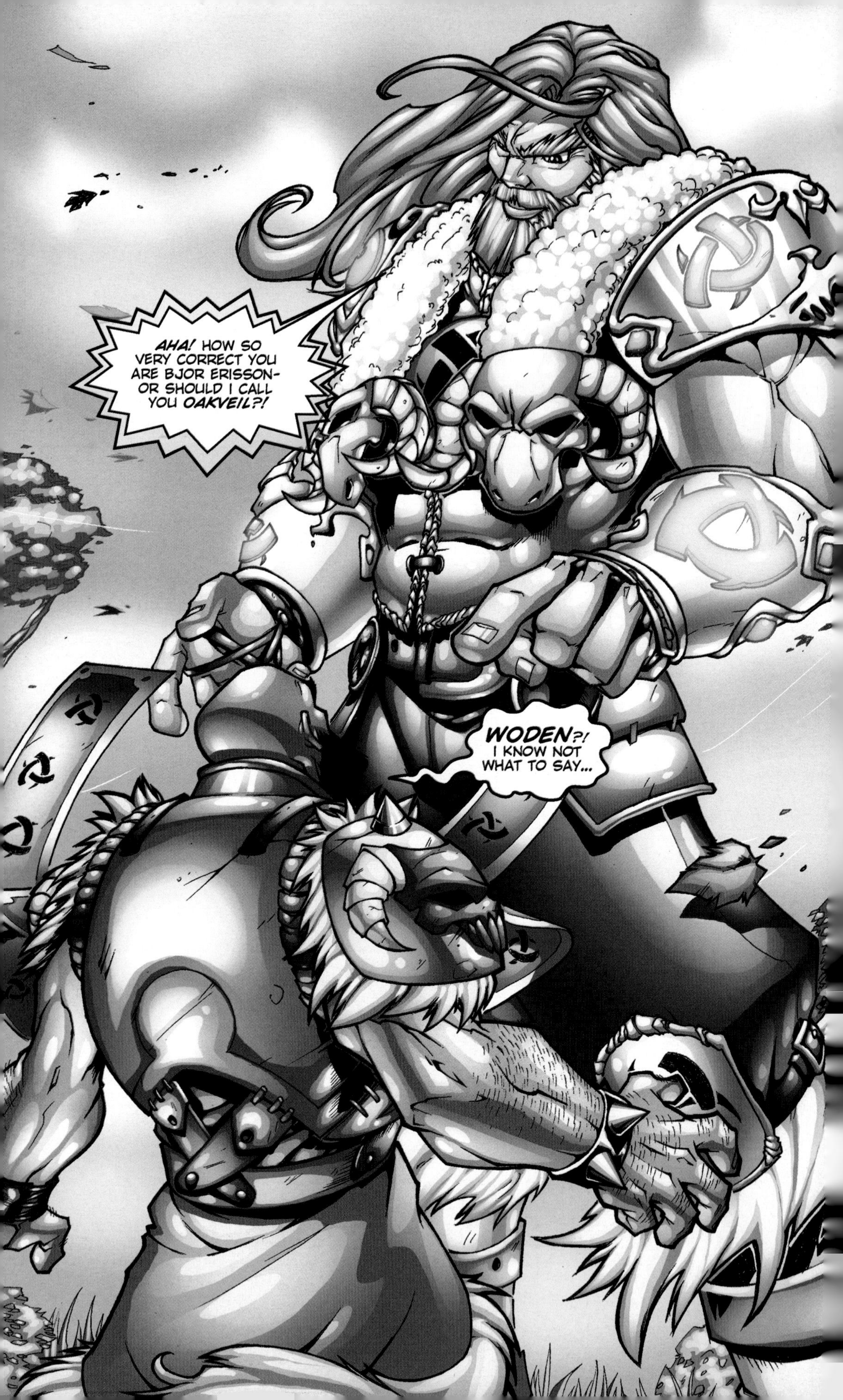
AHA! HOW SO VERY CORRECT YOU ARE BJOR ERISSON- OR SHOULD I CALL YOU OAKVEIL?!
WODEN?! I KNOW NOT WHAT TO SAY...

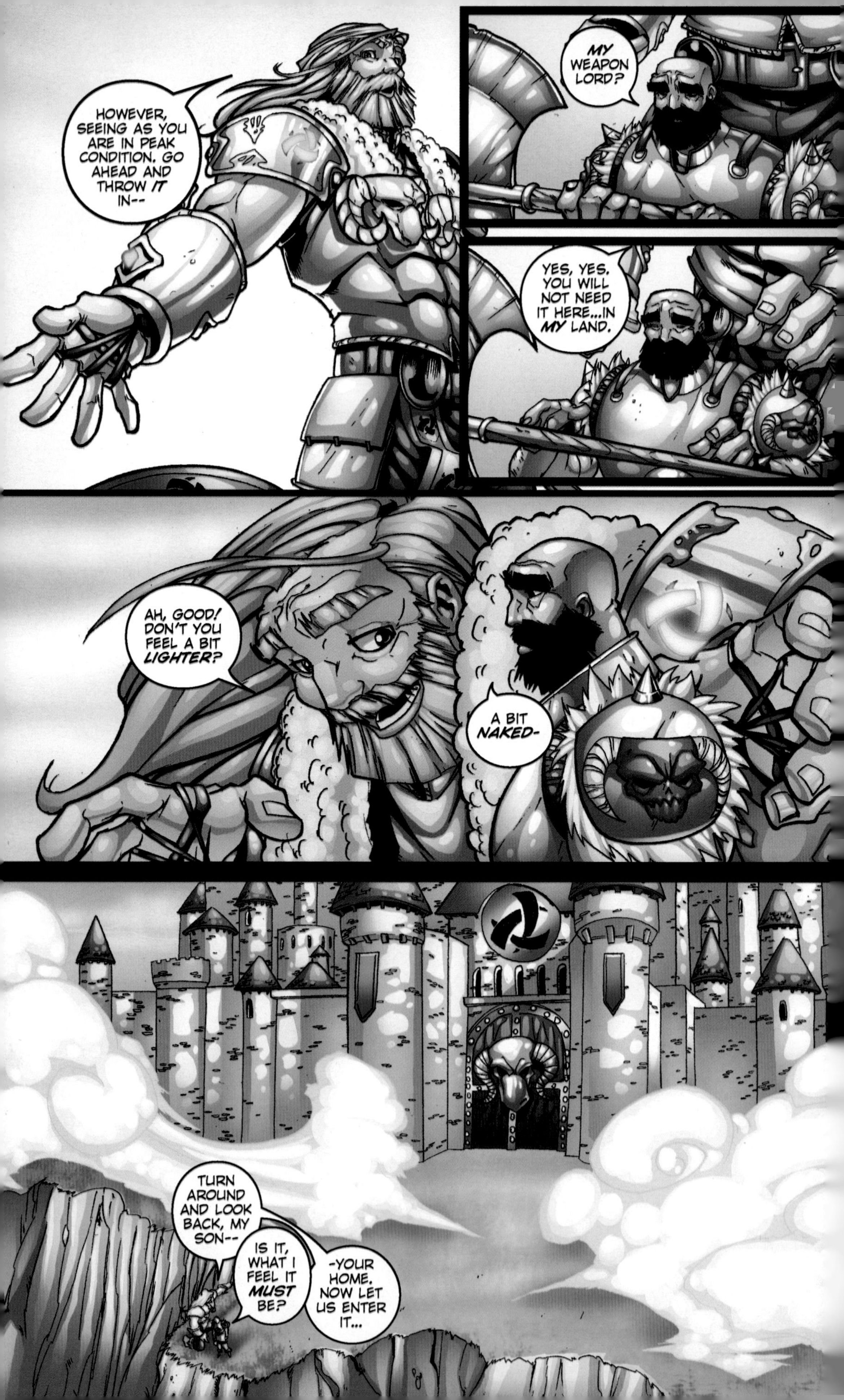
HOWEVER, SEEING AS YOU ARE IN PEAK CONDITION. GO AHEAD AND THROW *IT* IN--
MY WEAPON LORD?
YES, YES. YOU WILL NOT NEED IT HERE...IN *MY* LAND.
AH, GOOD! DON'T YOU FEEL A BIT *LIGHTER?*
A BIT *NAKED-*
TURN AROUND AND LOOK BACK, MY SON--
IS IT, WHAT I FEEL IT *MUST* BE?
-YOUR HOME. NOW LET US ENTER IT...

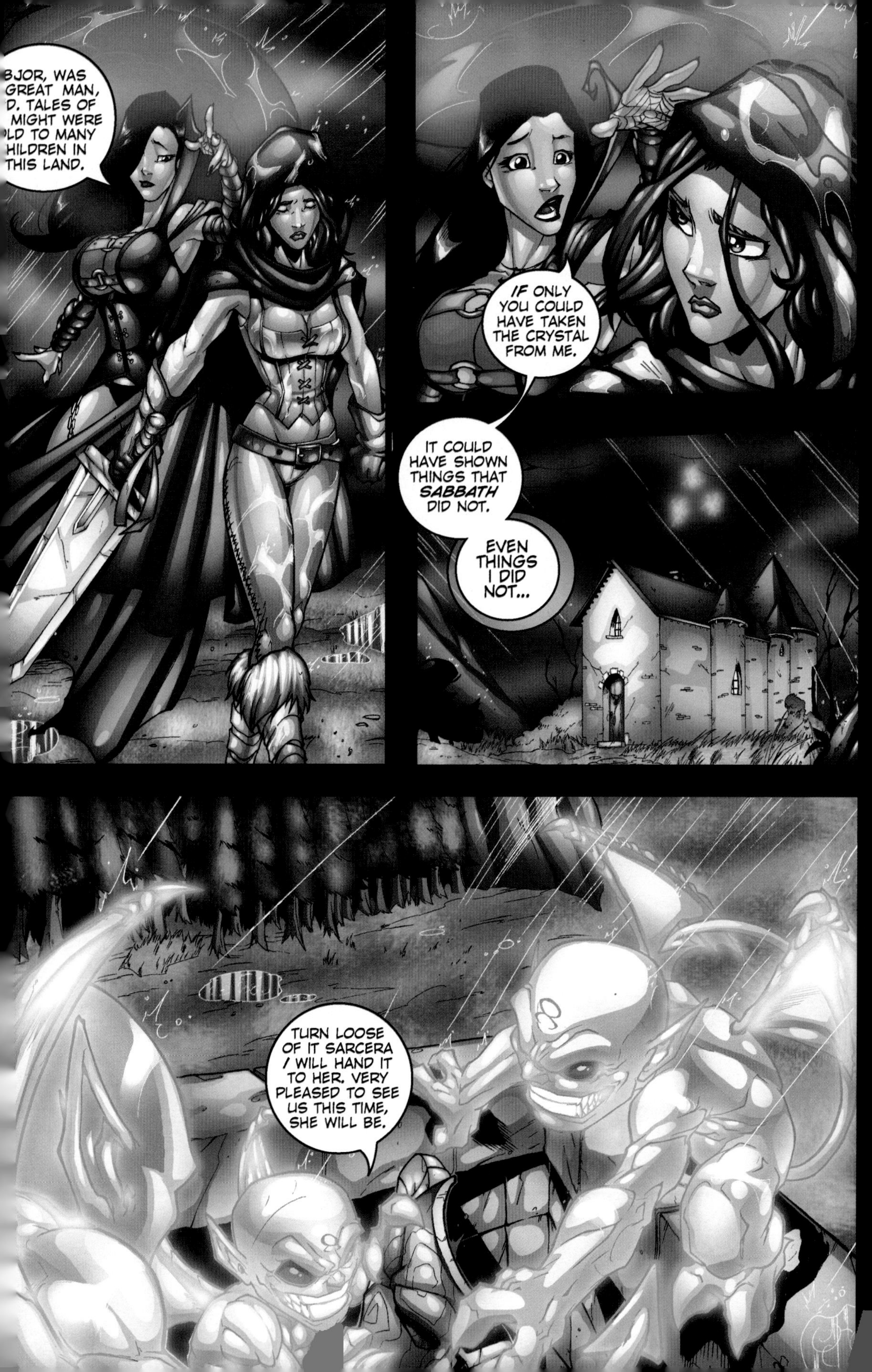

BJOR, WAS
GREAT MAN,
D. TALES OF
MIGHT WERE
LD TO MANY
HILDREN IN
THIS LAND.
IF ONLY YOU COULD HAVE TAKEN THE CRYSTAL FROM ME.
IT COULD HAVE SHOWN THINGS THAT SABBATH DID NOT.
EVEN THINGS I DID NOT...
TURN LOOSE OF IT SARCERA / WILL HAND IT TO HER. VERY PLEASED TO SEE US THIS TIME, SHE WILL BE.

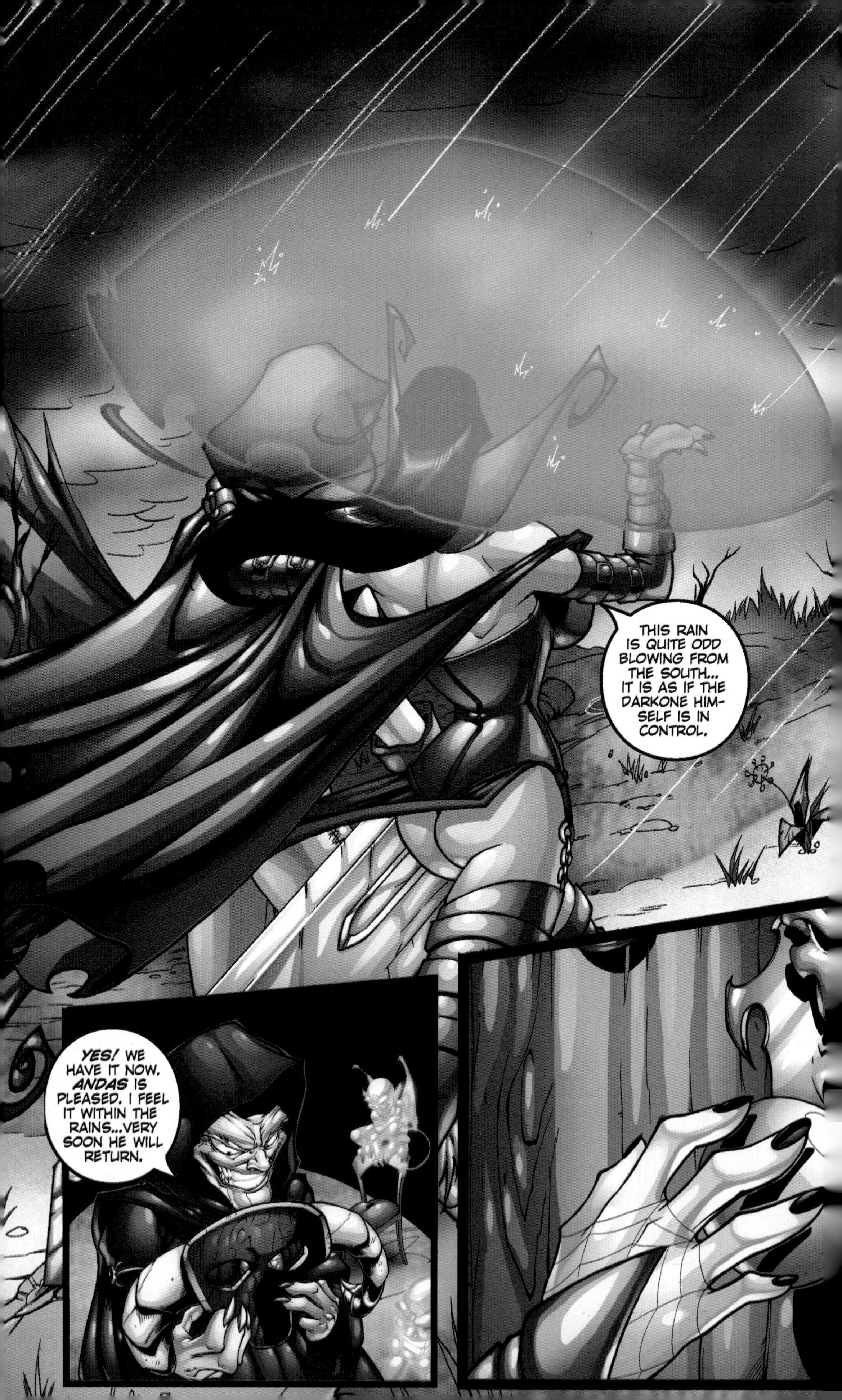
THIS RAIN IS QUITE ODD BLOWING FROM THE SOUTH... IT IS AS IF THE DARKONE HIM-SELF IS IN CONTROL.
YES! WE HAVE IT NOW. *ANDAS* IS PLEASED. I FEEL IT WITHIN THE RAINS...VERY SOON HE WILL RETURN.

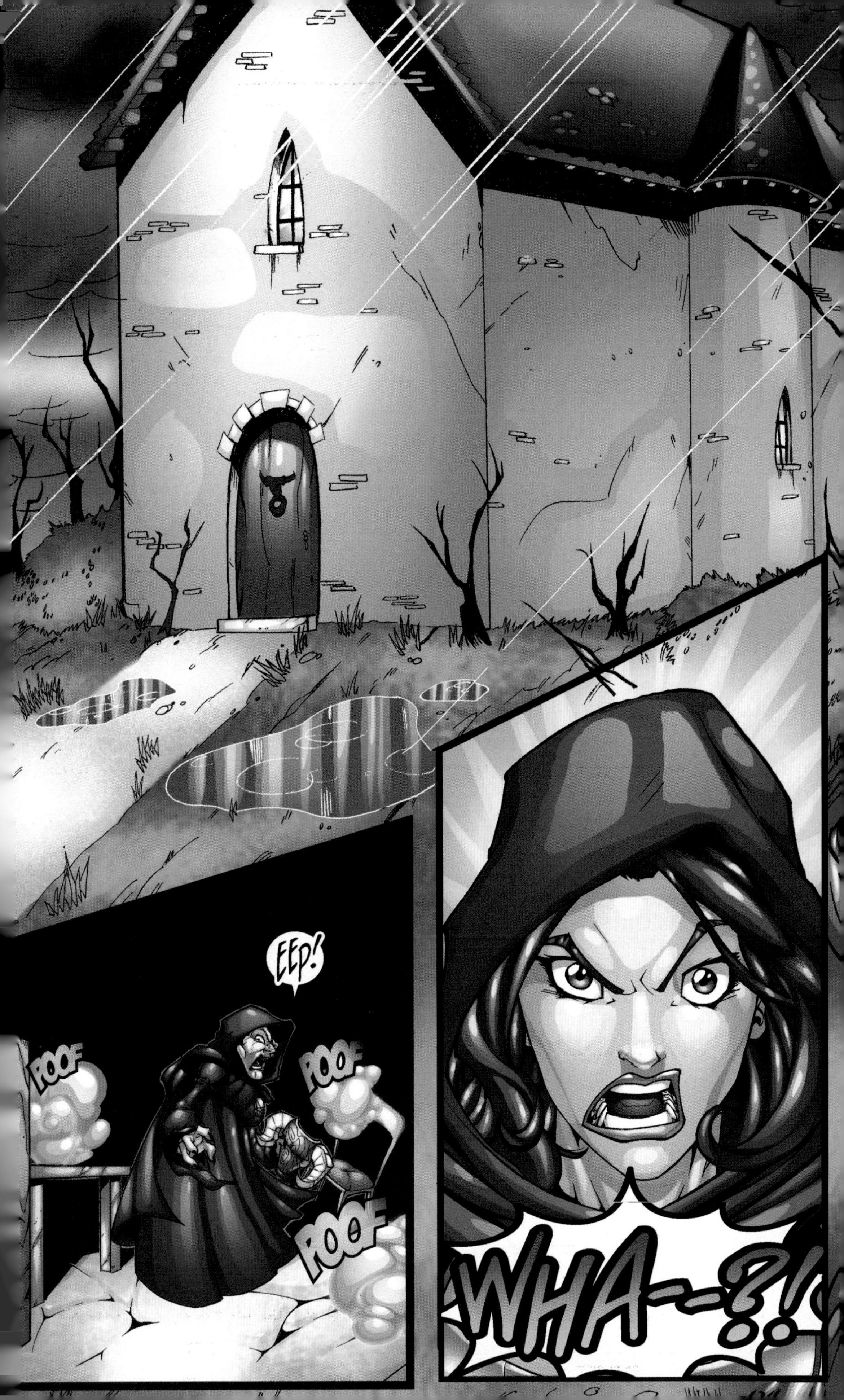
EEP!
POOF
POOF
POOF
WHA--?!

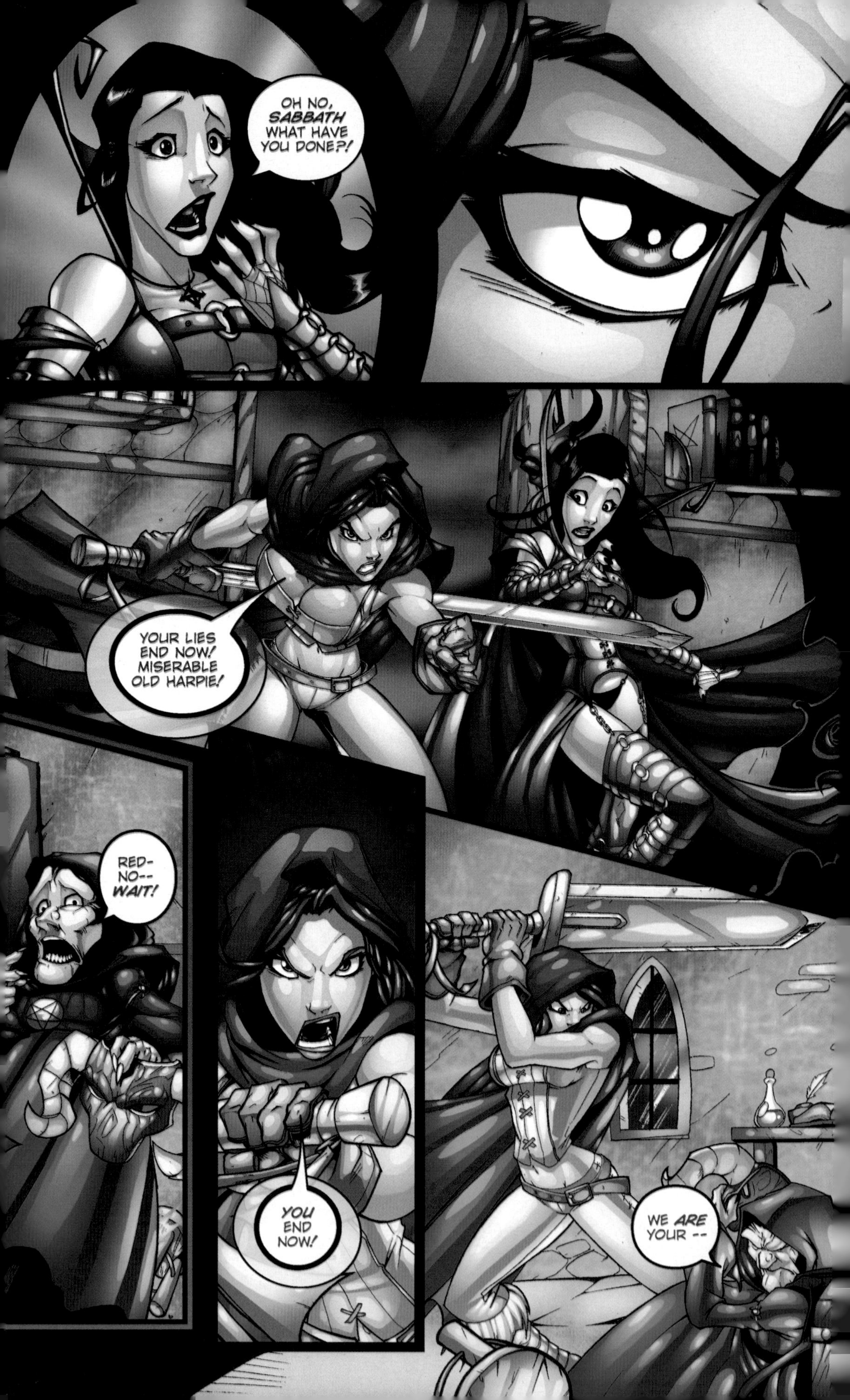
OH NO, SABBATH WHAT HAVE YOU DONE?!
YOUR LIES END NOW! MISERABLE OLD HARPIE!
RED- NO-- WAIT!
YOU END NOW!
WE ARE YOUR --

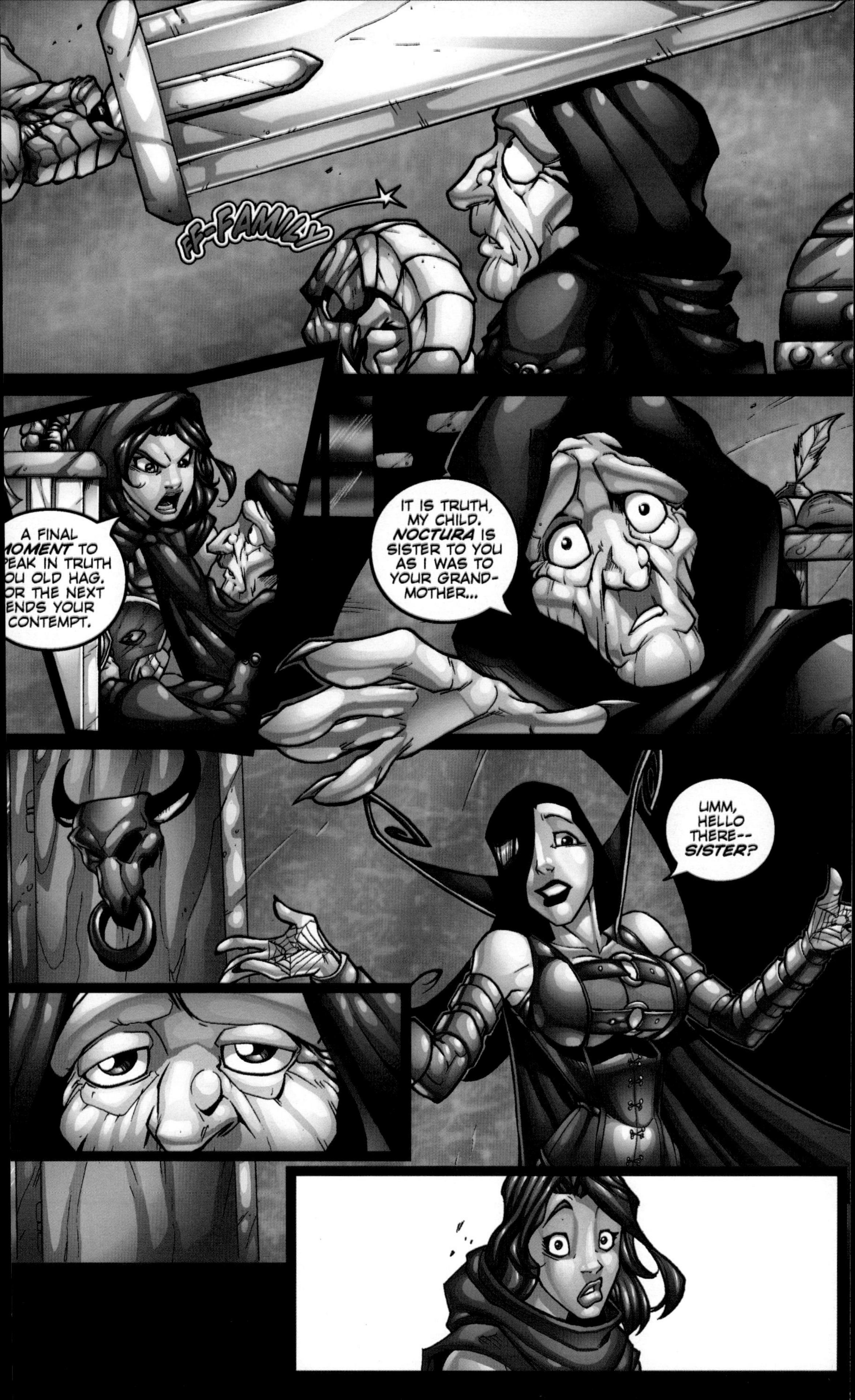

FF-FAMILY
A FINAL MOMENT TO PEAK IN TRUTH OU OLD HAG. OR THE NEXT ENDS YOUR CONTEMPT.
IT IS TRUTH, MY CHILD. NOCTURA IS SISTER TO YOU AS I WAS TO YOUR GRAND-MOTHER...
UMM, HELLO THERE-- SISTER?

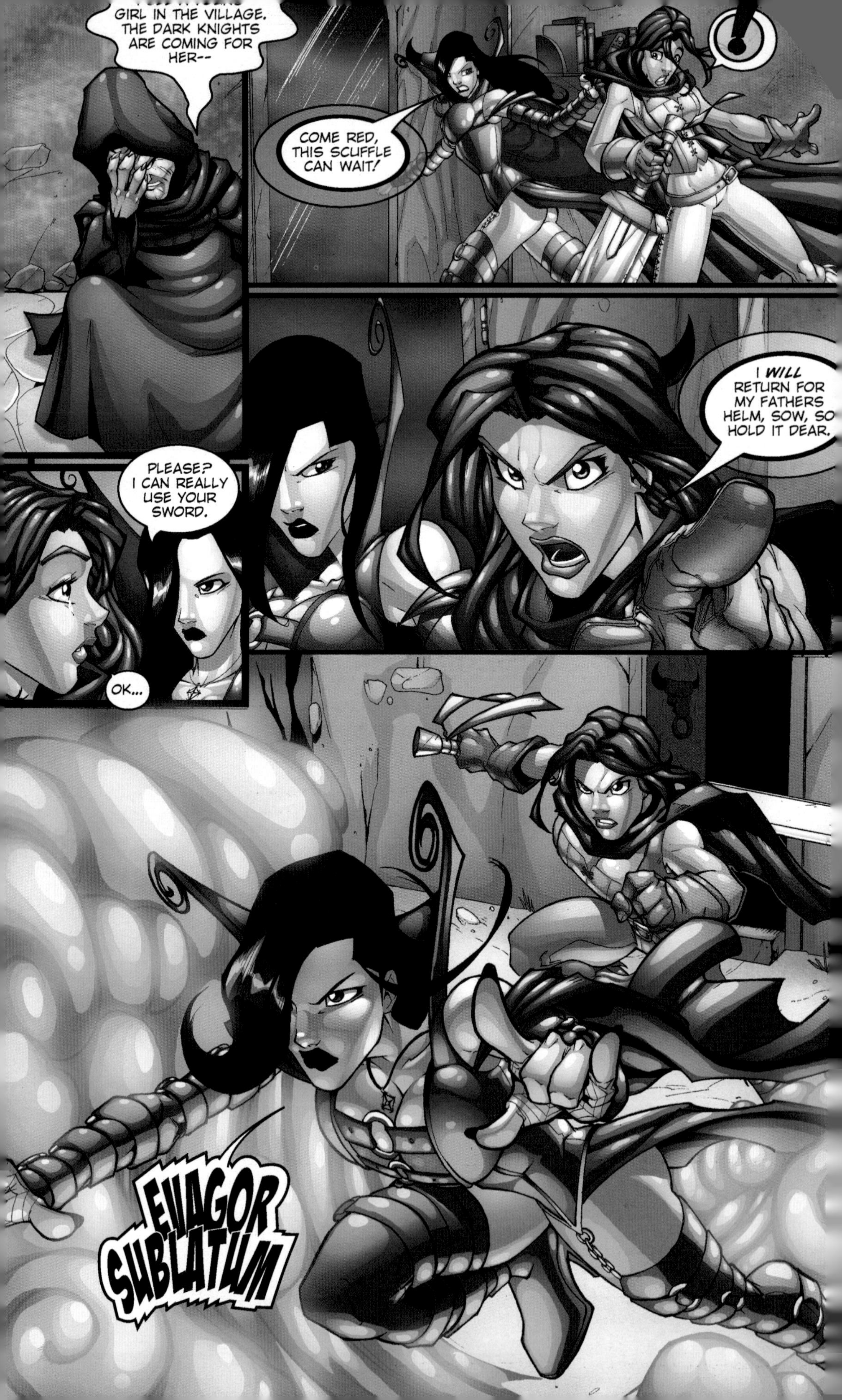

GIRL IN THE VILLAGE. THE DARK KNIGHTS ARE COMING FOR HER--
COME RED, THIS SCUFFLE CAN WAIT!
!
I WILL RETURN FOR MY FATHERS HELM, SOW, SO HOLD IT DEAR.
PLEASE? I CAN REALLY USE YOUR SWORD.
OK...
EVAGOR SUBLATUM

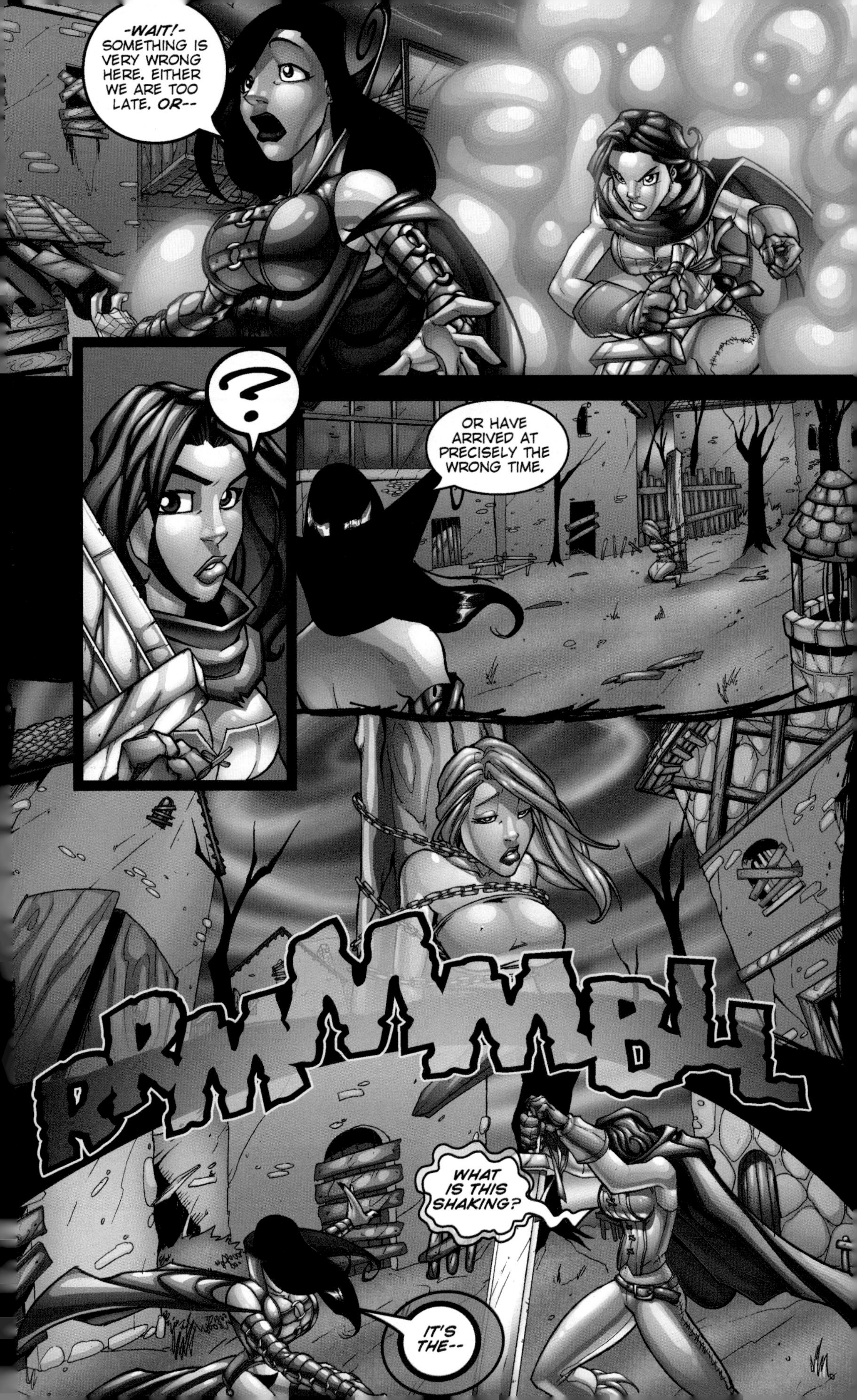
-WAIT!- SOMETHING IS VERY WRONG HERE. EITHER WE ARE TOO LATE. OR--
?
OR HAVE ARRIVED AT PRECISELY THE WRONG TIME.
RRMMMBLL
WHAT IS THIS SHAKING?
IT'S THE--

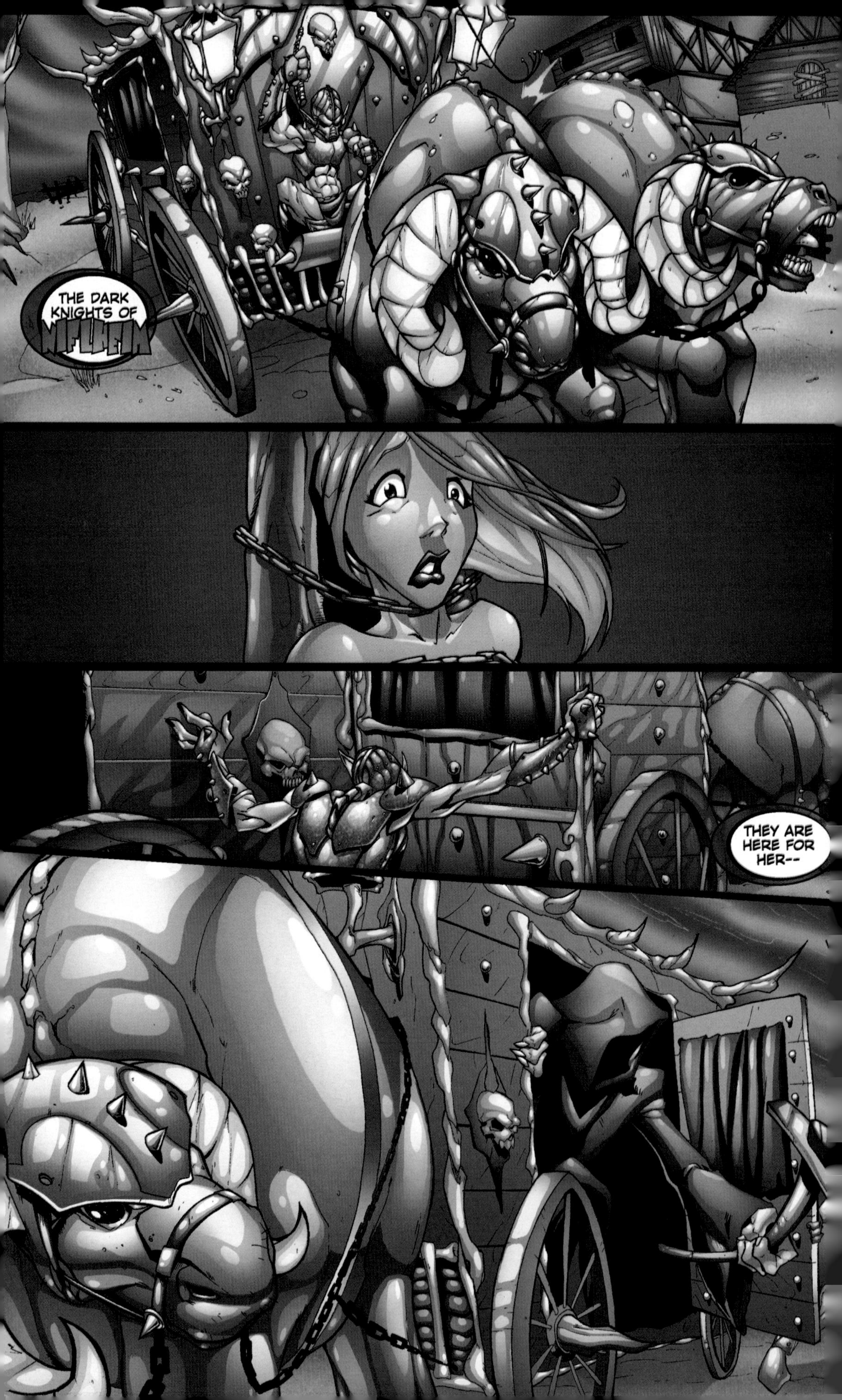
THE DARK KNIGHTS OF
NIFLHEIM
THEY ARE HERE FOR HER--

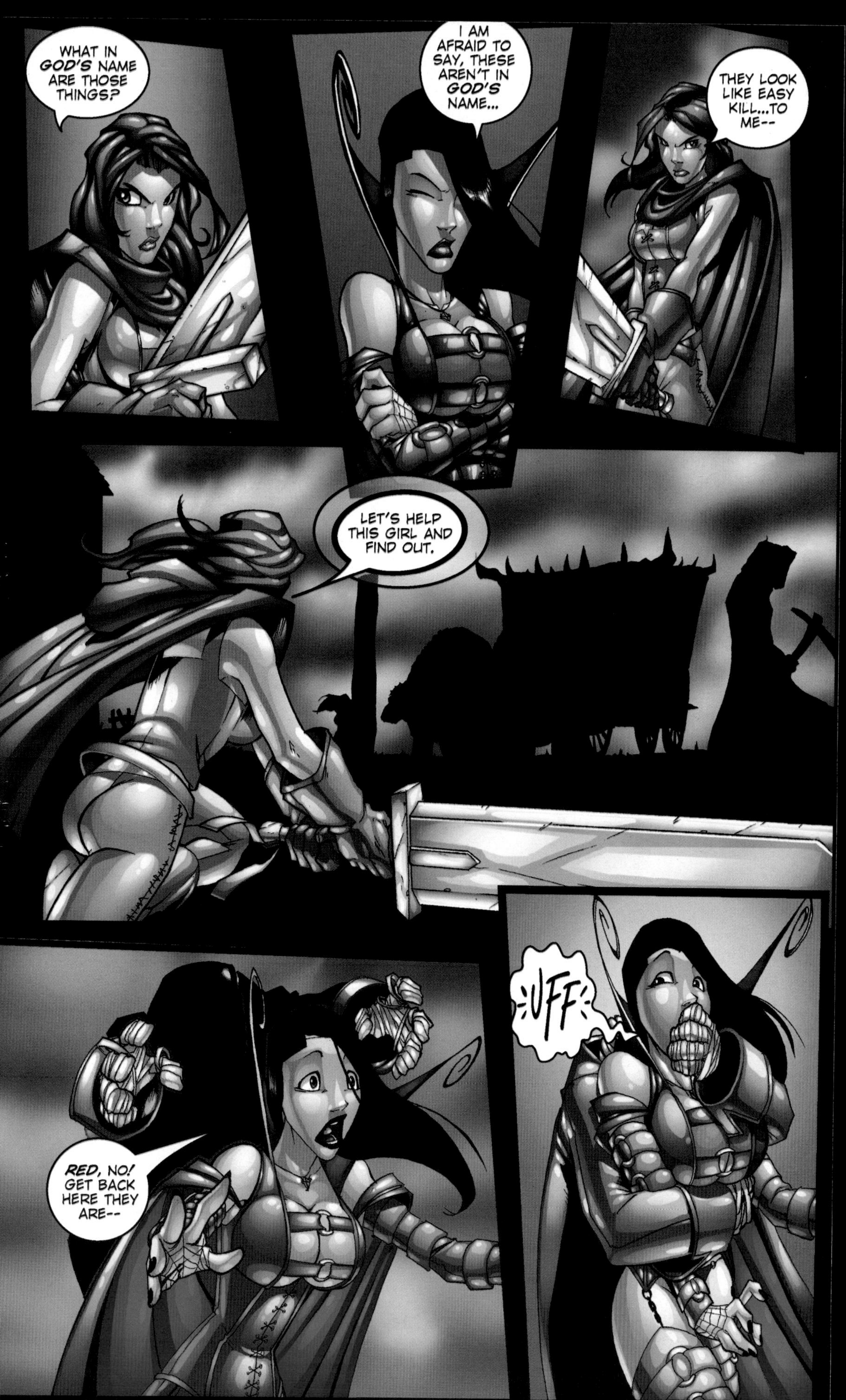
WHAT IN GOD'S NAME ARE THOSE THINGS?
I AM AFRAID TO SAY, THESE AREN'T IN GOD'S NAME...
THEY LOOK LIKE EASY KILL...TO ME--
LET'S HELP THIS GIRL AND FIND OUT.
RED, NO! GET BACK HERE THEY ARE--
UFF

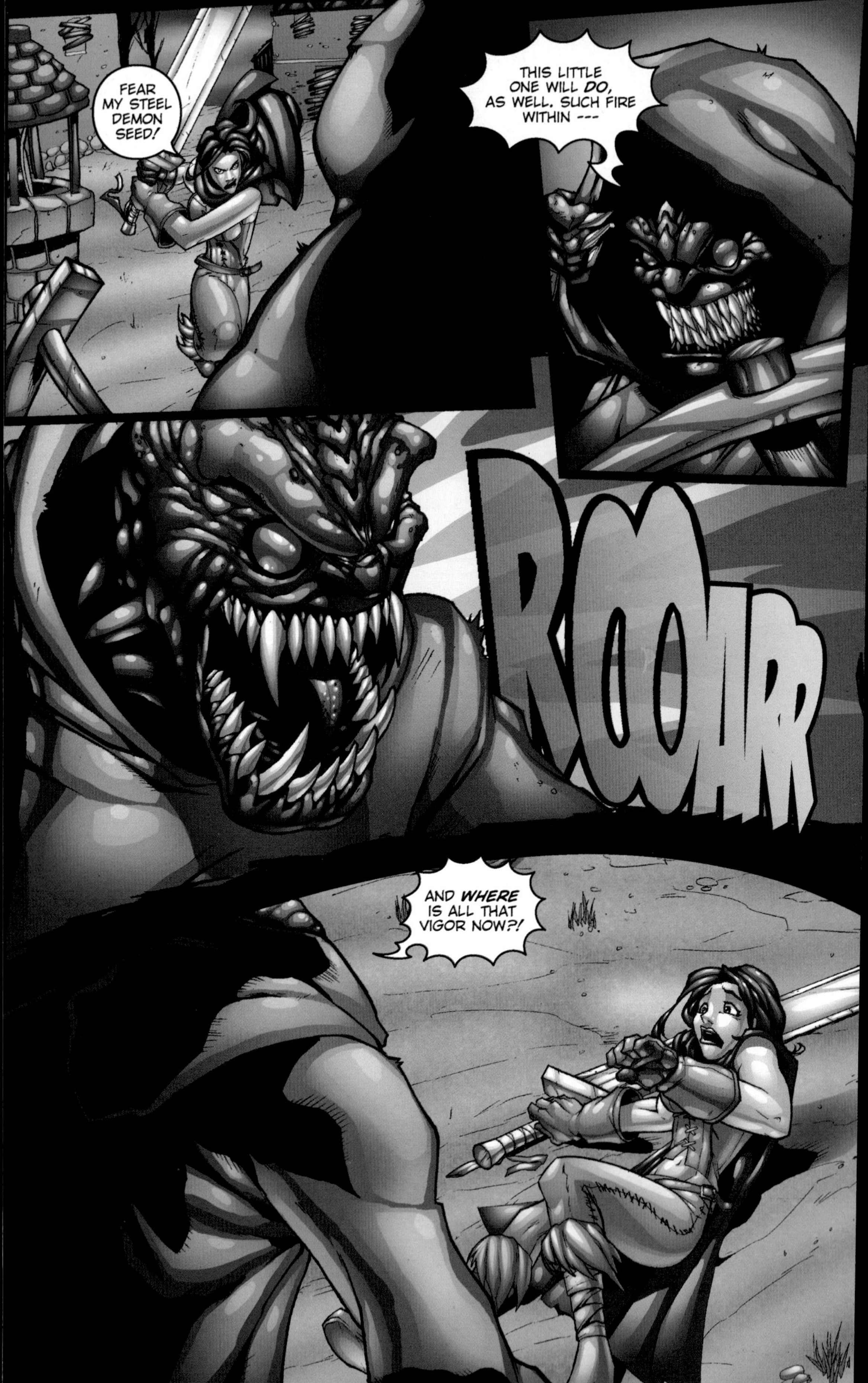
FEAR MY STEEL DEMON SEED!
THIS LITTLE ONE WILL DO, AS WELL. SUCH FIRE WITHIN ---
ROOAHRR
AND WHERE IS ALL THAT VIGOR NOW?!

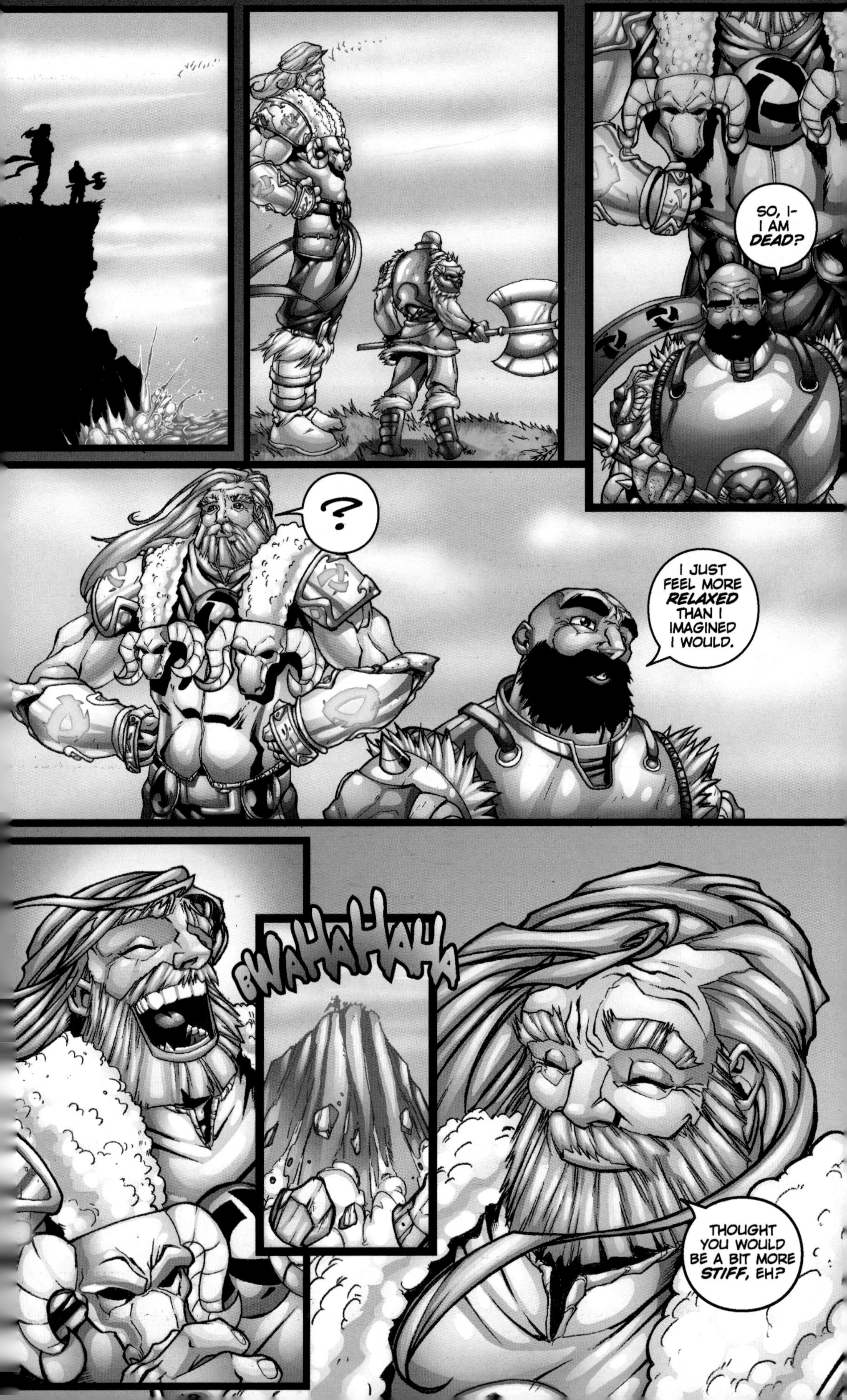
SO, I-
I AM DEAD?
?
I JUST FEEL MORE RELAXED THAN I IMAGINED I WOULD.
BWAHAHAHAHA
THOUGHT YOU WOULD BE A BIT MORE STIFF, EH?

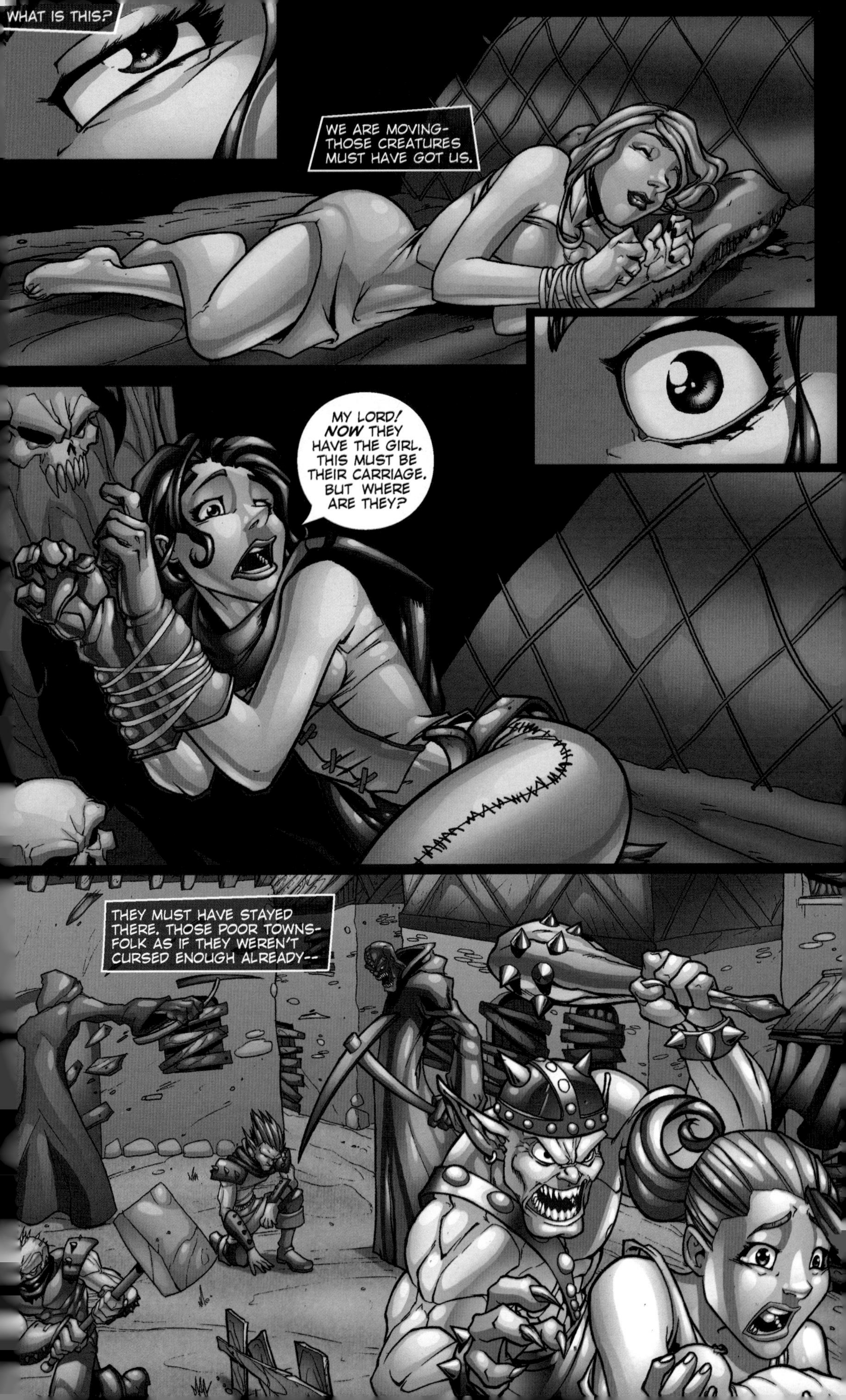

WHAT IS THIS?
WE ARE MOVING- THOSE CREATURES MUST HAVE GOT US.
MY LORD! NOW THEY HAVE THE GIRL. THIS MUST BE THEIR CARRIAGE. BUT WHERE ARE THEY?
THEY MUST HAVE STAYED THERE. THOSE POOR TOWNS-FOLK AS IF THEY WEREN'T CURSED ENOUGH ALREADY--

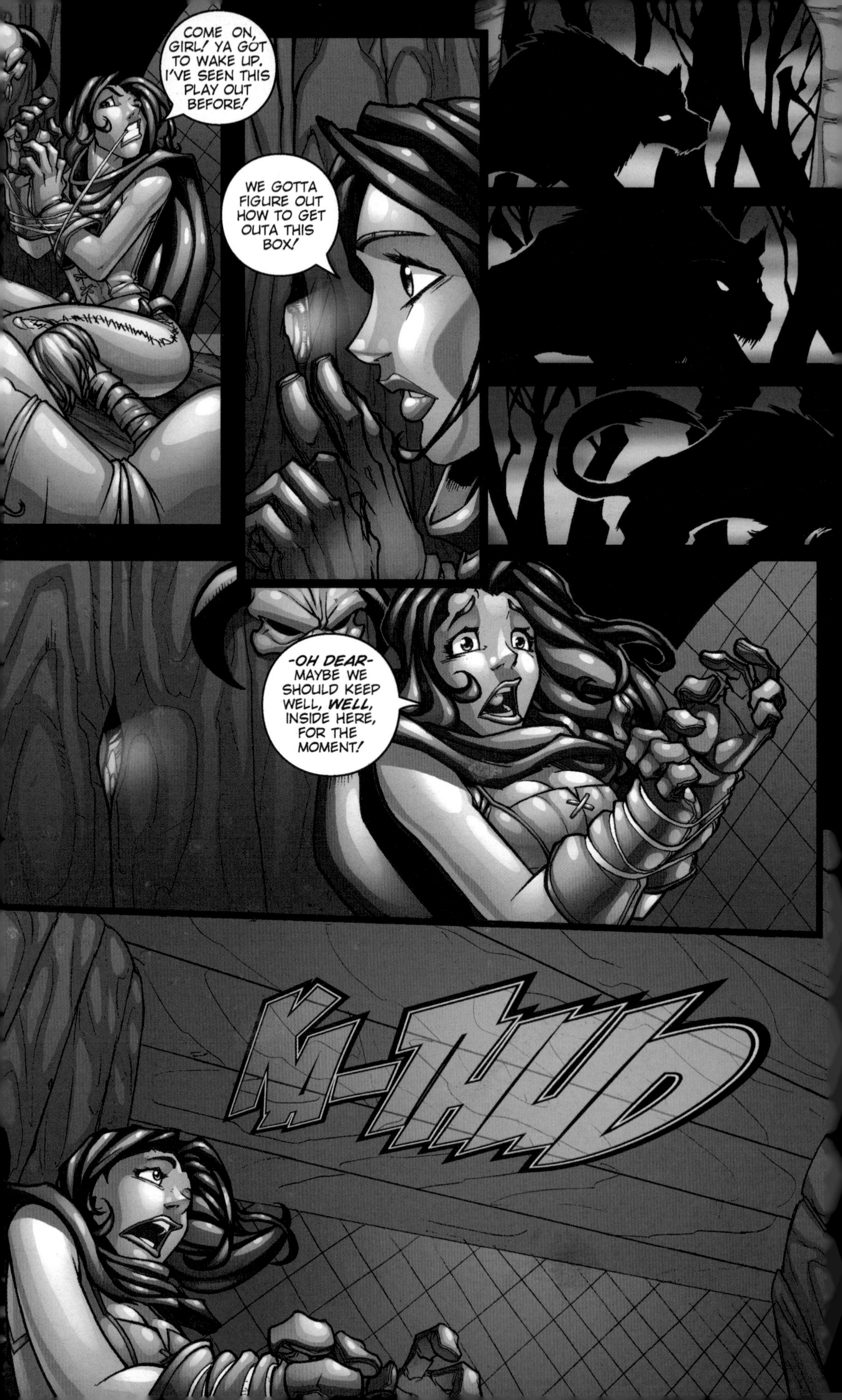
COME ON, GIRL! YA GOT TO WAKE UP. I'VE SEEN THIS PLAY OUT BEFORE!
WE GOTTA FIGURE OUT HOW TO GET OUTA THIS BOX!
-OH DEAR- MAYBE WE SHOULD KEEP WELL, WELL, INSIDE HERE, FOR THE MOMENT!
K-THUD

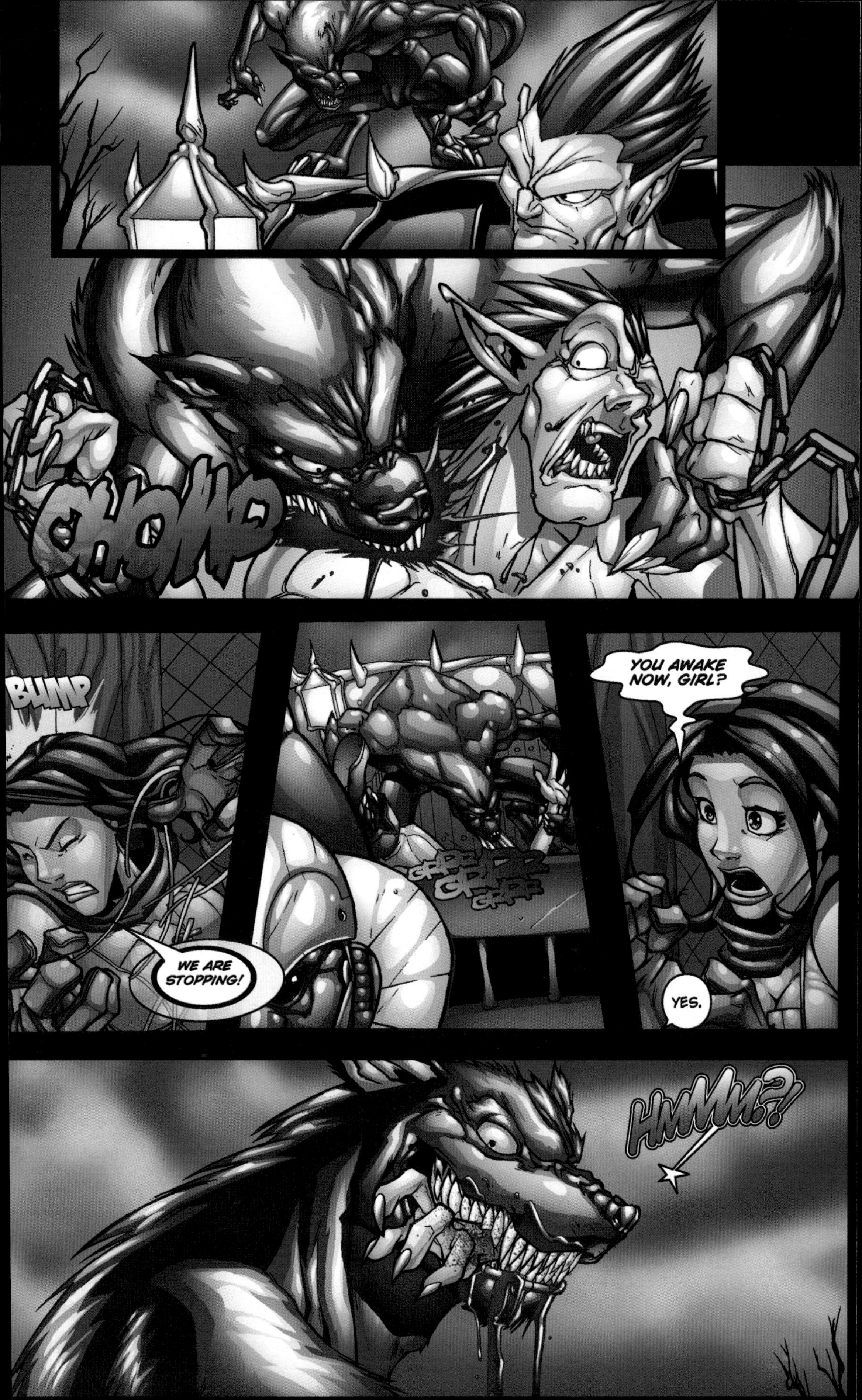
CHOMP
BUMP
WE ARE STOPPING!
YOU AWAKE NOW, GIRL?
YES.
HMMM?!

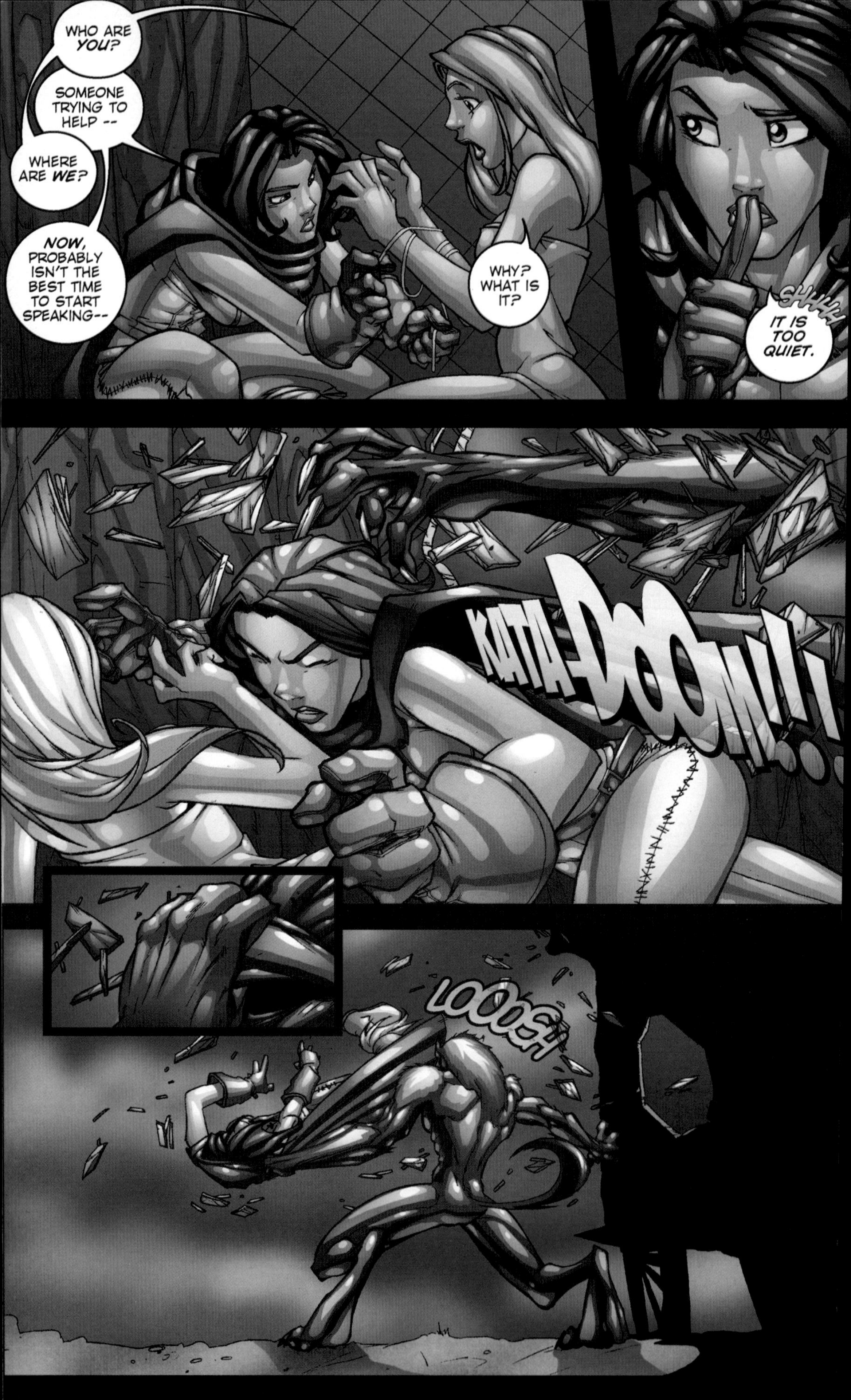
WHO ARE *YOU*?
SOMEONE TRYING TO HELP --
WHERE ARE *WE*?
NOW, PROBABLY ISN'T THE BEST TIME TO START SPEAKING--
WHY? WHAT IS IT?
SHHH
IT IS TOO QUIET.
KATA-DOOM!!!...
LOOOSH

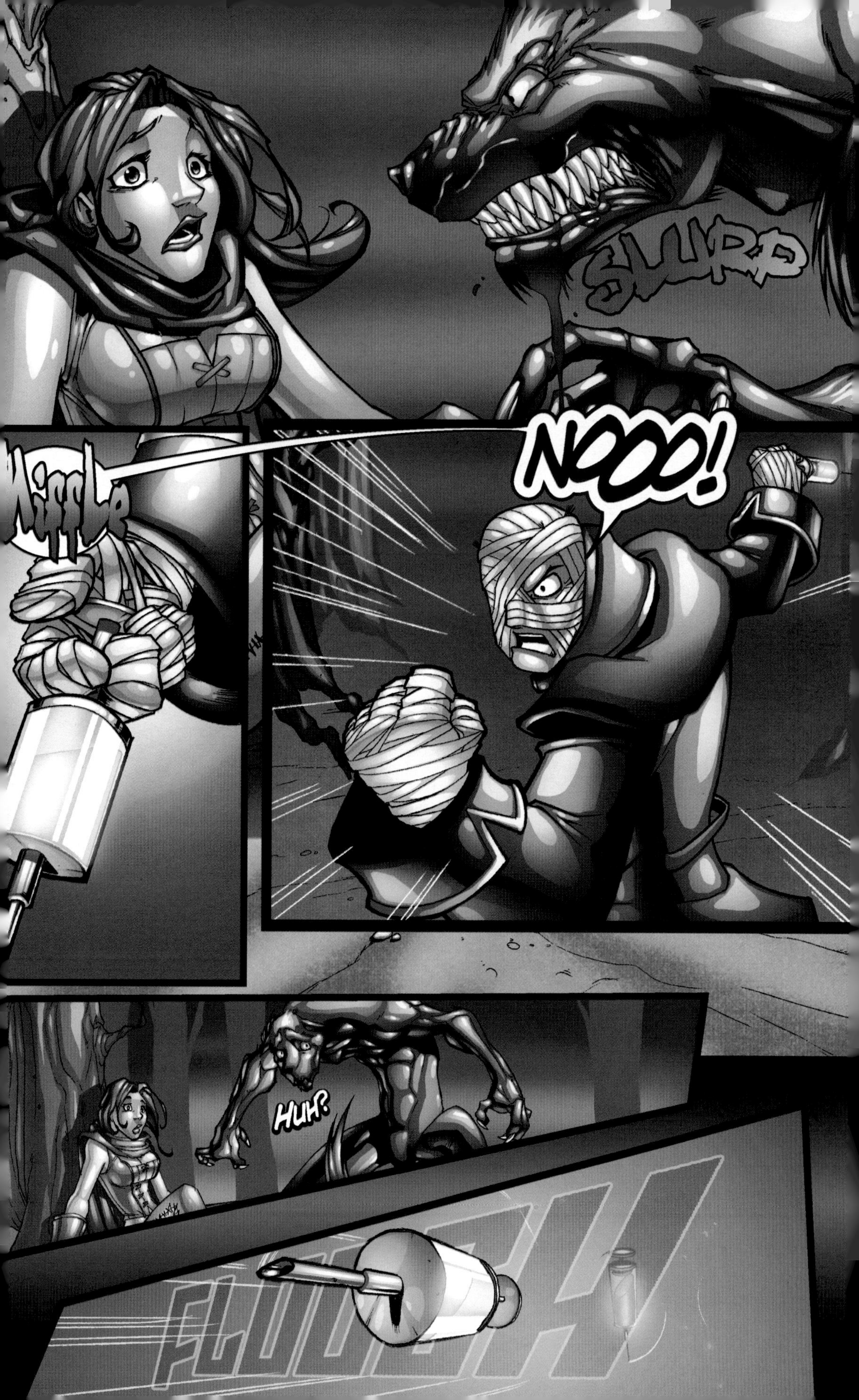
SLURP
NOOO!
HUH?

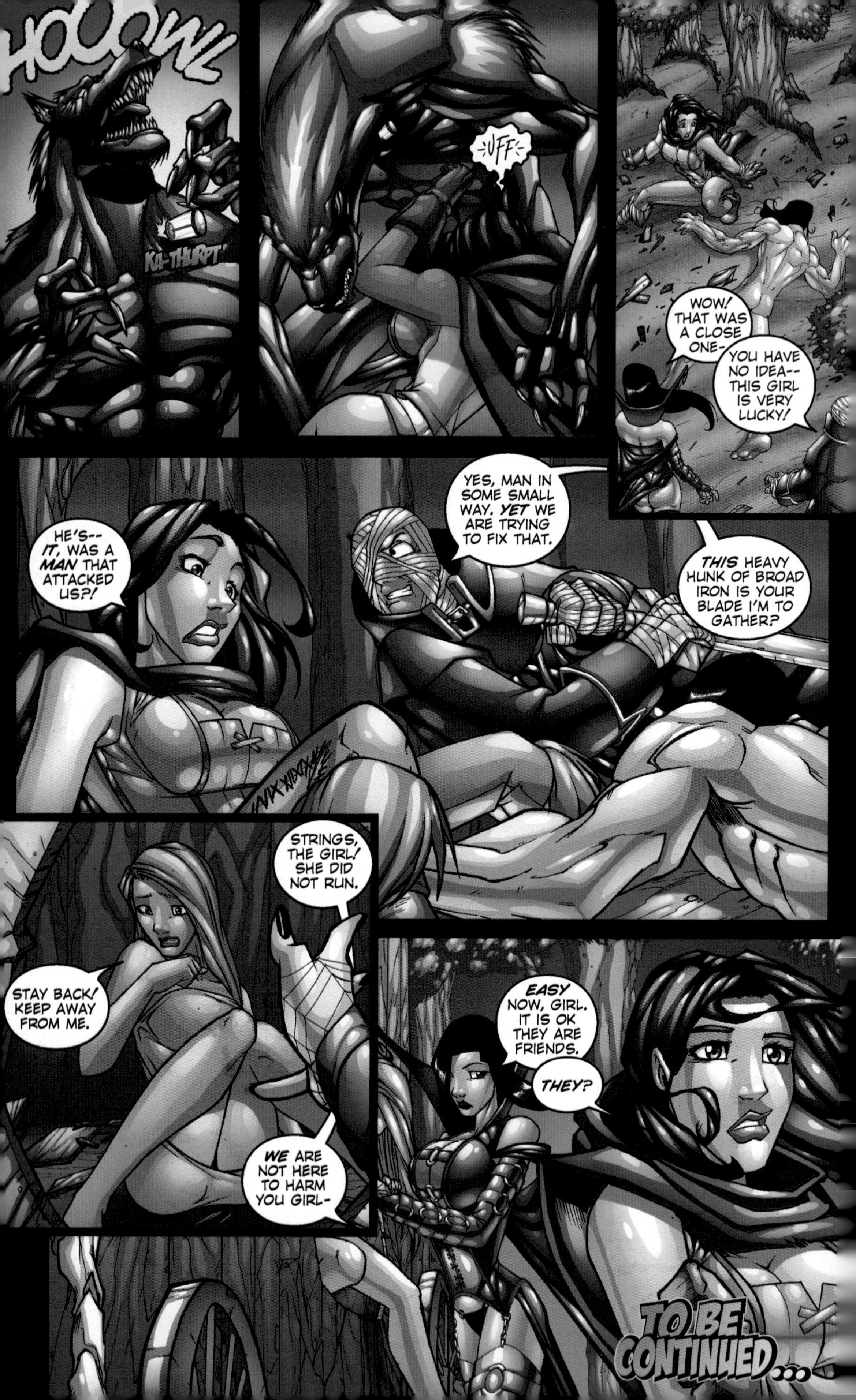
HOOOWL
KA-THURPT
UFF
WOW! THAT WAS A CLOSE ONE-
YOU HAVE NO IDEA-- THIS GIRL IS VERY LUCKY!
HE'S-- IT, WAS A MAN THAT ATTACKED US?!
YES, MAN IN SOME SMALL WAY. YET WE ARE TRYING TO FIX THAT.
THIS HEAVY HUNK OF BROAD IRON IS YOUR BLADE I'M TO GATHER?
STRINGS, THE GIRL! SHE DID NOT RUN.
STAY BACK! KEEP AWAY FROM ME.
WE ARE NOT HERE TO HARM YOU GIRL-
EASY NOW, GIRL. IT IS OK THEY ARE FRIENDS.
THEY?
TO BE CONTINUED...

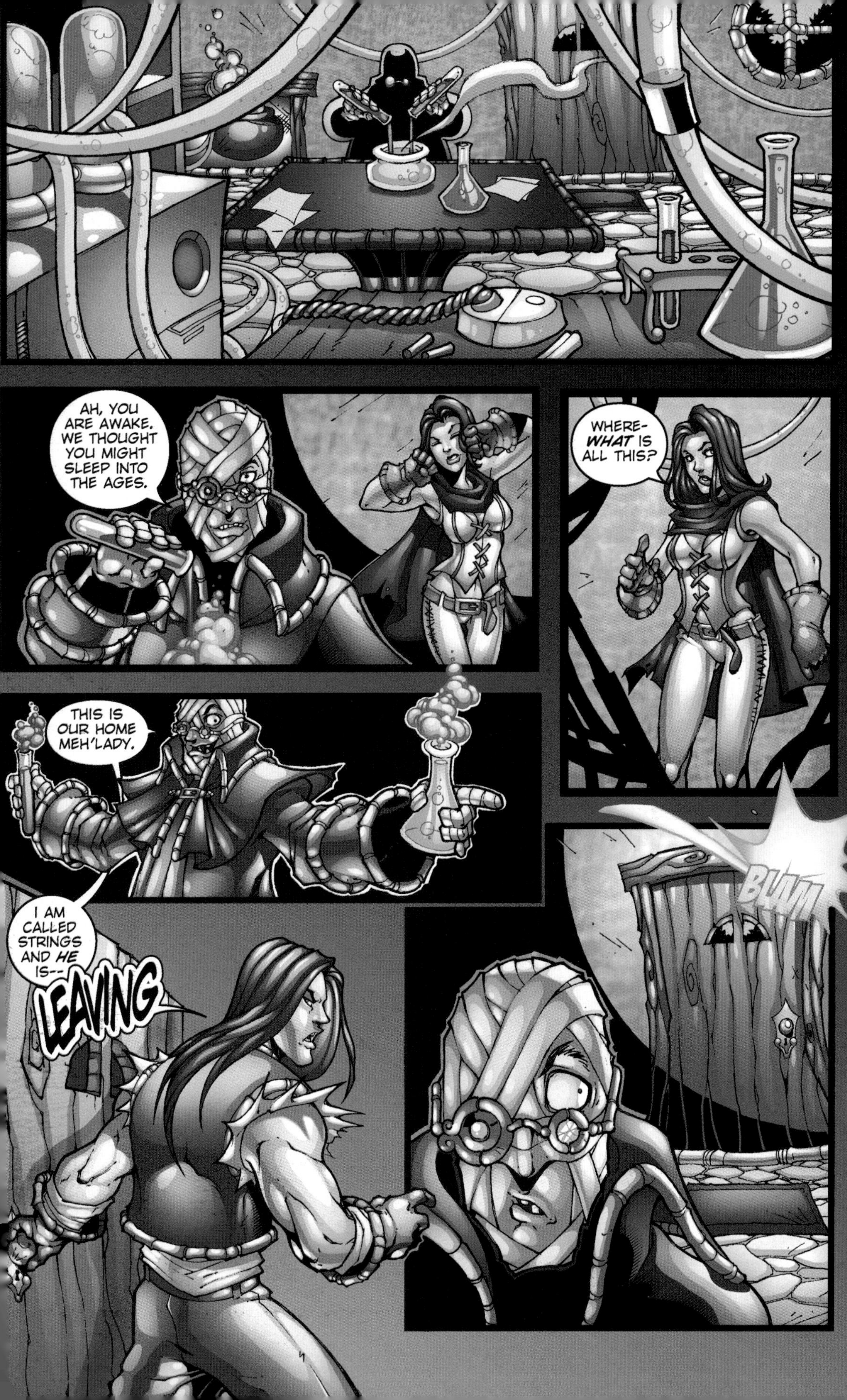
AH, YOU ARE AWAKE. WE THOUGHT YOU MIGHT SLEEP INTO THE AGES.
WHERE-*WHAT* IS ALL THIS?
THIS IS OUR HOME MEH'LADY.
I AM CALLED STRINGS AND *HE* IS--
LEAVING
BLAM

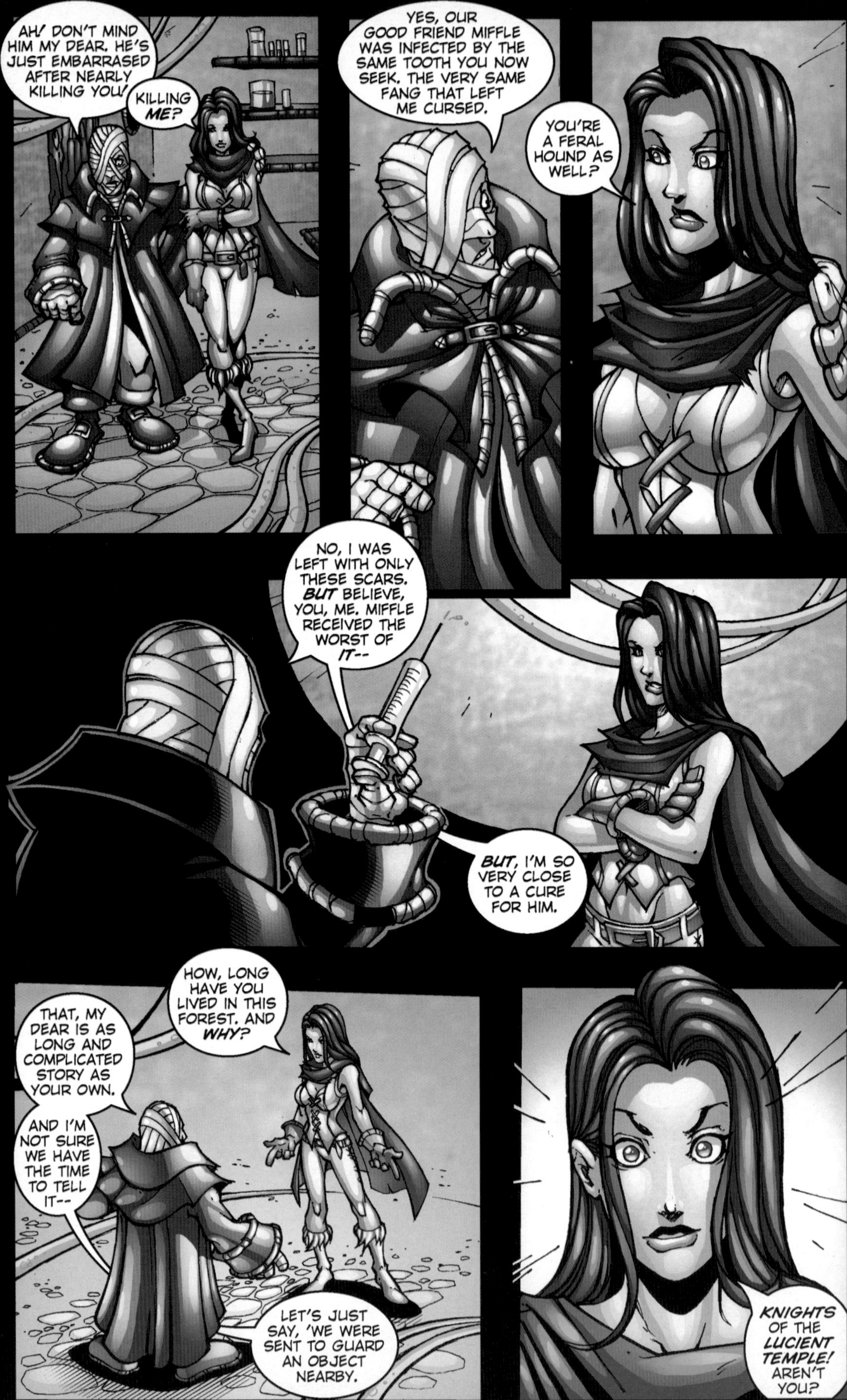
AH! DON'T MIND HIM MY DEAR. HE'S JUST EMBARRASED AFTER NEARLY KILLING YOU!
KILLING *ME*?
YES, OUR GOOD FRIEND MIFFLE WAS INFECTED BY THE SAME TOOTH YOU NOW SEEK. THE VERY SAME FANG THAT LEFT ME CURSED.
YOU'RE A FERAL HOUND AS WELL?
NO, I WAS LEFT WITH ONLY THESE SCARS. *BUT* BELIEVE, YOU, ME. MIFFLE RECEIVED THE WORST OF *IT*--
BUT, I'M SO VERY CLOSE TO A CURE FOR HIM.
HOW, LONG HAVE YOU LIVED IN THIS FOREST. AND *WHY*?
THAT, MY DEAR IS AS LONG AND COMPLICATED STORY AS YOUR OWN.
AND I'M NOT SURE WE HAVE THE TIME TO TELL IT--
LET'S JUST SAY, 'WE WERE SENT TO GUARD AN OBJECT NEARBY.
KNIGHTS OF THE *LUCIENT TEMPLE!* AREN'T YOU?

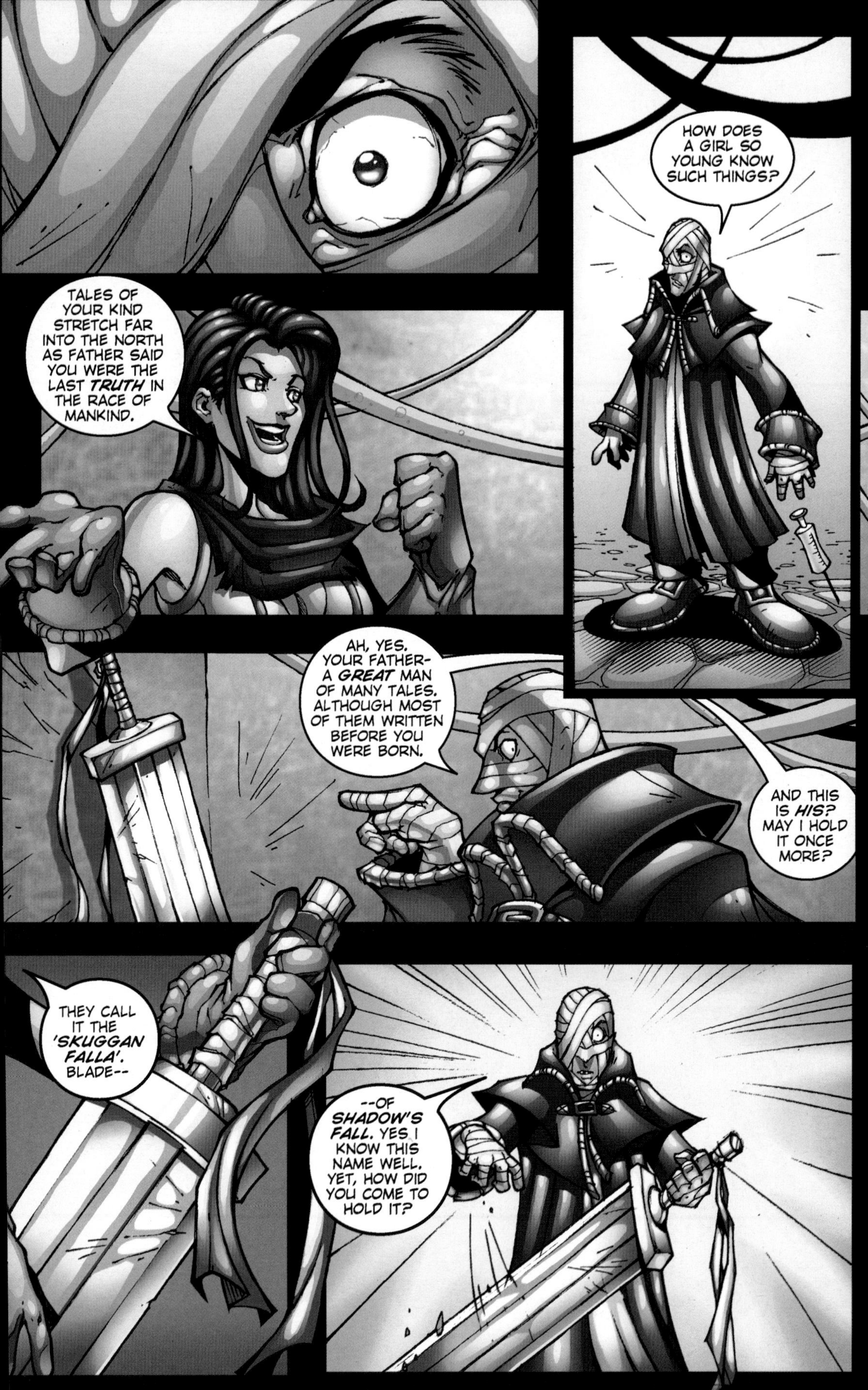
HOW DOES A GIRL SO YOUNG KNOW SUCH THINGS?
TALES OF YOUR KIND STRETCH FAR INTO THE NORTH AS FATHER SAID YOU WERE THE LAST TRUTH IN THE RACE OF MANKIND.
AH, YES. YOUR FATHER- A GREAT MAN OF MANY TALES. ALTHOUGH MOST OF THEM WRITTEN BEFORE YOU WERE BORN.
AND THIS IS HIS? MAY I HOLD IT ONCE MORE?
THEY CALL IT THE 'SKUGGAN FALLA'. BLADE--
--OF SHADOW'S FALL. YES I KNOW THIS NAME WELL. YET, HOW DID YOU COME TO HOLD IT?

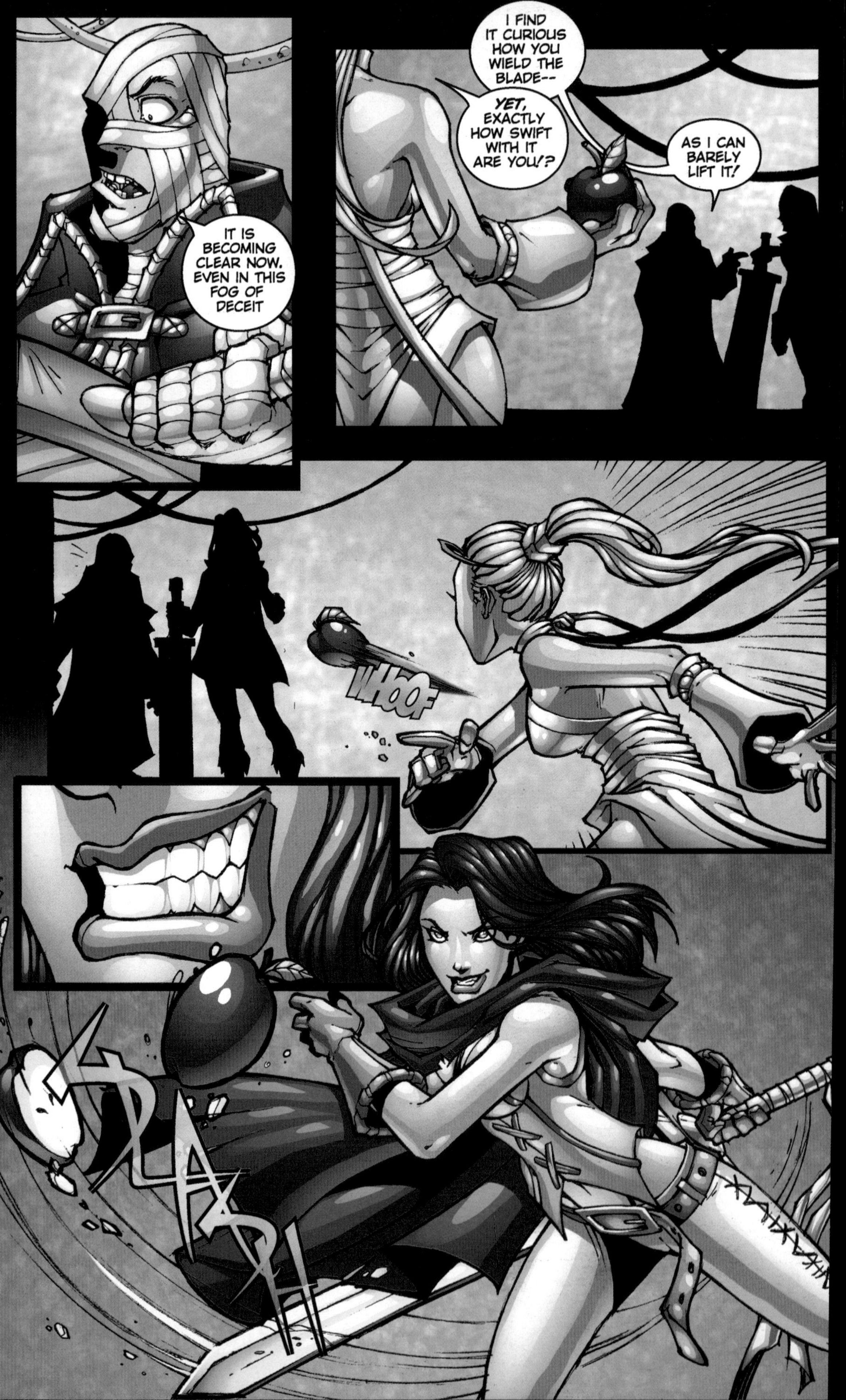
IT IS BECOMING CLEAR NOW. EVEN IN THIS FOG OF DECEIT
I FIND IT CURIOUS HOW YOU WIELD THE BLADE--
YET, EXACTLY HOW SWIFT WITH IT ARE YOU!?
AS I CAN BARELY LIFT IT!
WHOOF
CRASH!

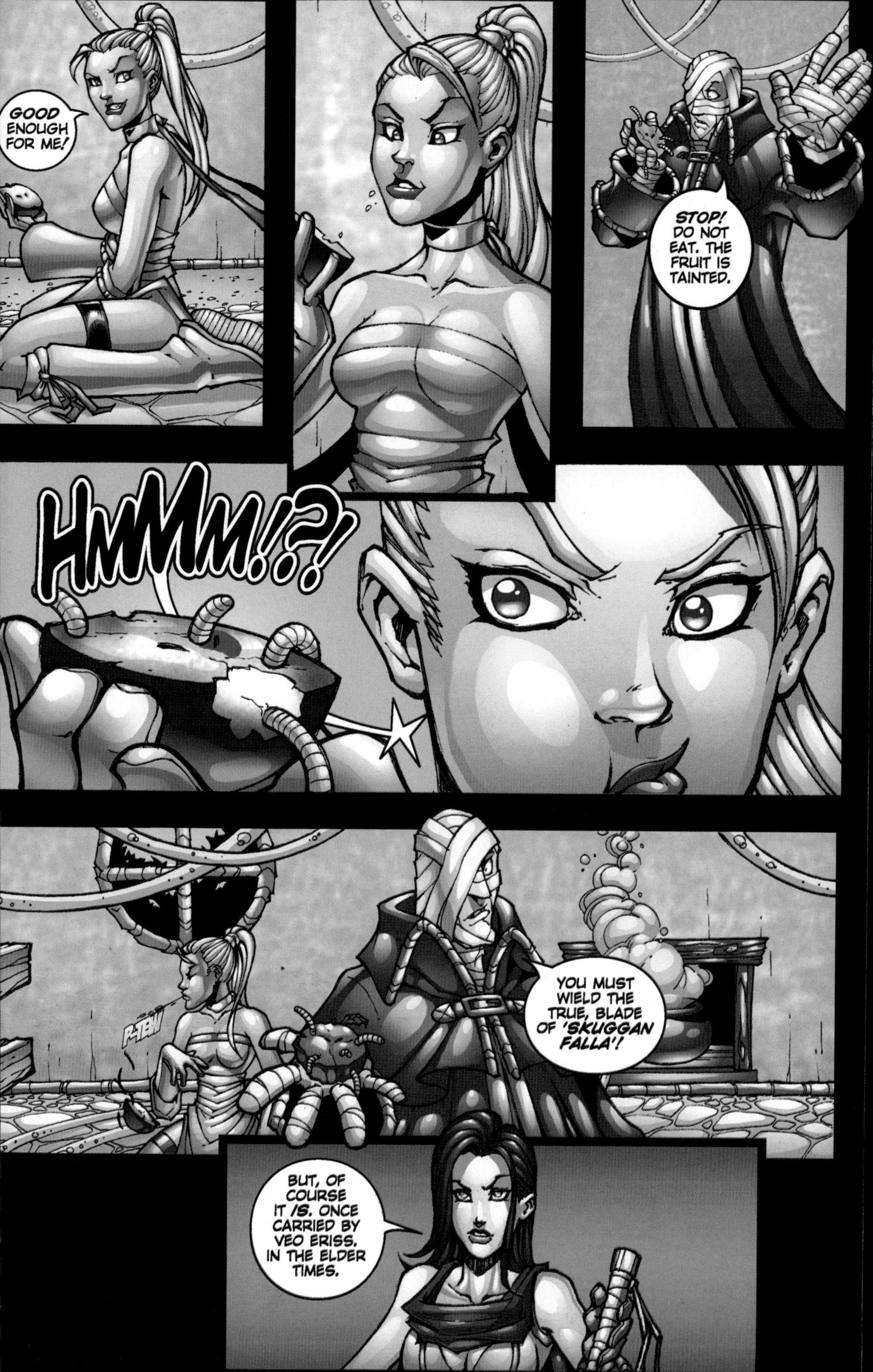
GOOD ENOUGH FOR ME!
STOP! DO NOT EAT. THE FRUIT IS TAINTED.
HMMM!?!
P-TEW
YOU MUST WIELD THE TRUE, BLADE OF 'SKUGGAN FALLA'!
BUT, OF COURSE IT IS. ONCE CARRIED BY VEO ERISS. IN THE ELDER TIMES.

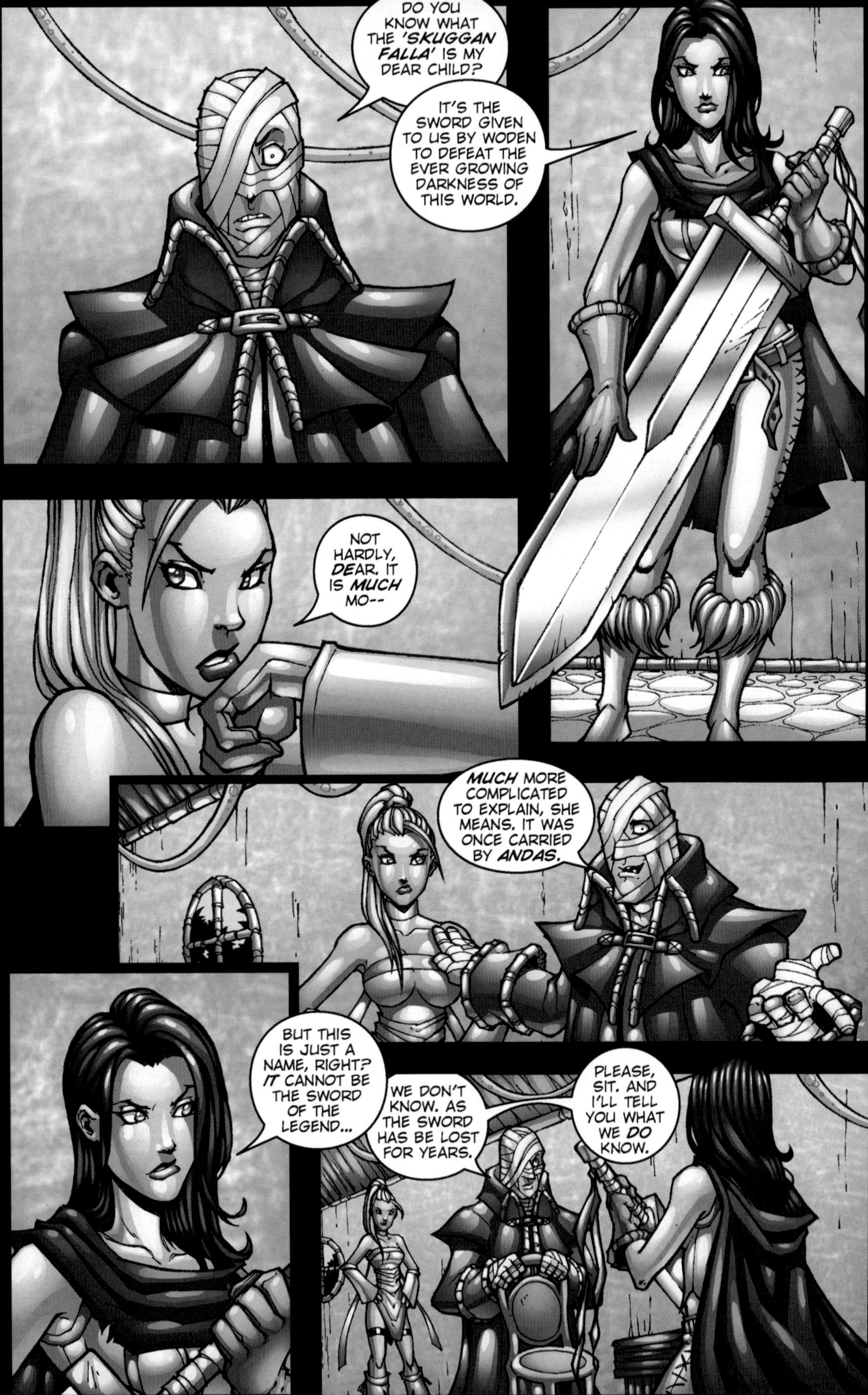
DO YOU KNOW WHAT THE 'SKUGGAN FALLA' IS MY DEAR CHILD?
IT'S THE SWORD GIVEN TO US BY WODEN TO DEFEAT THE EVER GROWING DARKNESS OF THIS WORLD.
NOT HARDLY, DEAR. IT IS MUCH MO--
MUCH MORE COMPLICATED TO EXPLAIN, SHE MEANS. IT WAS ONCE CARRIED BY ANDAS.
BUT THIS IS JUST A NAME, RIGHT? IT CANNOT BE THE SWORD OF THE LEGEND...
WE DON'T KNOW. AS THE SWORD HAS BE LOST FOR YEARS.
PLEASE, SIT. AND I'LL TELL YOU WHAT WE DO KNOW.

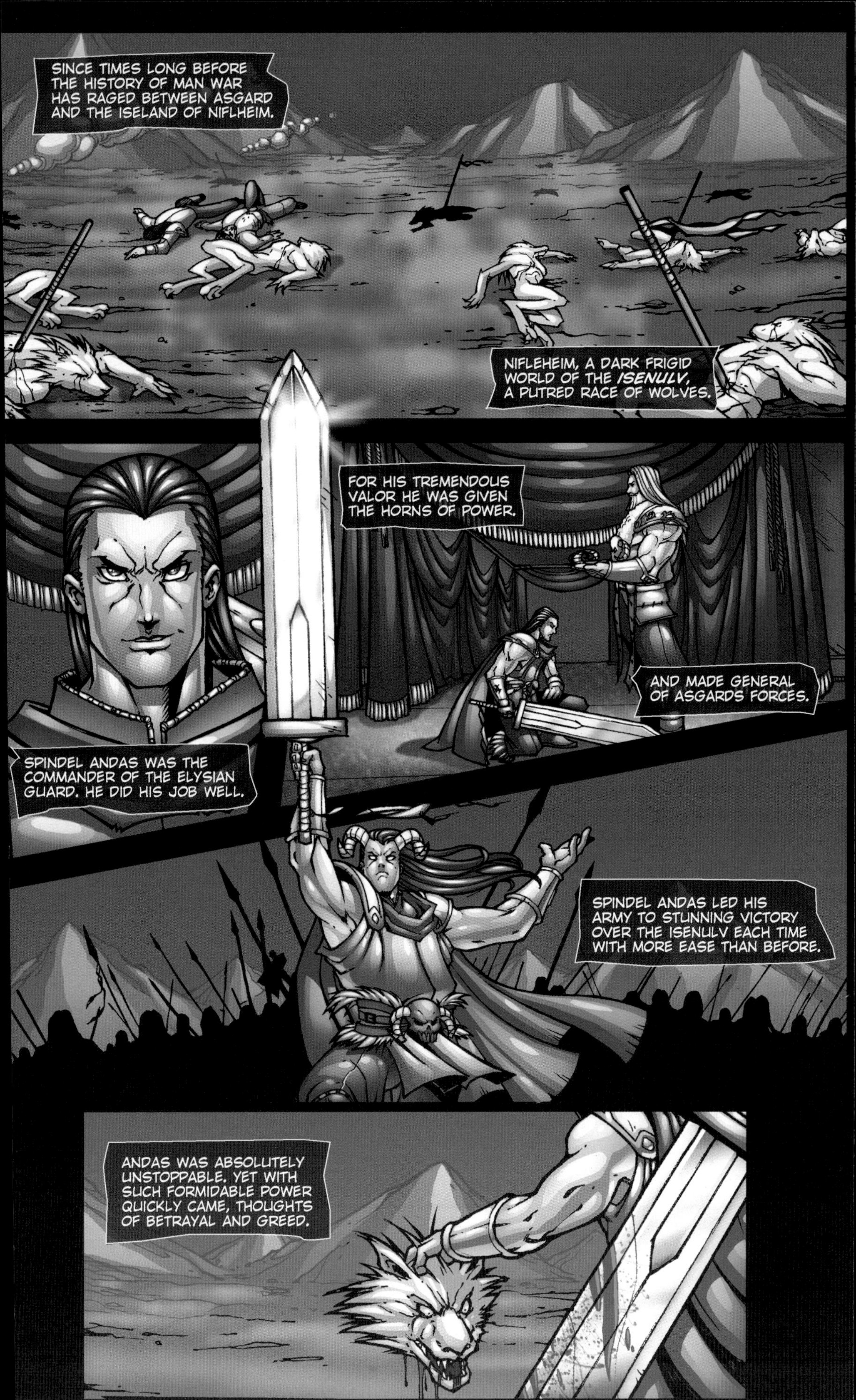
SINCE TIMES LONG BEFORE THE HISTORY OF MAN WAR HAS RAGED BETWEEN ASGARD AND THE ISELAND OF NIFLHEIM.
NIFLEHEIM, A DARK FRIGID WORLD OF THE *ISENULV*, A PUTRED RACE OF WOLVES.
SPINDEL ANDAS WAS THE COMMANDER OF THE ELYSIAN GUARD. HE DID HIS JOB WELL.
FOR HIS TREMENDOUS VALOR HE WAS GIVEN THE HORNS OF POWER.
AND MADE GENERAL OF ASGARDS FORCES.
SPINDEL ANDAS LED HIS ARMY TO STUNNING VICTORY OVER THE ISENULV EACH TIME WITH MORE EASE THAN BEFORE.
ANDAS WAS ABSOLUTELY UNSTOPPABLE. YET WITH SUCH FORMIDABLE POWER QUICKLY CAME, THOUGHTS OF BETRAYAL AND GREED.

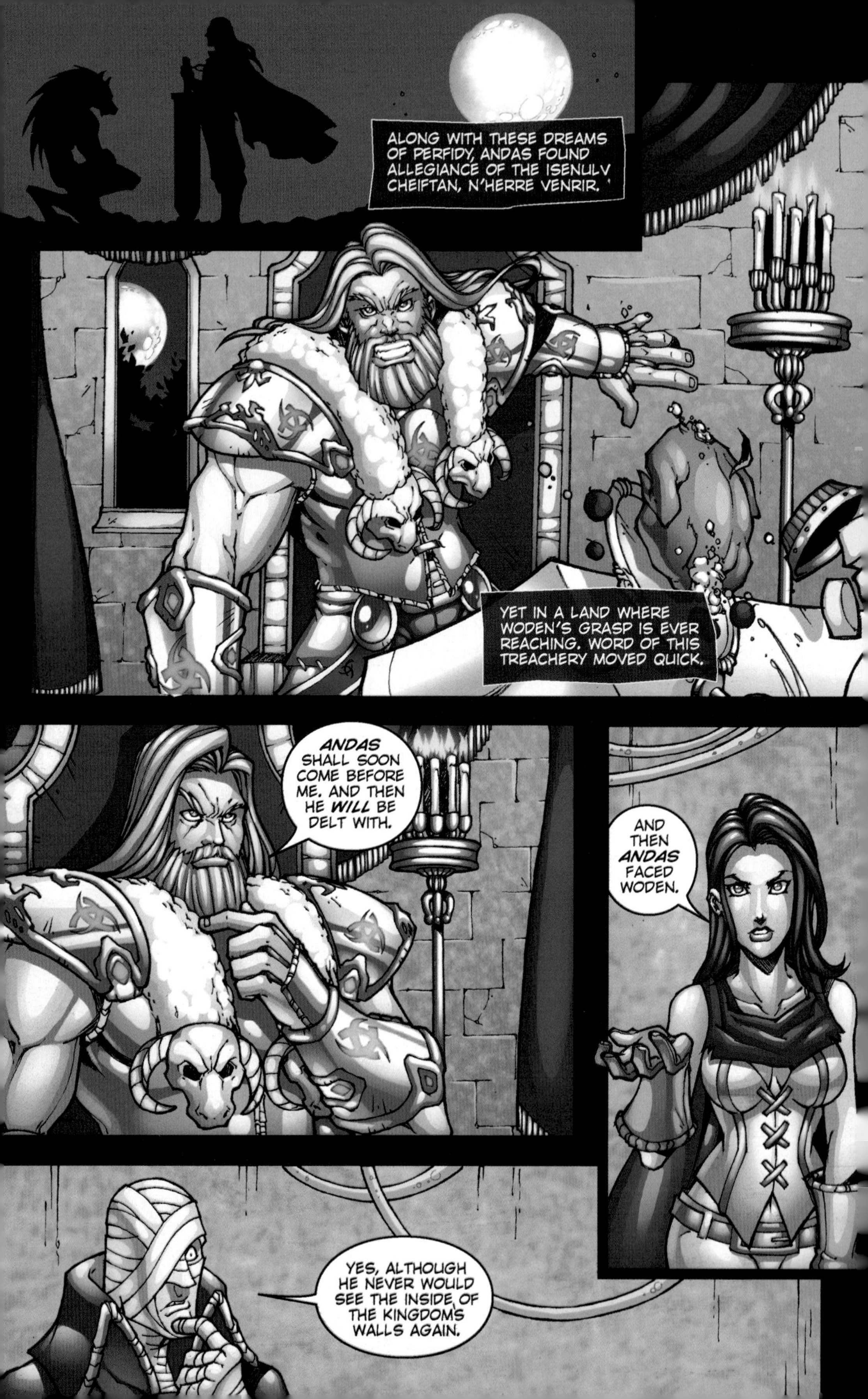
ALONG WITH THESE DREAMS OF PERFIDY, ANDAS FOUND ALLEGIANCE OF THE ISENULV CHEIFTAN, N'HERRE VENRIR.
YET IN A LAND WHERE WODEN'S GRASP IS EVER REACHING. WORD OF THIS TREACHERY MOVED QUICK.
ANDAS SHALL SOON COME BEFORE ME. AND THEN HE WILL BE DELT WITH.
AND THEN ANDAS FACED WODEN.
YES, ALTHOUGH HE NEVER WOULD SEE THE INSIDE OF THE KINGDOM'S WALLS AGAIN.

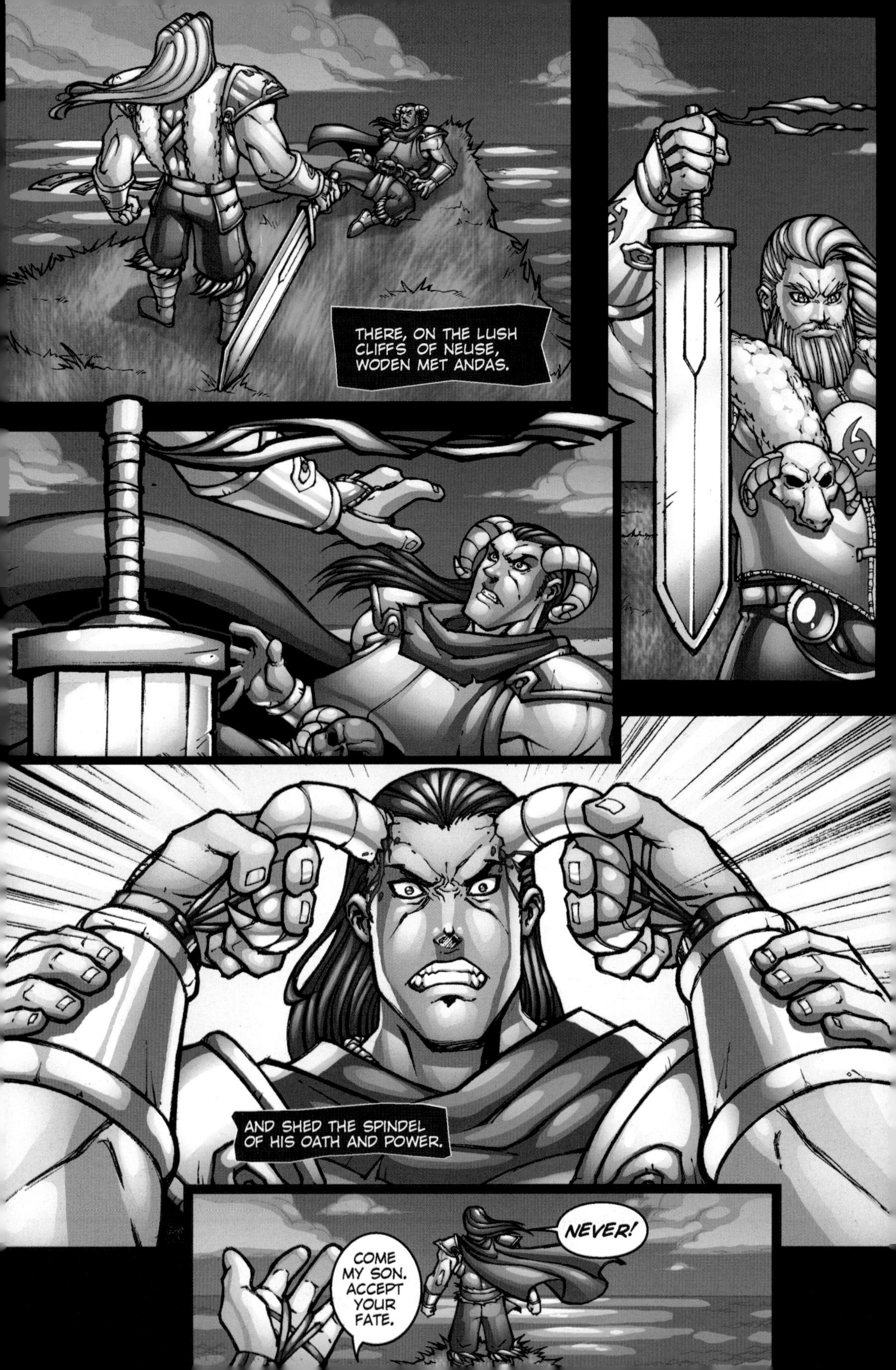
THERE, ON THE LUSH CLIFFS OF NEUSE, WODEN MET ANDAS.
AND SHED THE SPINDEL OF HIS OATH AND POWER.
COME MY SON. ACCEPT YOUR FATE.
NEVER!

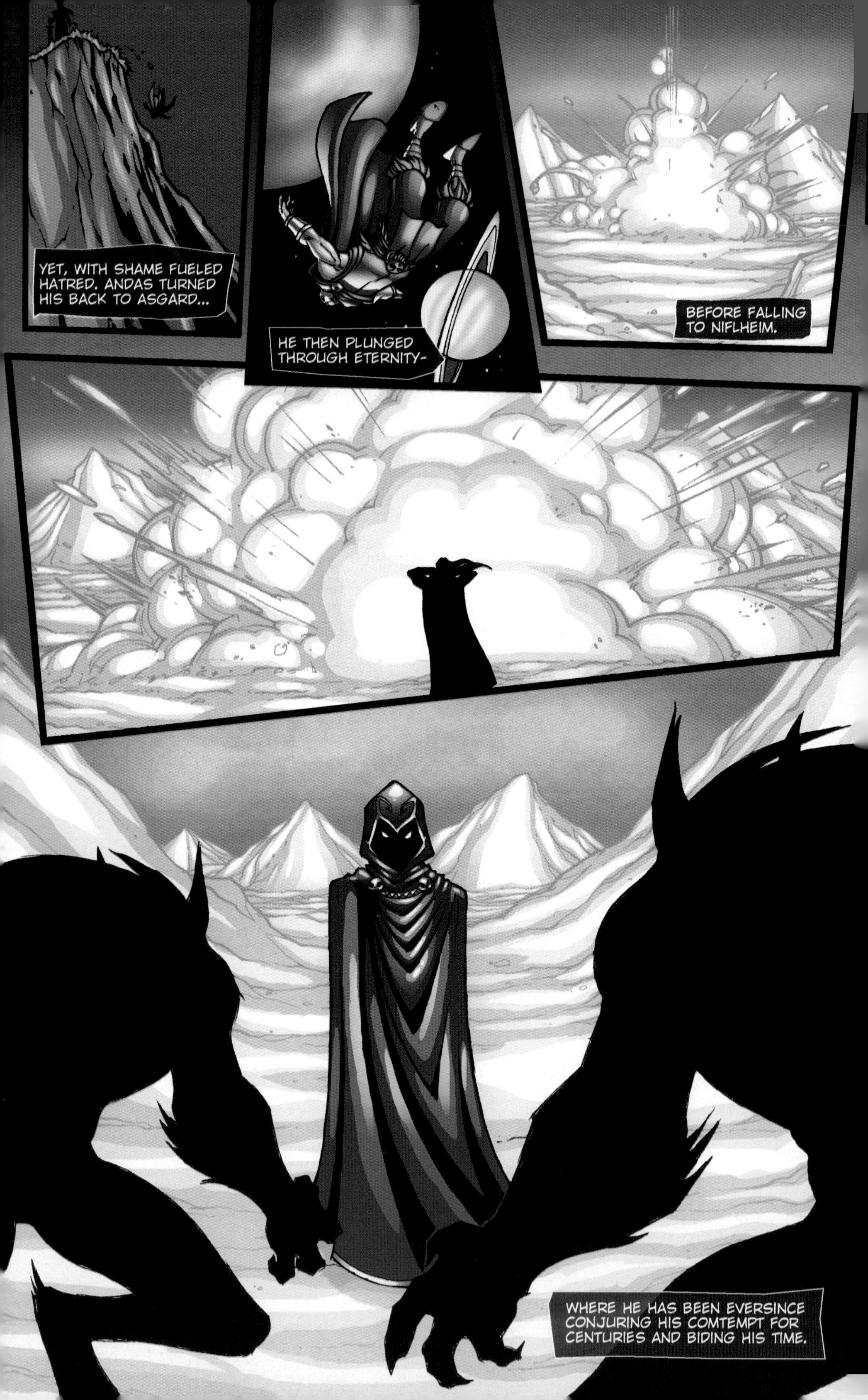
YET, WITH SHAME FUELED HATRED. ANDAS TURNED HIS BACK TO ASGARD...
HE THEN PLUNGED THROUGH ETERNITY-
BEFORE FALLING TO NIFLHEIM.
WHERE HE HAS BEEN EVERSINCE CONJURING HIS COMTEMPT FOR CENTURIES AND BIDING HIS TIME.

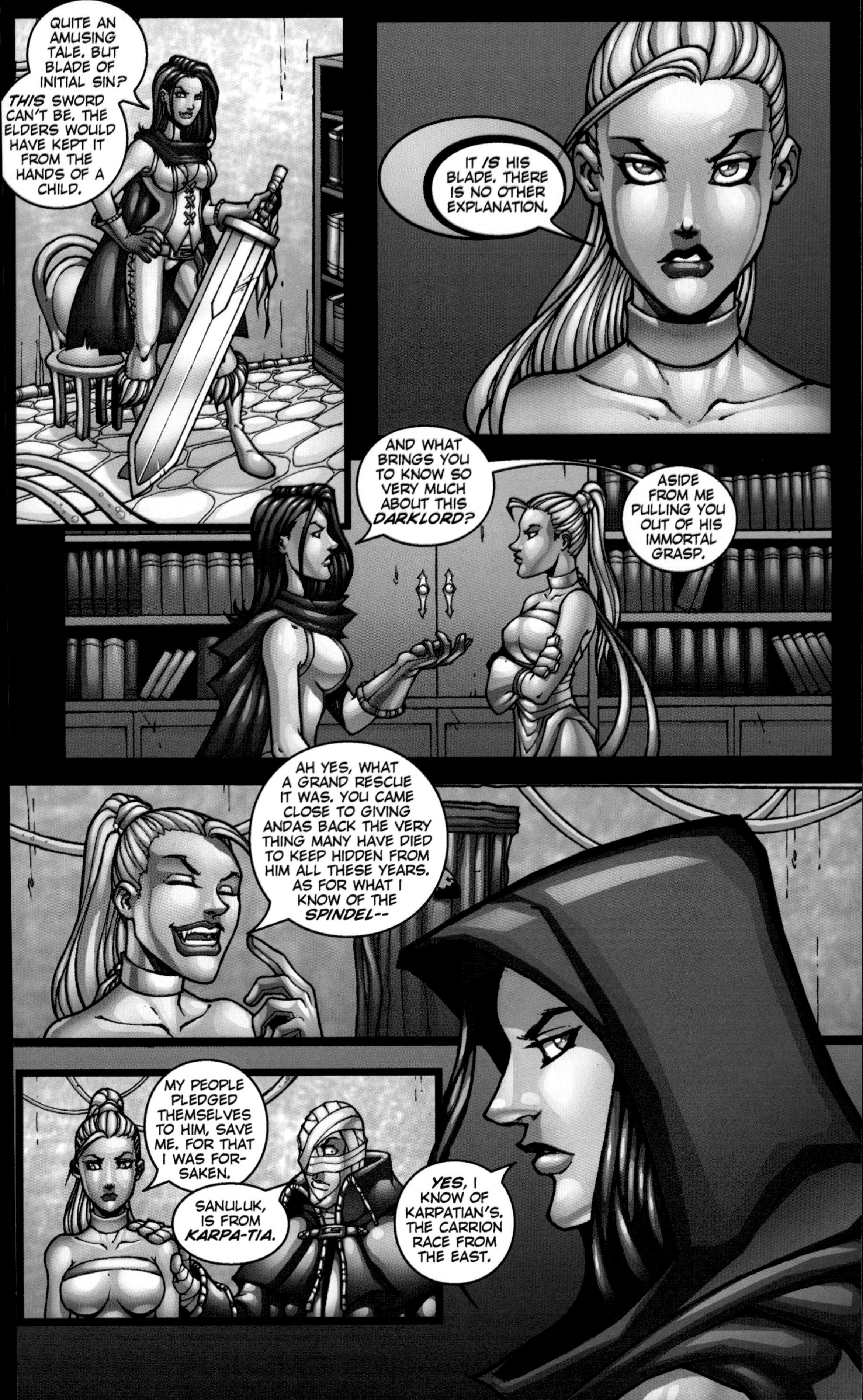
QUITE AN AMUSING TALE. BUT BLADE OF INITIAL SIN? *THIS* SWORD CAN'T BE. THE ELDERS WOULD HAVE KEPT IT FROM THE HANDS OF A CHILD.
IT *IS* HIS BLADE. THERE IS NO OTHER EXPLANATION.
AND WHAT BRINGS YOU TO KNOW SO VERY MUCH ABOUT THIS *DARKLORD*?
ASIDE FROM ME PULLING YOU OUT OF HIS IMMORTAL GRASP.
AH YES, WHAT A GRAND RESCUE IT WAS. YOU CAME CLOSE TO GIVING ANDAS BACK THE VERY THING MANY HAVE DIED TO KEEP HIDDEN FROM HIM ALL THESE YEARS. AS FOR WHAT I KNOW OF THE *SPINDEL*--
MY PEOPLE PLEDGED THEMSELVES TO HIM, SAVE ME. FOR THAT I WAS FOR-SAKEN.
SANULUK, IS FROM *KARPA-TIA*.
YES, I KNOW OF KARPATIAN'S. THE CARRION RACE FROM THE EAST.

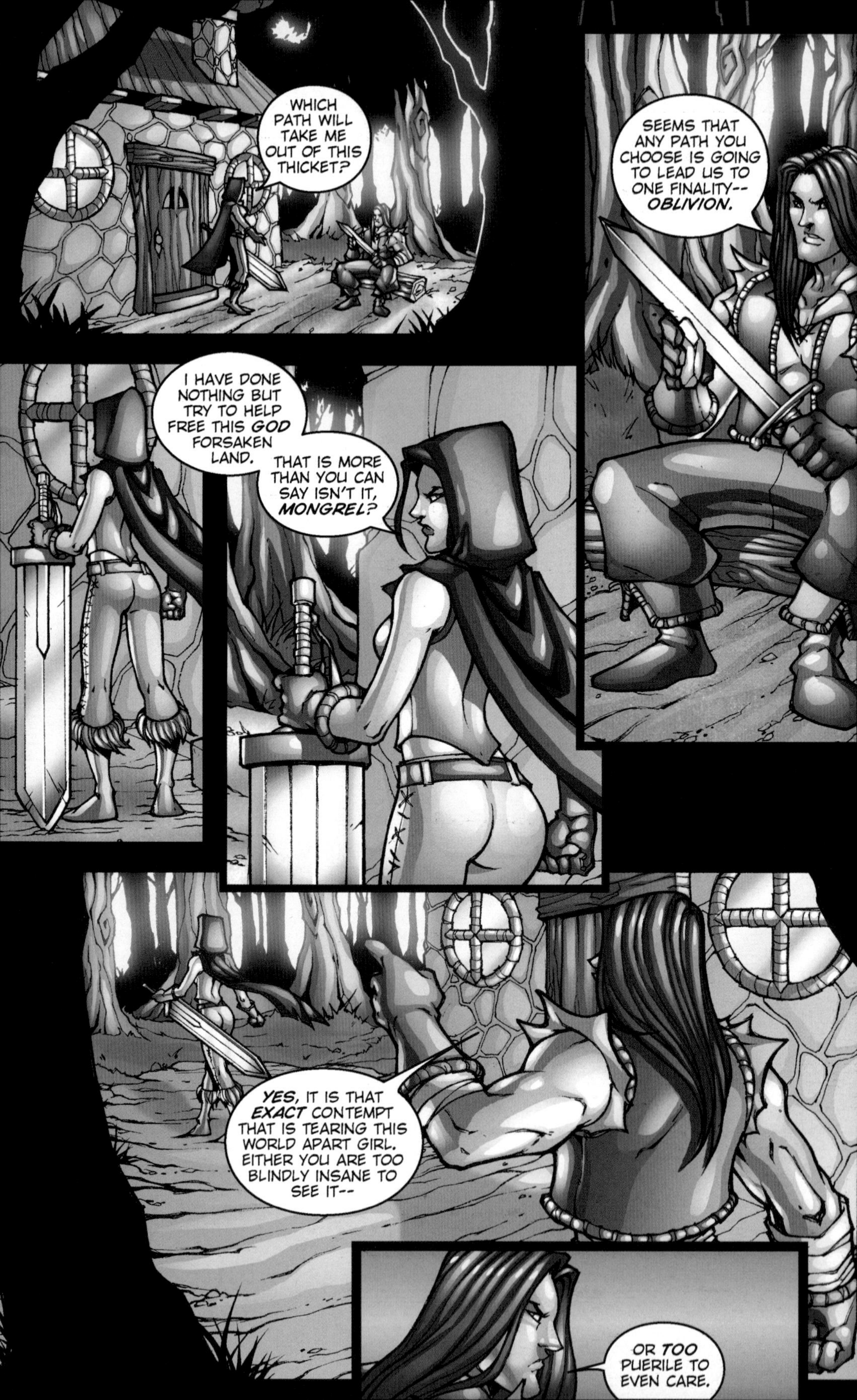

WHICH PATH WILL TAKE ME OUT OF THIS THICKET?
SEEMS THAT ANY PATH YOU CHOOSE IS GOING TO LEAD US TO ONE FINALITY-- OBLIVION.
I HAVE DONE NOTHING BUT TRY TO HELP FREE THIS GOD FORSAKEN LAND.
THAT IS MORE THAN YOU CAN SAY ISN'T IT, MONGREL?
YES, IT IS THAT EXACT CONTEMPT THAT IS TEARING THIS WORLD APART GIRL. EITHER YOU ARE TOO BLINDLY INSANE TO SEE IT--
OR TOO PUERILE TO EVEN CARE.

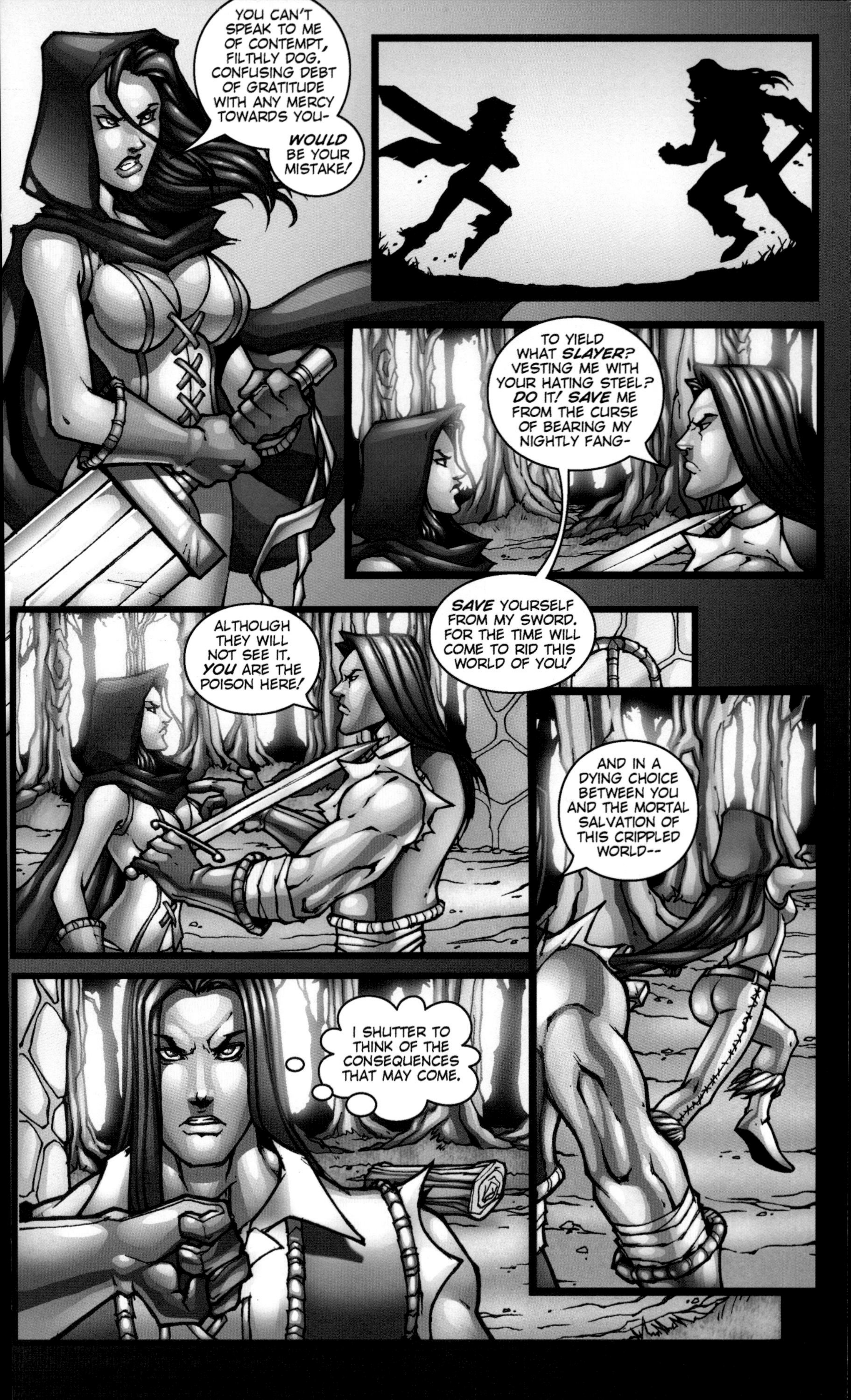
YOU CAN'T SPEAK TO ME OF CONTEMPT, FILTHLY DOG. CONFUSING DEBT OF GRATITUDE WITH ANY MERCY TOWARDS YOU-
WOULD BE YOUR MISTAKE!
TO YIELD WHAT SLAYER? VESTING ME WITH YOUR HATING STEEL? DO IT! SAVE ME FROM THE CURSE OF BEARING MY NIGHTLY FANG-
SAVE YOURSELF FROM MY SWORD. FOR THE TIME WILL COME TO RID THIS WORLD OF YOU!
ALTHOUGH THEY WILL NOT SEE IT. YOU ARE THE POISON HERE!
AND IN A DYING CHOICE BETWEEN YOU AND THE MORTAL SALVATION OF THIS CRIPPLED WORLD--
I SHUTTER TO THINK OF THE CONSEQUENCES THAT MAY COME.

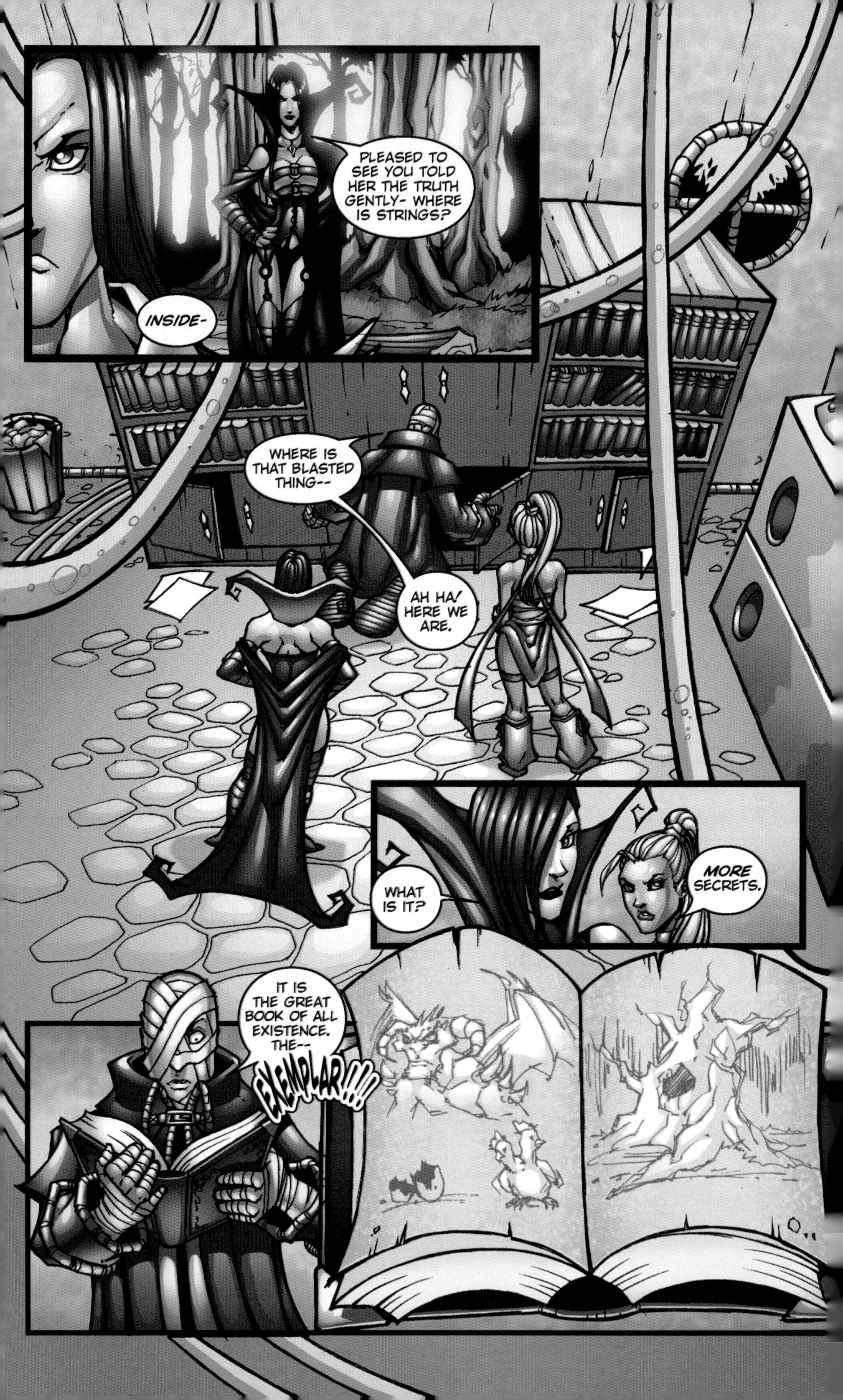
PLEASED TO SEE YOU TOLD HER THE TRUTH GENTLY- WHERE IS STRINGS?
INSIDE-
WHERE IS THAT BLASTED THING--
AH HA! HERE WE ARE.
WHAT IS IT?
MORE SECRETS.
IT IS THE GREAT BOOK OF ALL EXISTENCE. THE--
EXEMPLAR!!!!

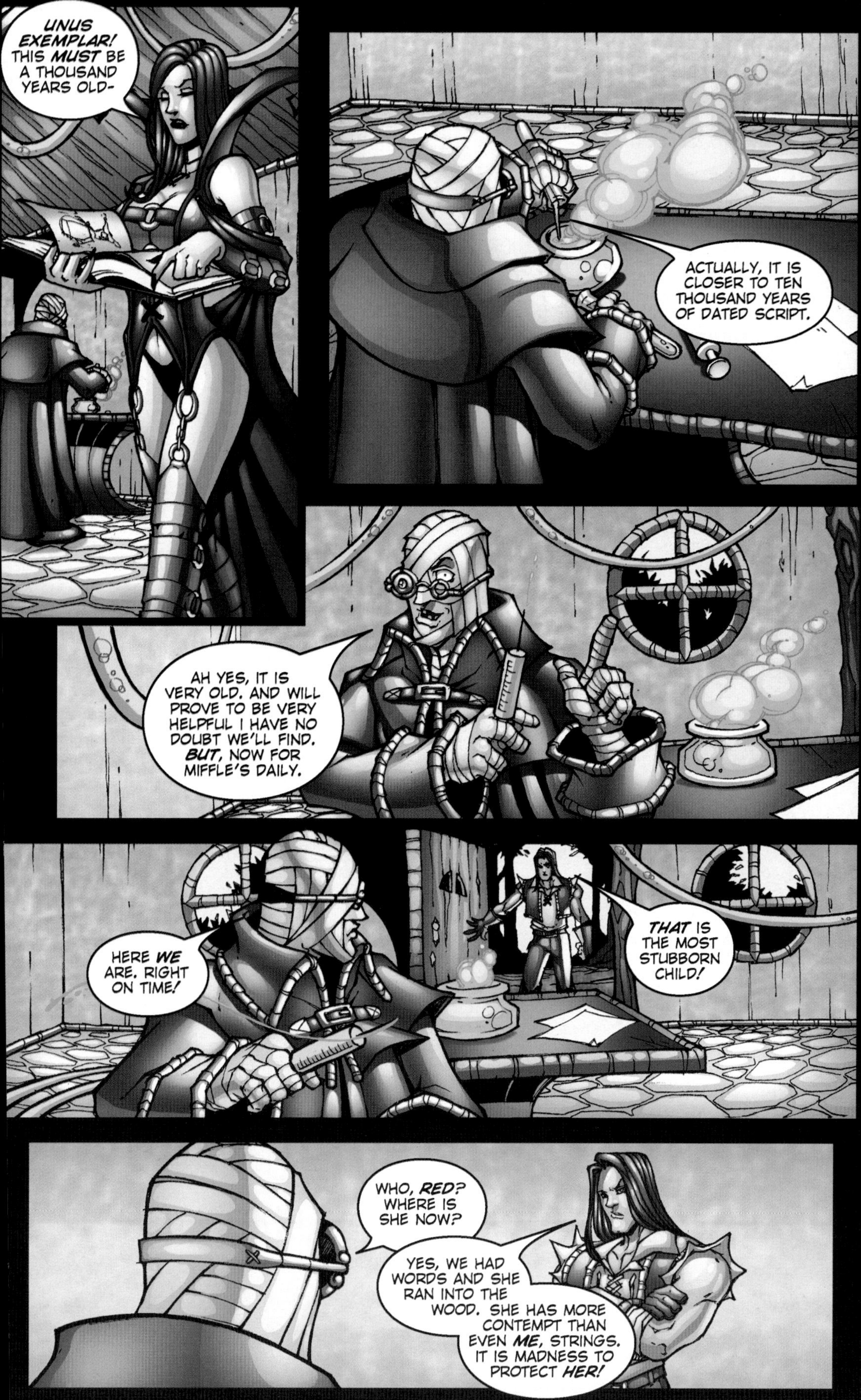
UNUS EXEMPLAR! THIS MUST BE A THOUSAND YEARS OLD-
ACTUALLY, IT IS CLOSER TO TEN THOUSAND YEARS OF DATED SCRIPT.
AH YES, IT IS VERY OLD. AND WILL PROVE TO BE VERY HELPFUL I HAVE NO DOUBT WE'LL FIND. BUT, NOW FOR MIFFLE'S DAILY.
HERE WE ARE. RIGHT ON TIME!
THAT IS THE MOST STUBBORN CHILD!
WHO, RED? WHERE IS SHE NOW?
YES, WE HAD WORDS AND SHE RAN INTO THE WOOD. SHE HAS MORE CONTEMPT THAN EVEN ME, STRINGS. IT IS MADNESS TO PROTECT HER!

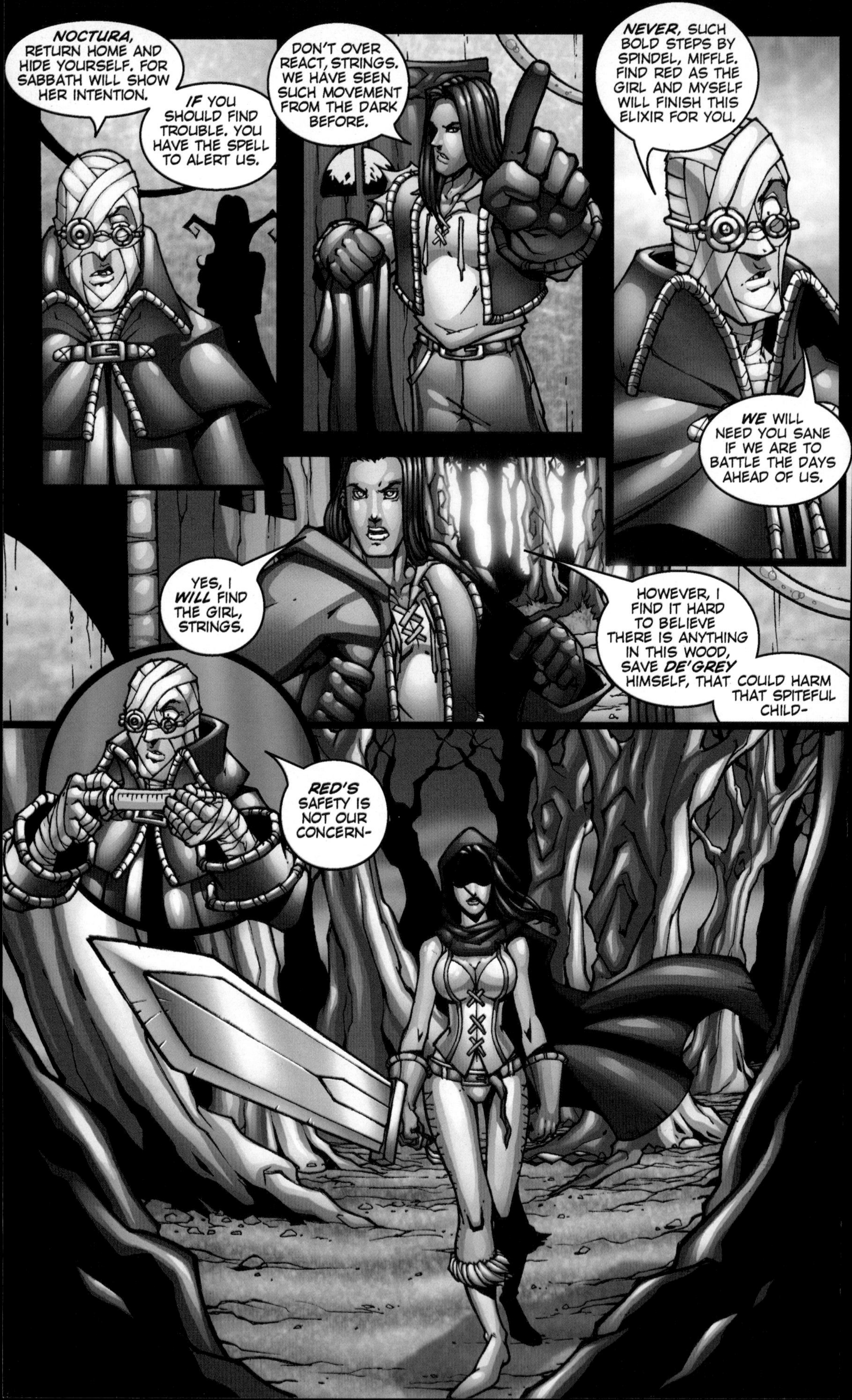
NOCTURA, RETURN HOME AND HIDE YOURSELF. FOR SABBATH WILL SHOW HER INTENTION.
IF YOU SHOULD FIND TROUBLE. YOU HAVE THE SPELL TO ALERT US.
DON'T OVER REACT, STRINGS. WE HAVE SEEN SUCH MOVEMENT FROM THE DARK BEFORE.
NEVER, SUCH BOLD STEPS BY SPINDEL, MIFFLE. FIND RED AS THE GIRL AND MYSELF WILL FINISH THIS ELIXIR FOR YOU.
WE WILL NEED YOU SANE IF WE ARE TO BATTLE THE DAYS AHEAD OF US.
YES, I WILL FIND THE GIRL, STRINGS.
HOWEVER, I FIND IT HARD TO BELIEVE THERE IS ANYTHING IN THIS WOOD, SAVE DE'GREY HIMSELF, THAT COULD HARM THAT SPITEFUL CHILD-
RED'S SAFETY IS NOT OUR CONCERN-

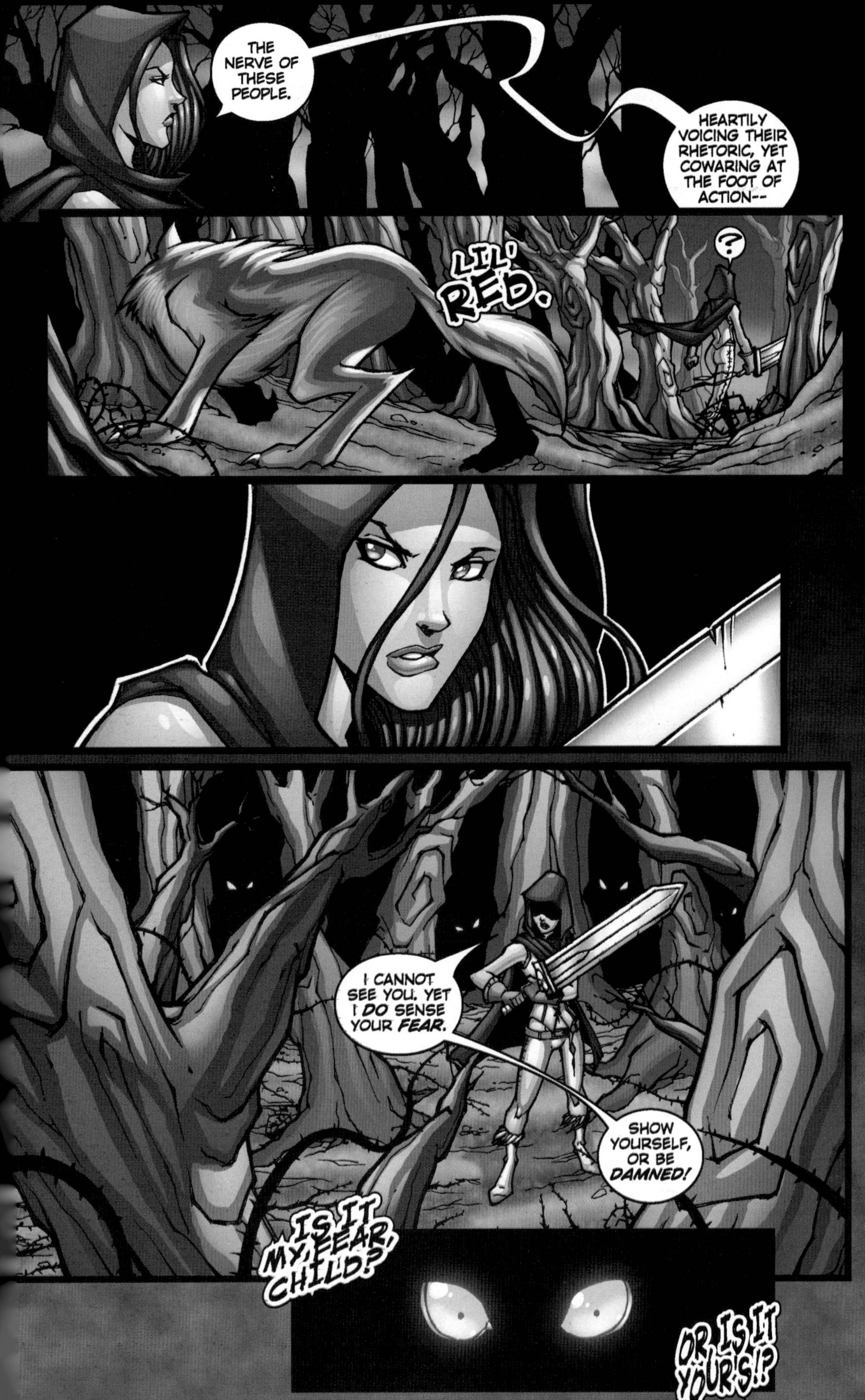
THE NERVE OF THESE PEOPLE.
HEARTILY VOICING THEIR RHETORIC, YET COWARING AT THE FOOT OF ACTION--
LIL' RED.
?
I CANNOT SEE YOU. YET I DO SENSE YOUR FEAR.
SHOW YOURSELF, OR BE DAMNED!
IS IT MY FEAR, CHILD?
OR IS IT YOURS!?

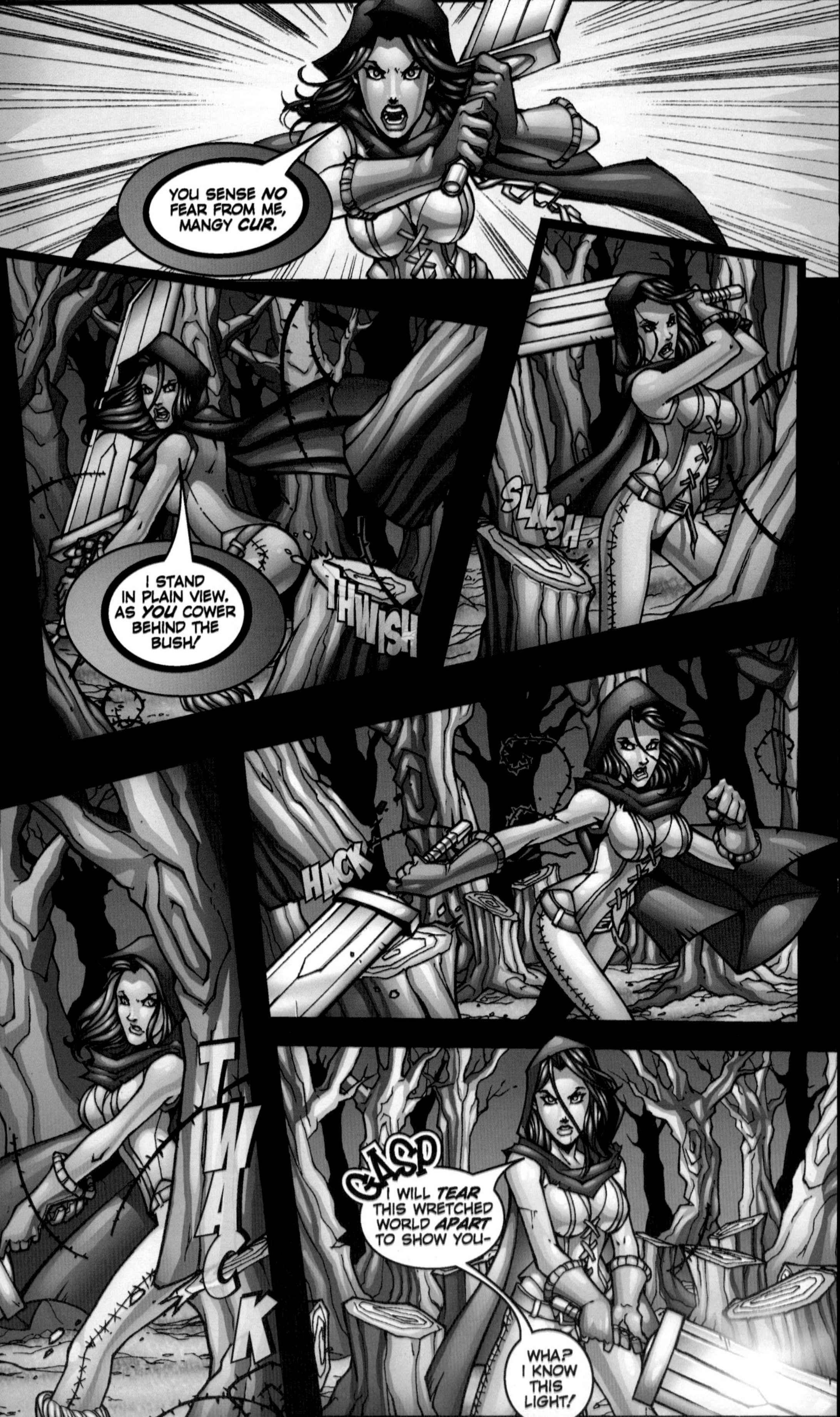
YOU SENSE NO FEAR FROM ME, MANGY CUR.
I STAND IN PLAIN VIEW. AS YOU COWER BEHIND THE BUSH!
THWISH
SLASH
HACK
TWACK
GASP
I WILL TEAR THIS WRETCHED WORLD APART TO SHOW YOU-
WHA? I KNOW THIS LIGHT!

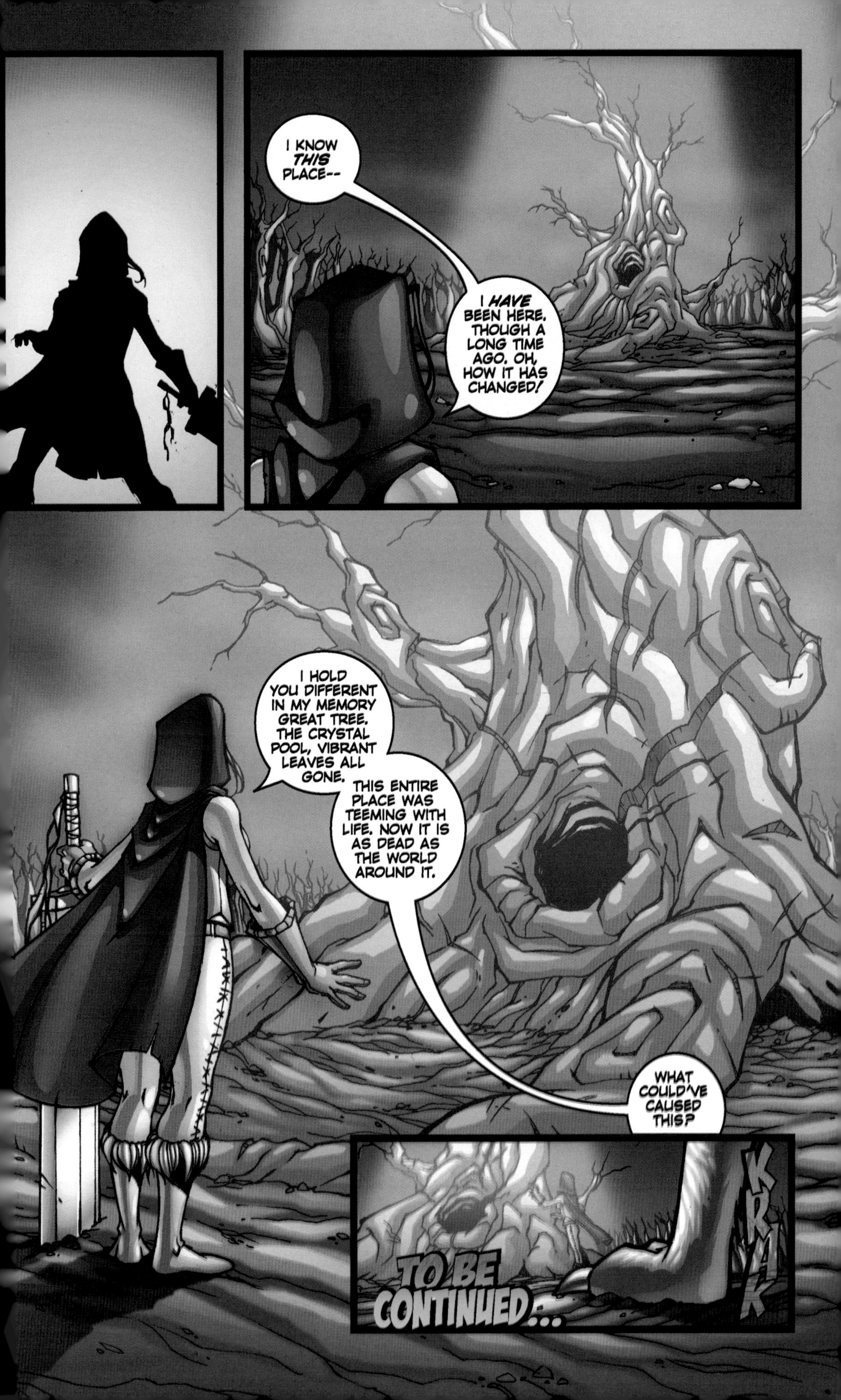
I KNOW *THIS* PLACE--
I *HAVE* BEEN HERE. THOUGH A LONG TIME AGO. OH, HOW IT HAS CHANGED!
I HOLD YOU DIFFERENT IN MY MEMORY GREAT TREE. THE CRYSTAL POOL, VIBRANT LEAVES ALL GONE.
THIS ENTIRE PLACE WAS TEEMING WITH LIFE. NOW IT IS AS DEAD AS THE WORLD AROUND IT.
WHAT COULD'VE CAUSED THIS?
KRAK
TO BE CONTINUED...

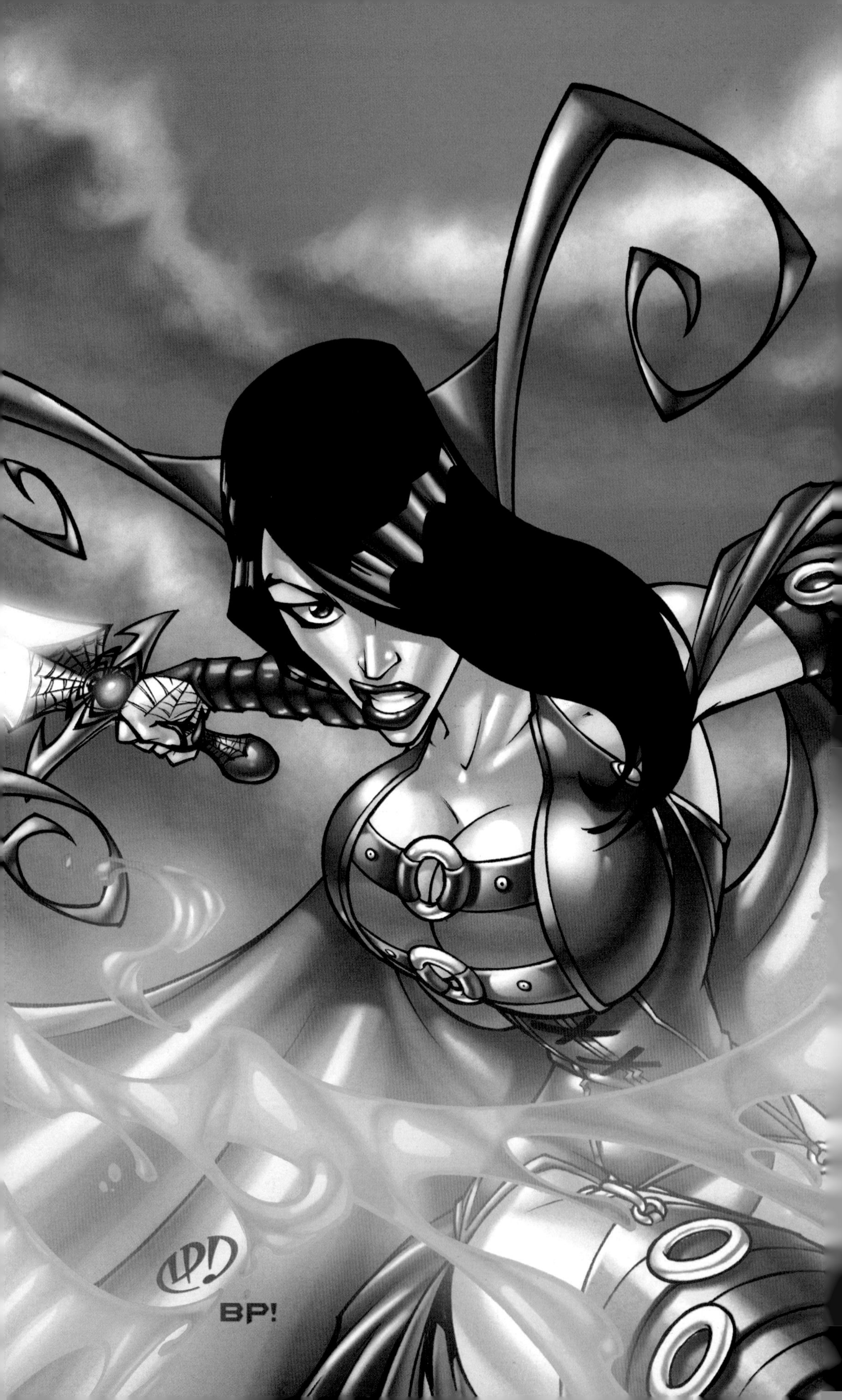
BP!

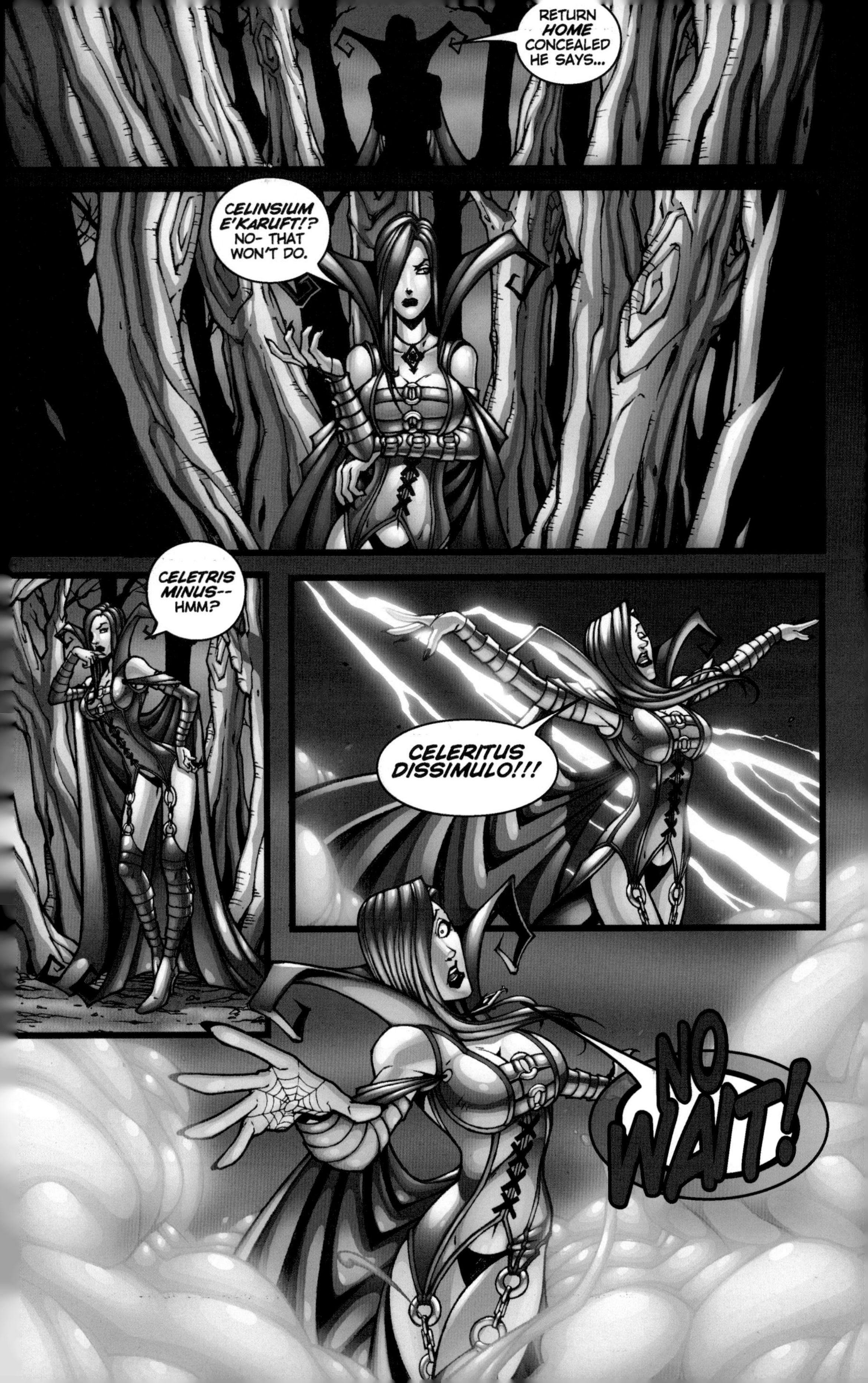
RETURN HOME CONCEALED HE SAYS...
CELINSIUM E'KARUFT!? NO- THAT WON'T DO.
CELETRIS MINUS-- HMM?
CELERITUS DISSIMULO!!!
NO WAIT!

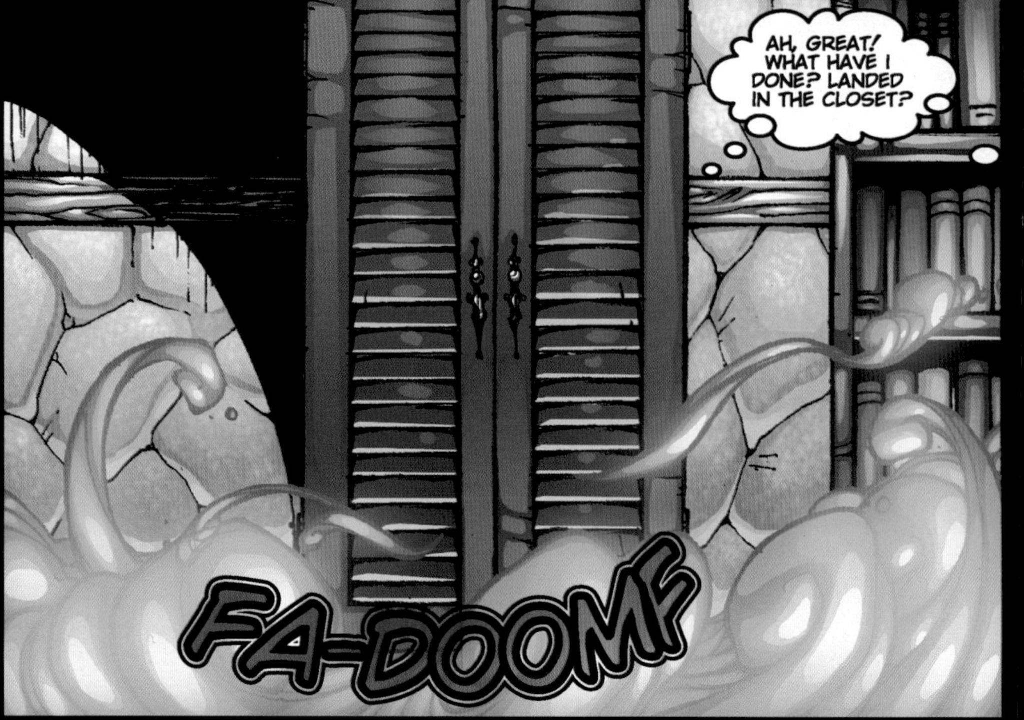
AH, GREAT! WHAT HAVE I DONE? LANDED IN THE CLOSET?
FA-DOOMF

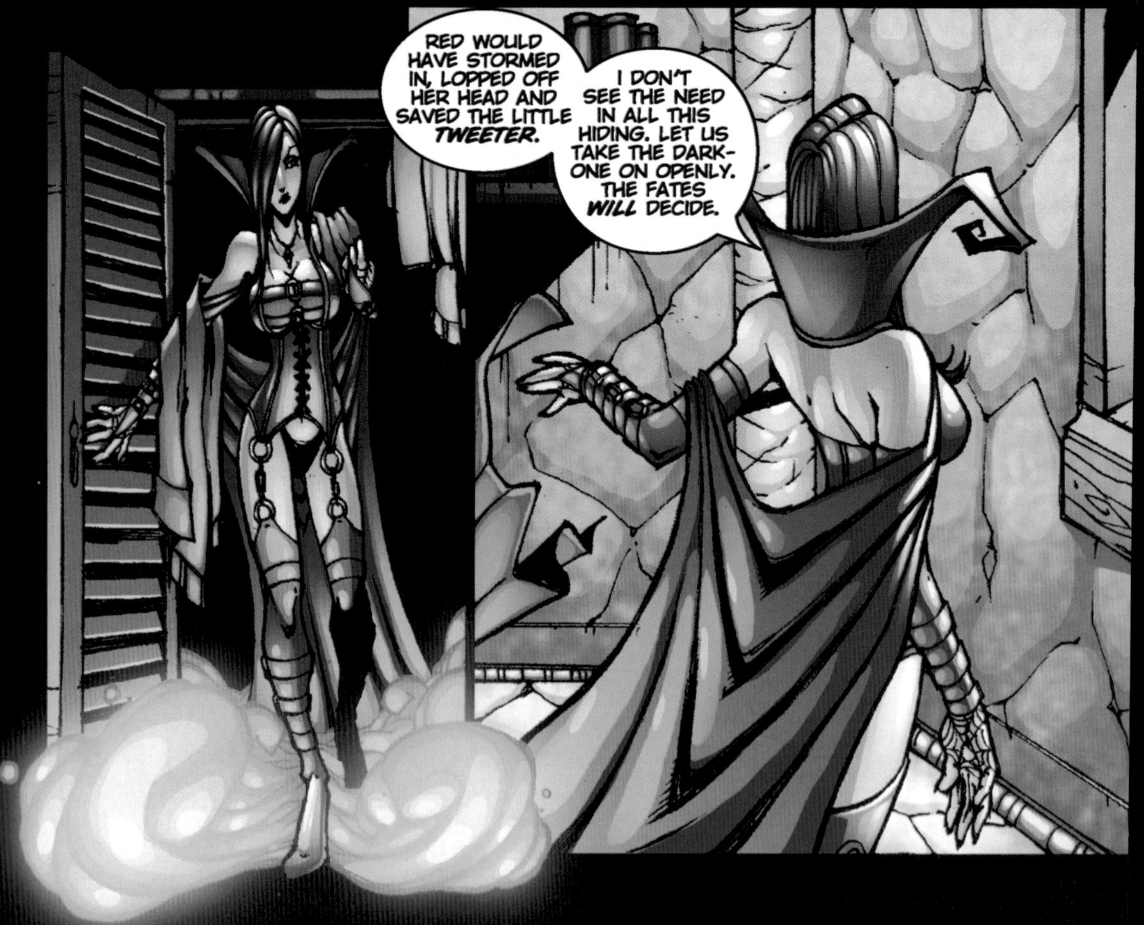
RED WOULD HAVE STORMED IN, LOPPED OFF HER HEAD AND SAVED THE LITTLE ***TWEETER***.
I DON'T SEE THE NEED IN ALL THIS HIDING. LET US TAKE THE DARK-ONE ON OPENLY. THE FATES ***WILL*** DECIDE.

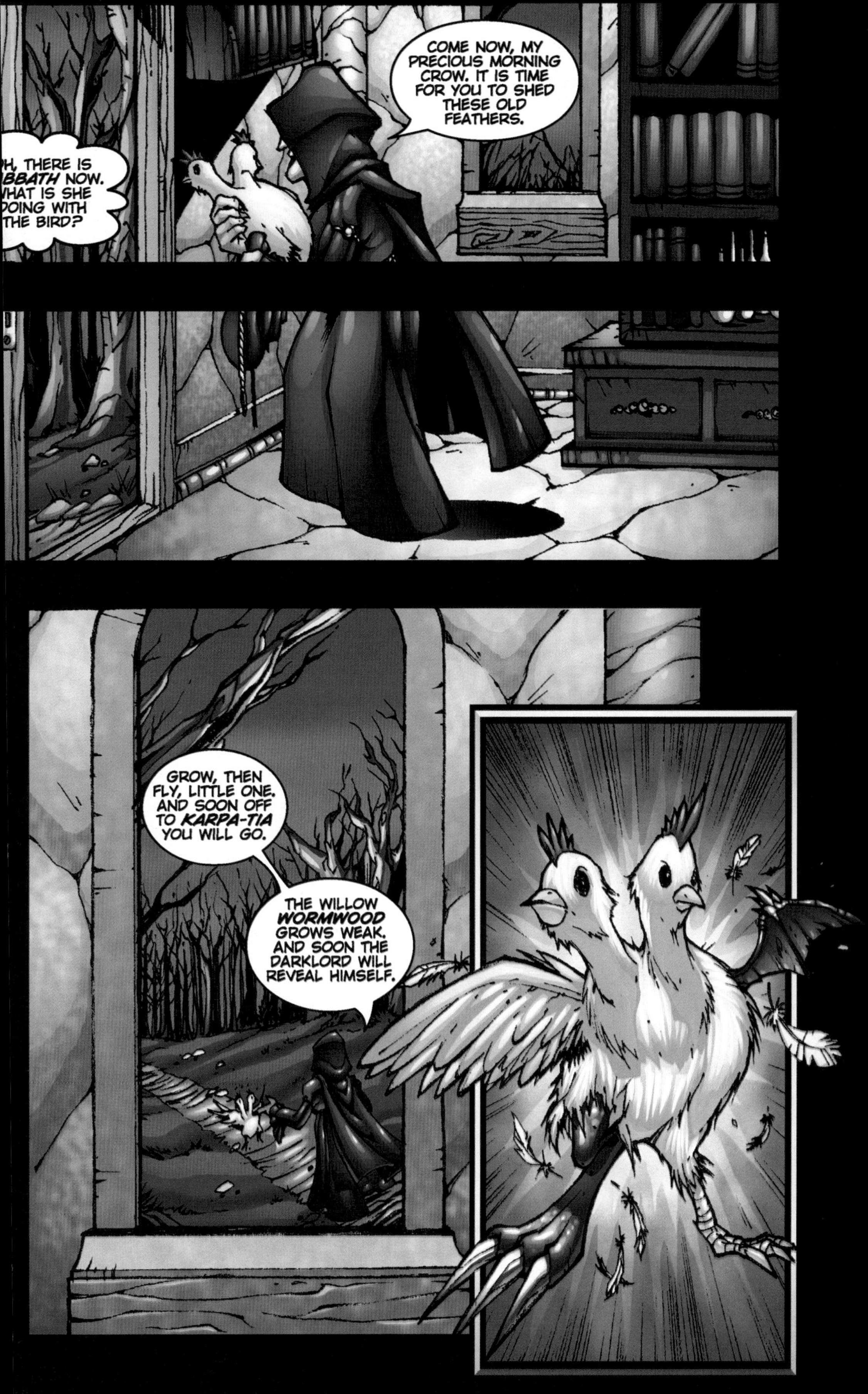

..H, THERE IS ..BBATH NOW. ..WHAT IS SHE ..DOING WITH THE BIRD?
COME NOW, MY PRECIOUS MORNING CROW. IT IS TIME FOR YOU TO SHED THESE OLD FEATHERS.
GROW, THEN FLY, LITTLE ONE. AND SOON OFF TO KARPA-TIA YOU WILL GO.
THE WILLOW WORMWOOD GROWS WEAK. AND SOON THE DARKLORD WILL REVEAL HIMSELF.

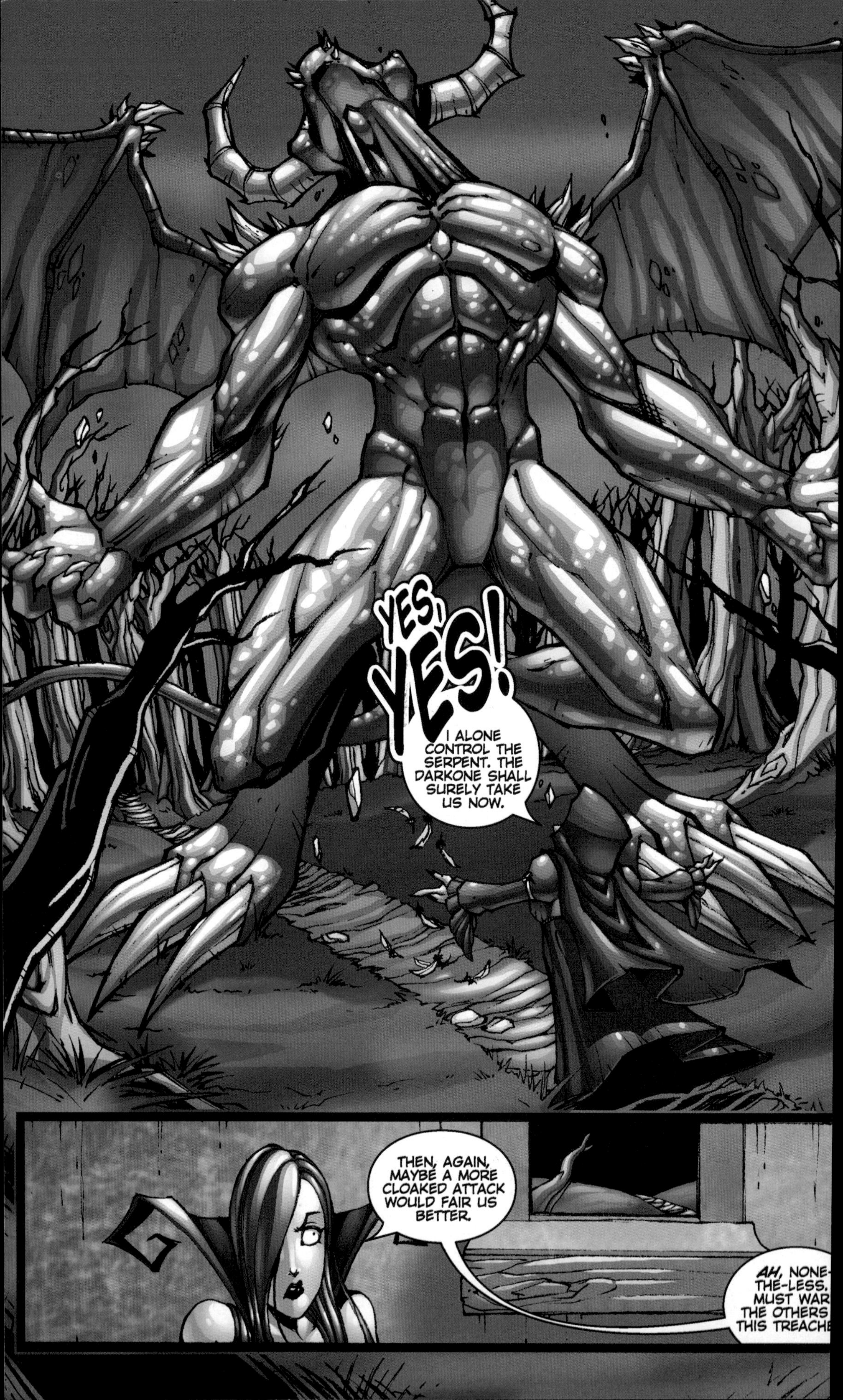
YES, YES!
I ALONE CONTROL THE SERPENT. THE DARKONE SHALL SURELY TAKE US NOW.
THEN, AGAIN, MAYBE A MORE CLOAKED ATTACK WOULD FAIR US BETTER.
AH, NONE-THE-LESS, MUST WAR THE OTHERS THIS TREACHE

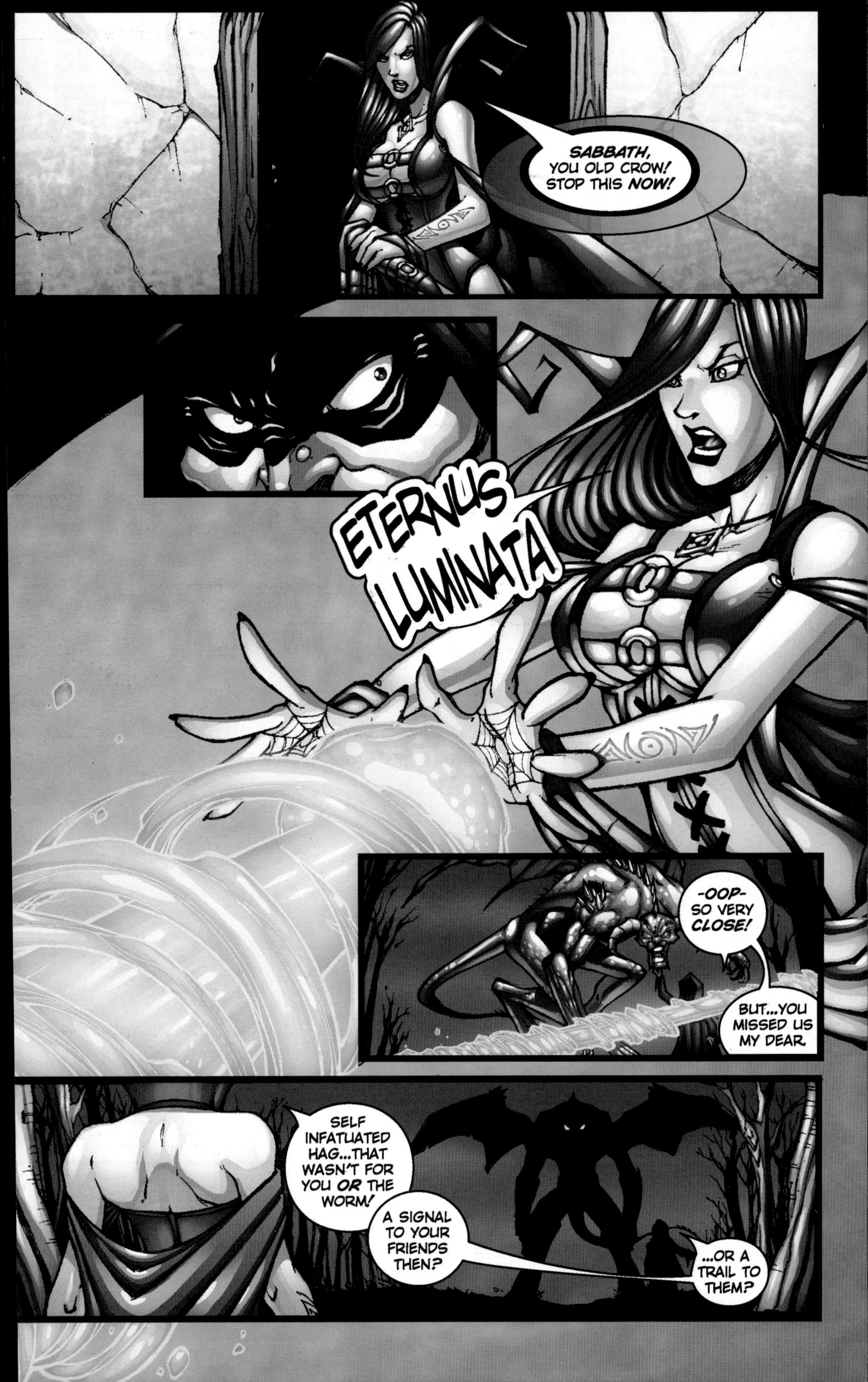
SABBATH, YOU OLD CROW! STOP THIS NOW!
ETERNUS LUMINATA
-OOP- SO VERY CLOSE!
BUT...YOU MISSED US MY DEAR.
SELF INFATUATED HAG...THAT WASN'T FOR YOU OR THE WORM!
A SIGNAL TO YOUR FRIENDS THEN?
...OR A TRAIL TO THEM?

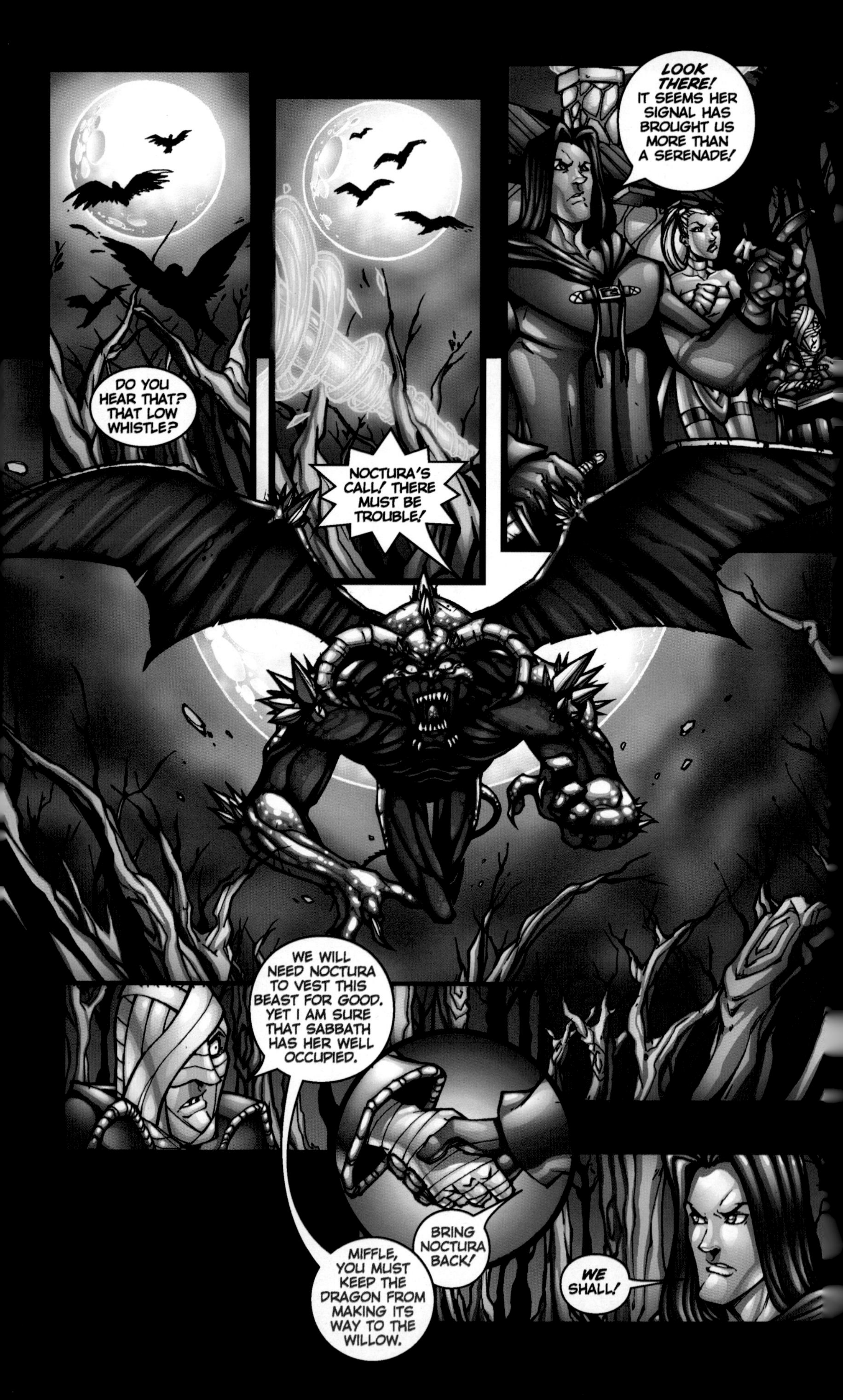
DO YOU HEAR THAT? THAT LOW WHISTLE?
NOCTURA'S CALL! THERE MUST BE TROUBLE!
LOOK THERE! IT SEEMS HER SIGNAL HAS BROUGHT US MORE THAN A SERENADE!
WE WILL NEED NOCTURA TO VEST THIS BEAST FOR GOOD. YET I AM SURE THAT SABBATH HAS HER WELL OCCUPIED.
MIFFLE, YOU MUST KEEP THE DRAGON FROM MAKING ITS WAY TO THE WILLOW.
BRING NOCTURA BACK!
WE SHALL!

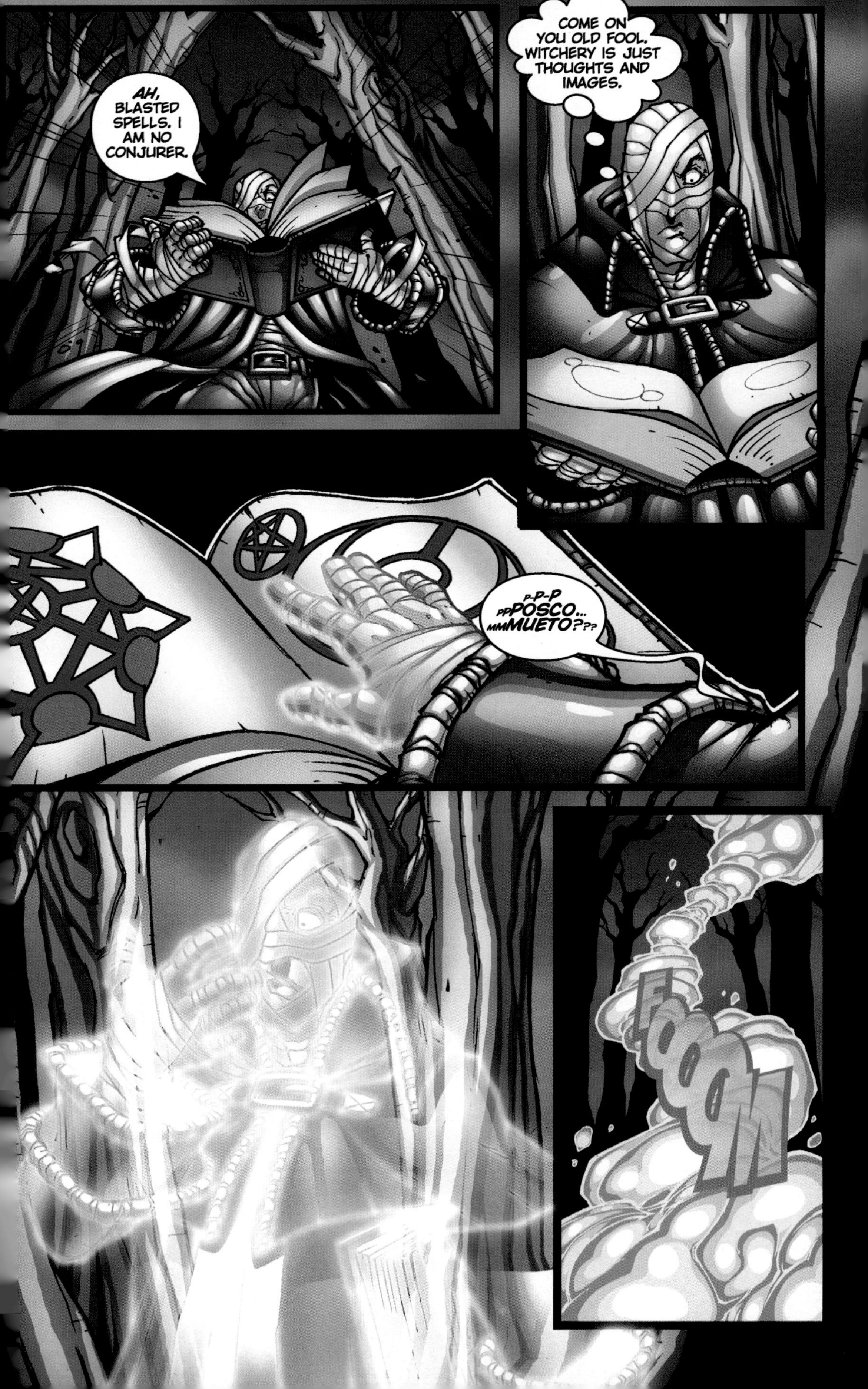
AH, BLASTED SPELLS. I AM NO CONJURER.
COME ON YOU OLD FOOL. WITCHERY IS JUST THOUGHTS AND IMAGES.
P-P-P PPPOSCO... MMMUETO???
FOOOM

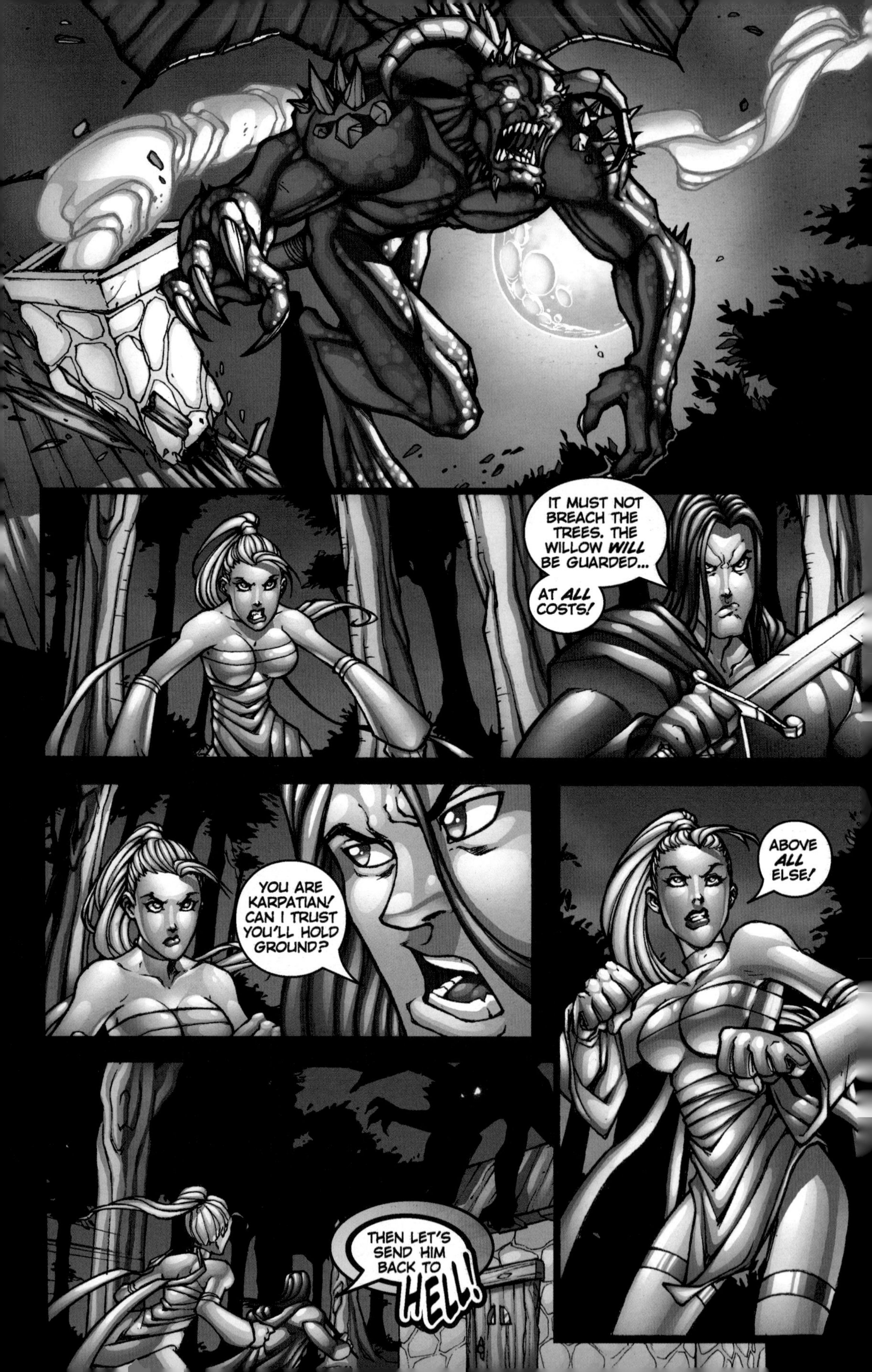
IT MUST NOT BREACH THE TREES. THE WILLOW WILL BE GUARDED...
AT ALL COSTS!
YOU ARE KARPATIAN! CAN I TRUST YOU'LL HOLD GROUND?
ABOVE ALL ELSE!
THEN LET'S SEND HIM BACK TO HELL!

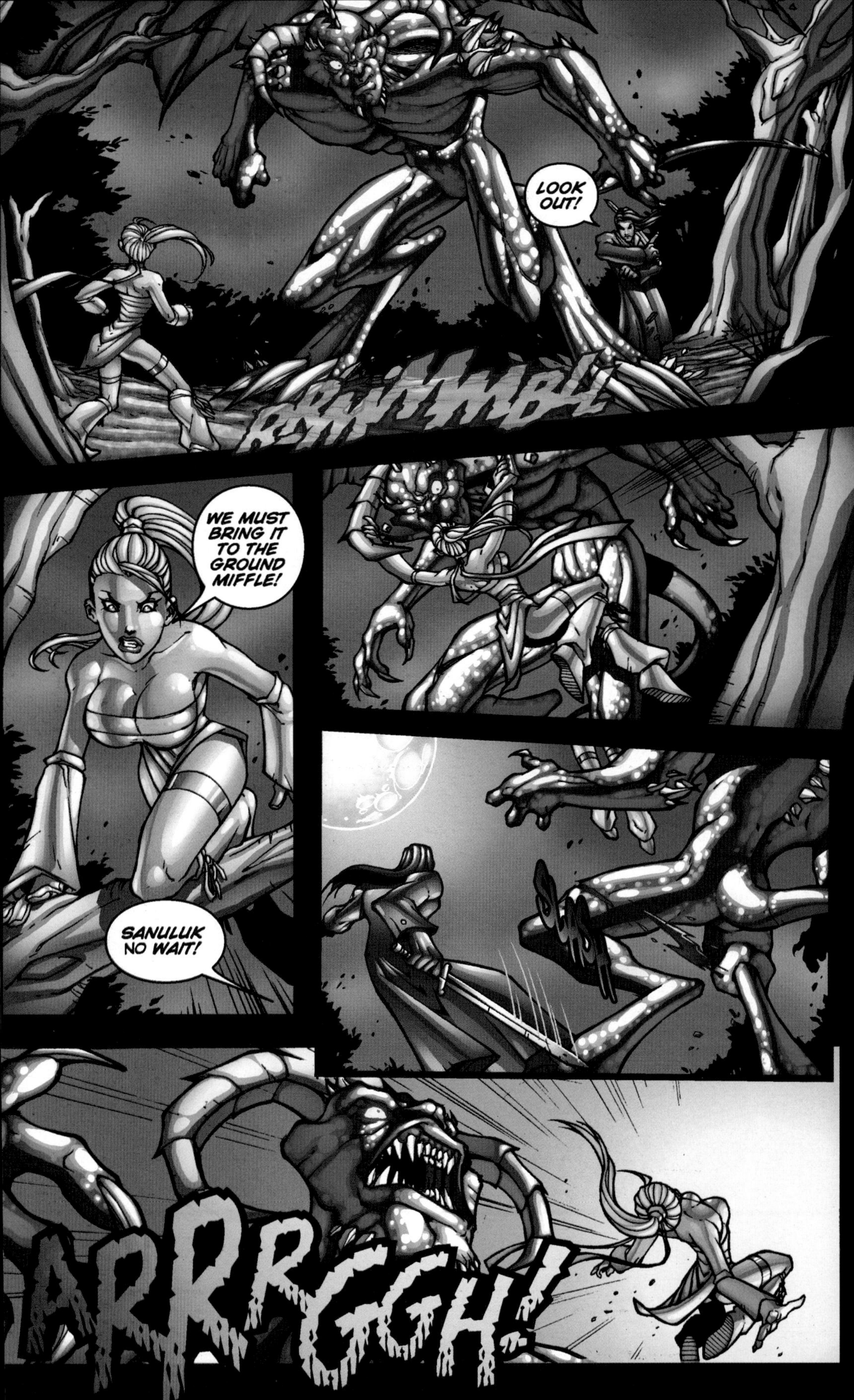
LOOK OUT!
RRUMBLE
WE MUST BRING IT TO THE GROUND MIFFLE!
SANULUK NO WAIT!
ARRRGGH!

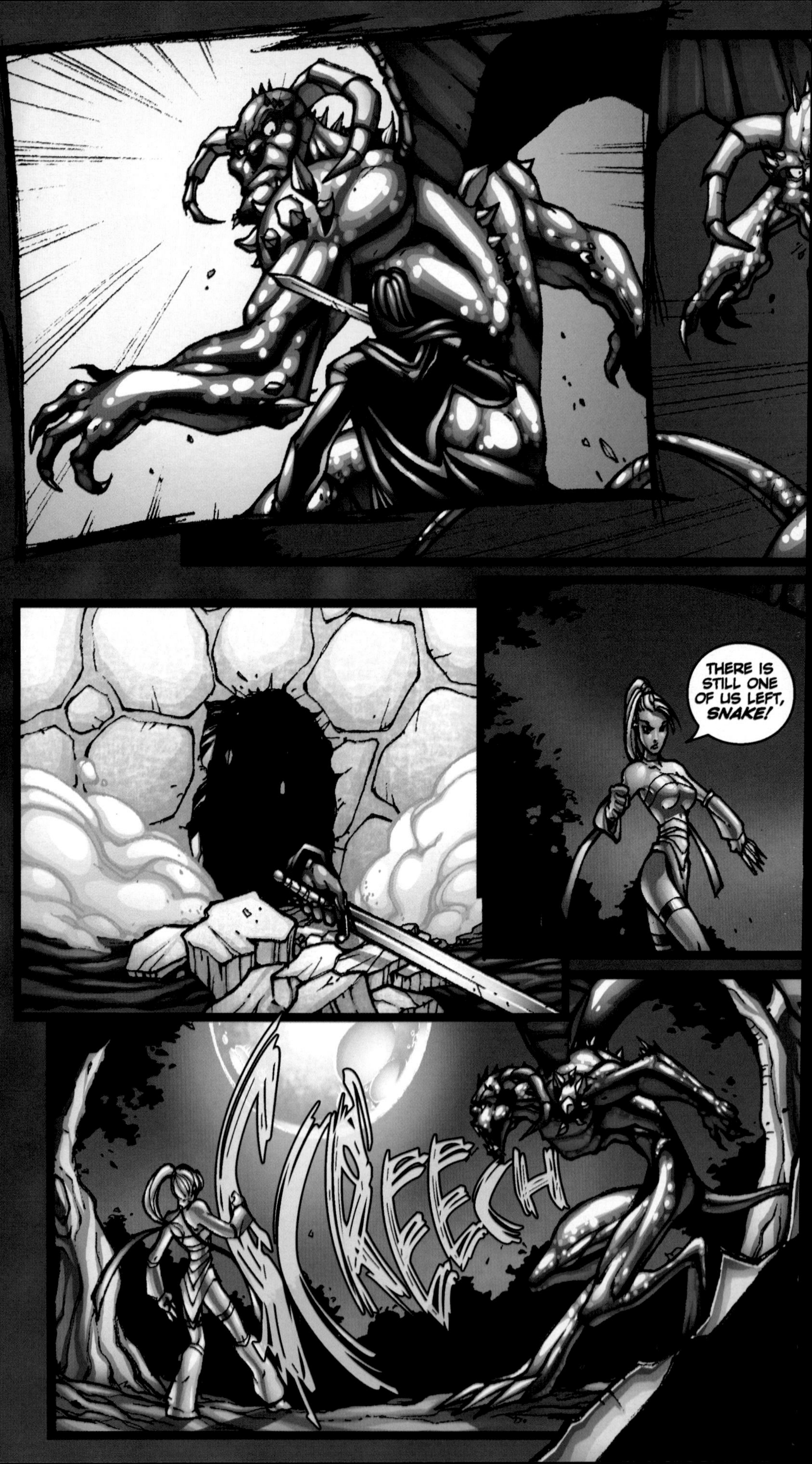
THERE IS STILL ONE OF US LEFT, SNAKE!
SKREECH

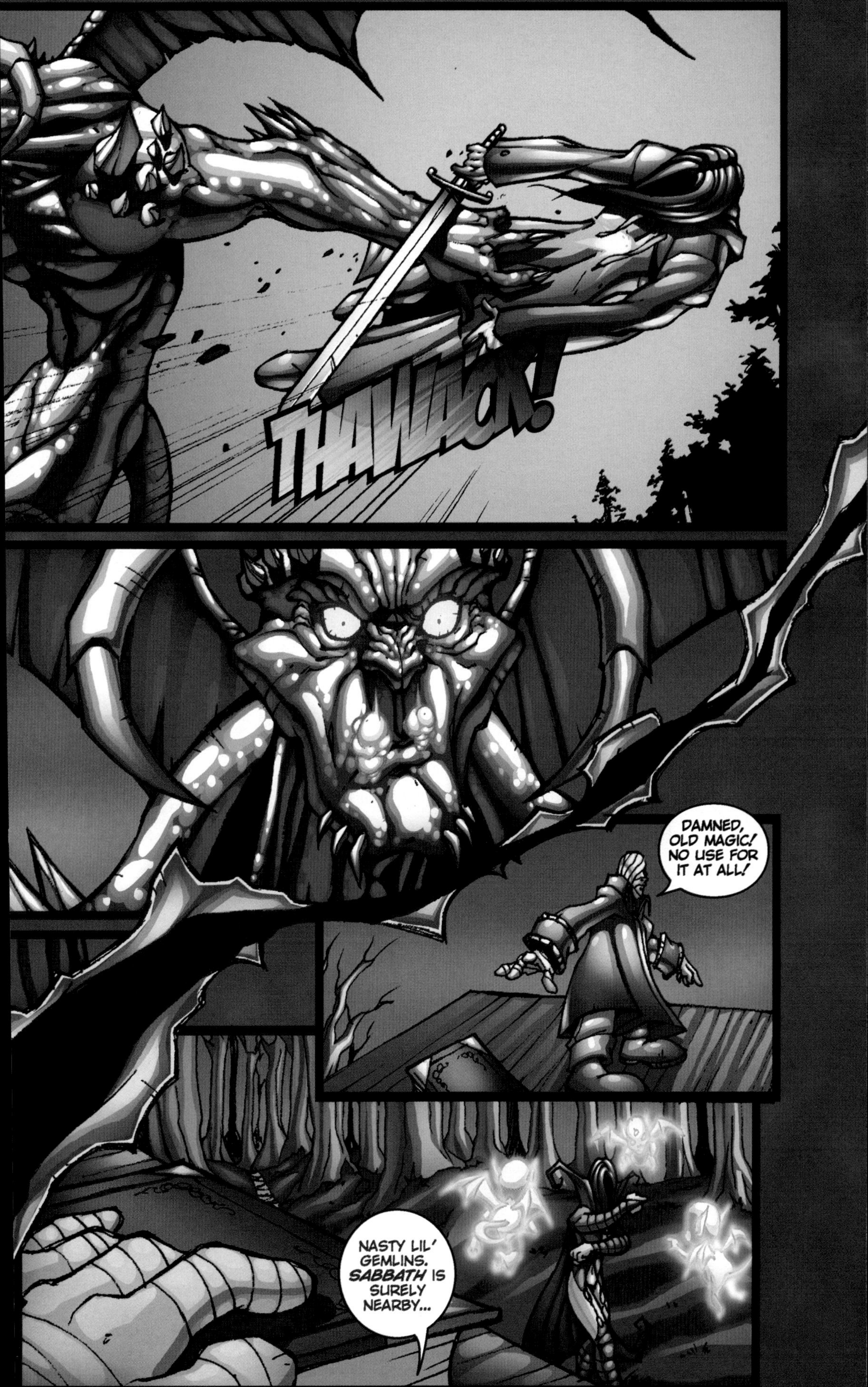
THAWACK!
DAMNED, OLD MAGIC! NO USE FOR IT AT ALL!
NASTY LIL' GEMLINS. SABBATH IS SURELY NEARBY...

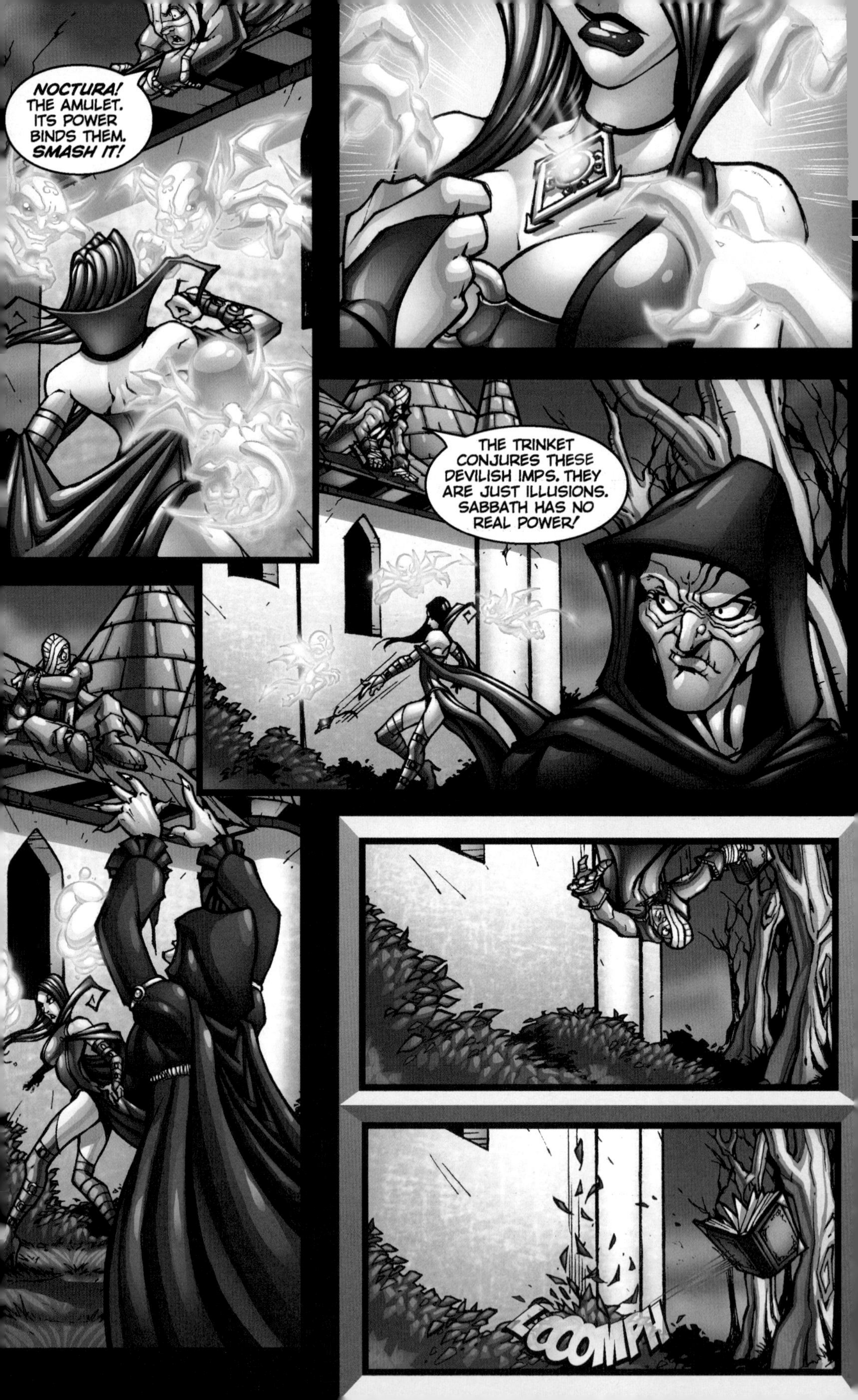
NOCTURA! THE AMULET. ITS POWER BINDS THEM. SMASH IT!
THE TRINKET CONJURES THESE DEVILISH IMPS. THEY ARE JUST ILLUSIONS. SABBATH HAS NO REAL POWER!
WOOOMPH

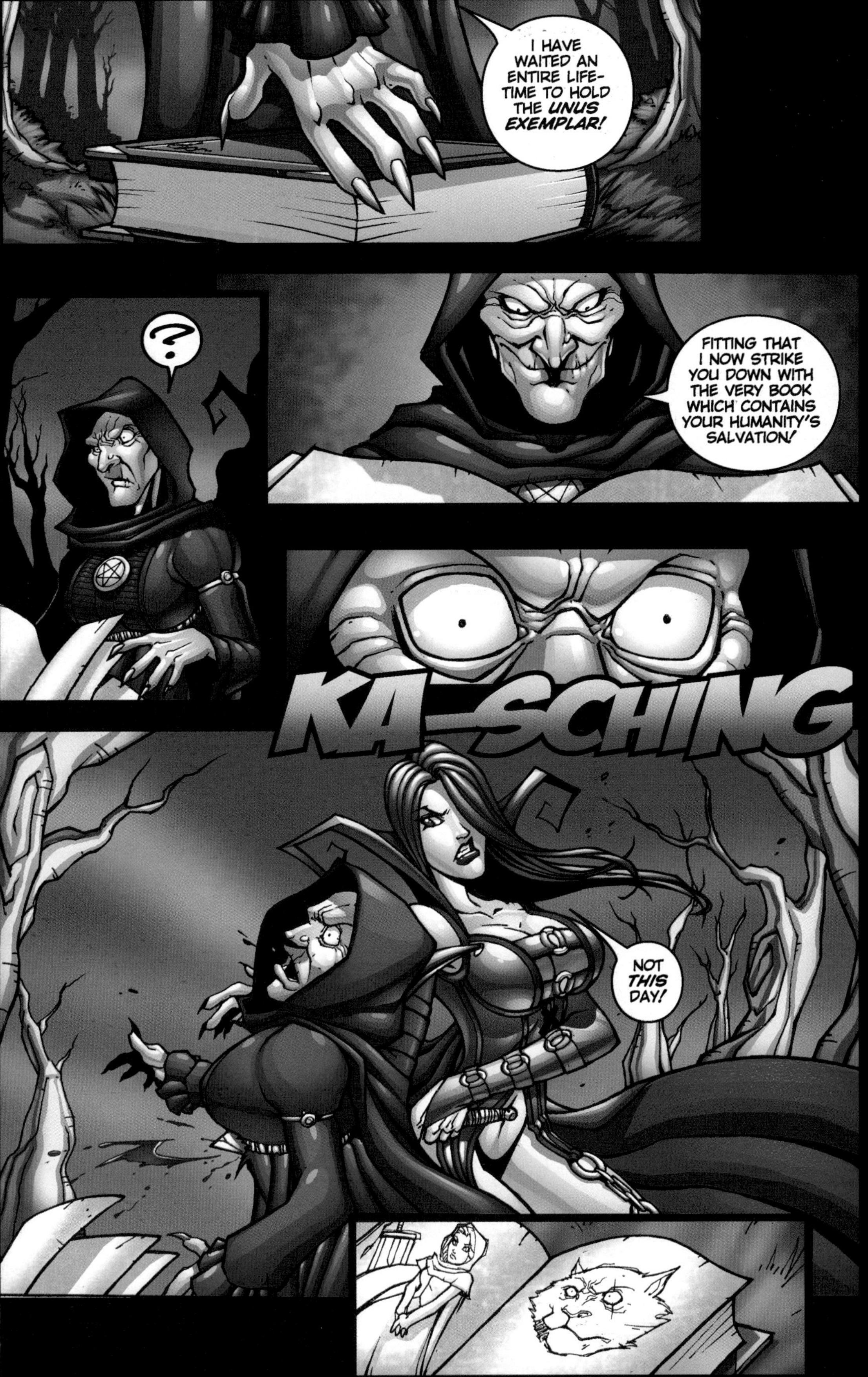
I HAVE WAITED AN ENTIRE LIFE-TIME TO HOLD THE *UNUS EXEMPLAR!*
?
FITTING THAT I NOW STRIKE YOU DOWN WITH THE VERY BOOK WHICH CONTAINS YOUR HUMANITY'S SALVATION!
KA-SCHING
NOT *THIS* DAY!

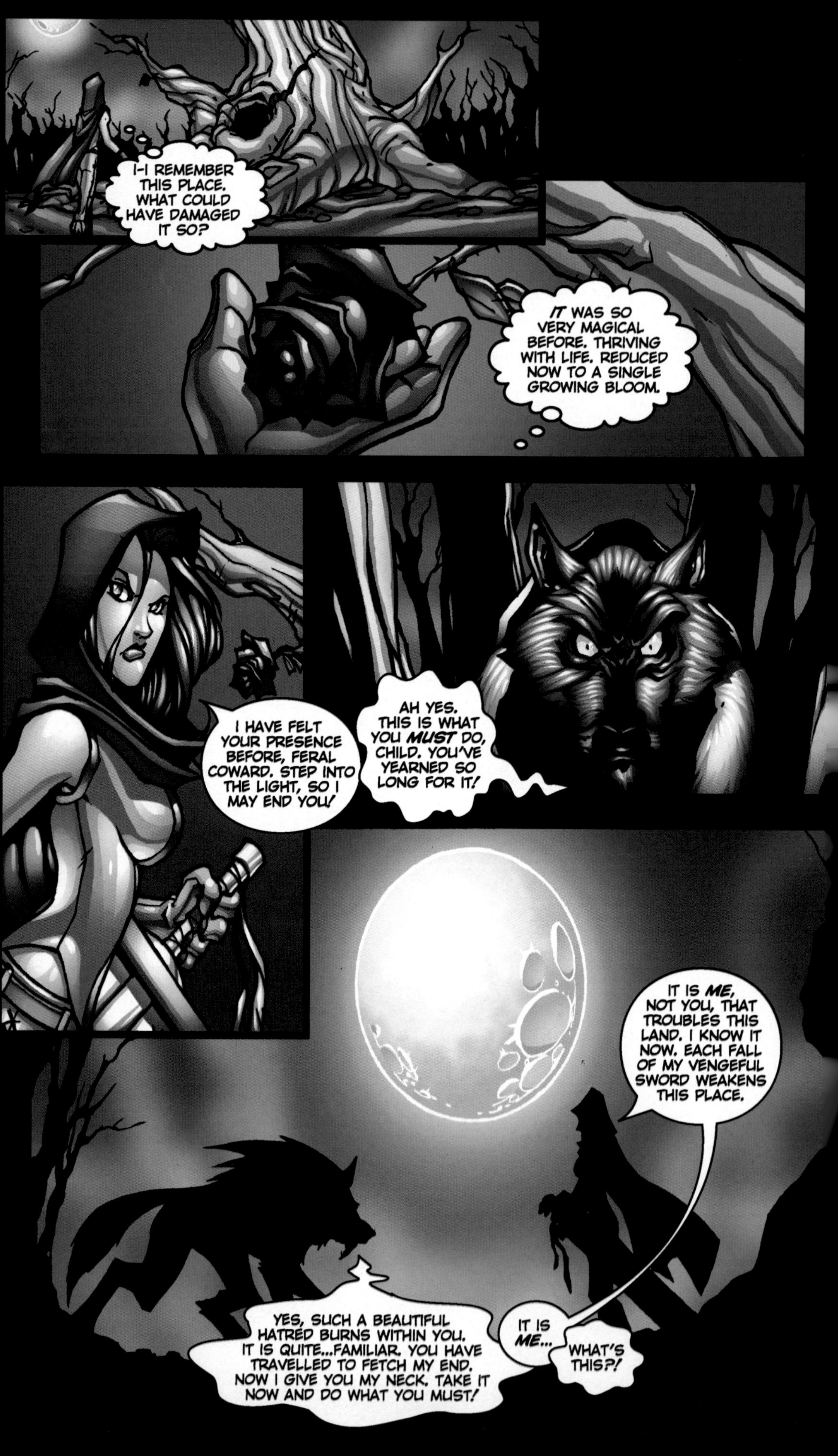
I-I REMEMBER THIS PLACE. WHAT COULD HAVE DAMAGED IT SO?
IT WAS SO VERY MAGICAL BEFORE. THRIVING WITH LIFE. REDUCED NOW TO A SINGLE GROWING BLOOM.
I HAVE FELT YOUR PRESENCE BEFORE, FERAL COWARD. STEP INTO THE LIGHT, SO I MAY END YOU!
AH YES. THIS IS WHAT YOU MUST DO, CHILD. YOU'VE YEARNED SO LONG FOR IT!
IT IS ME, NOT YOU, THAT TROUBLES THIS LAND. I KNOW IT NOW. EACH FALL OF MY VENGEFUL SWORD WEAKENS THIS PLACE.
YES, SUCH A BEAUTIFUL HATRED BURNS WITHIN YOU. IT IS QUITE...FAMILIAR. YOU HAVE TRAVELLED TO FETCH MY END. NOW I GIVE YOU MY NECK. TAKE IT NOW AND DO WHAT YOU MUST!
IT IS ME...
WHAT'S THIS?!

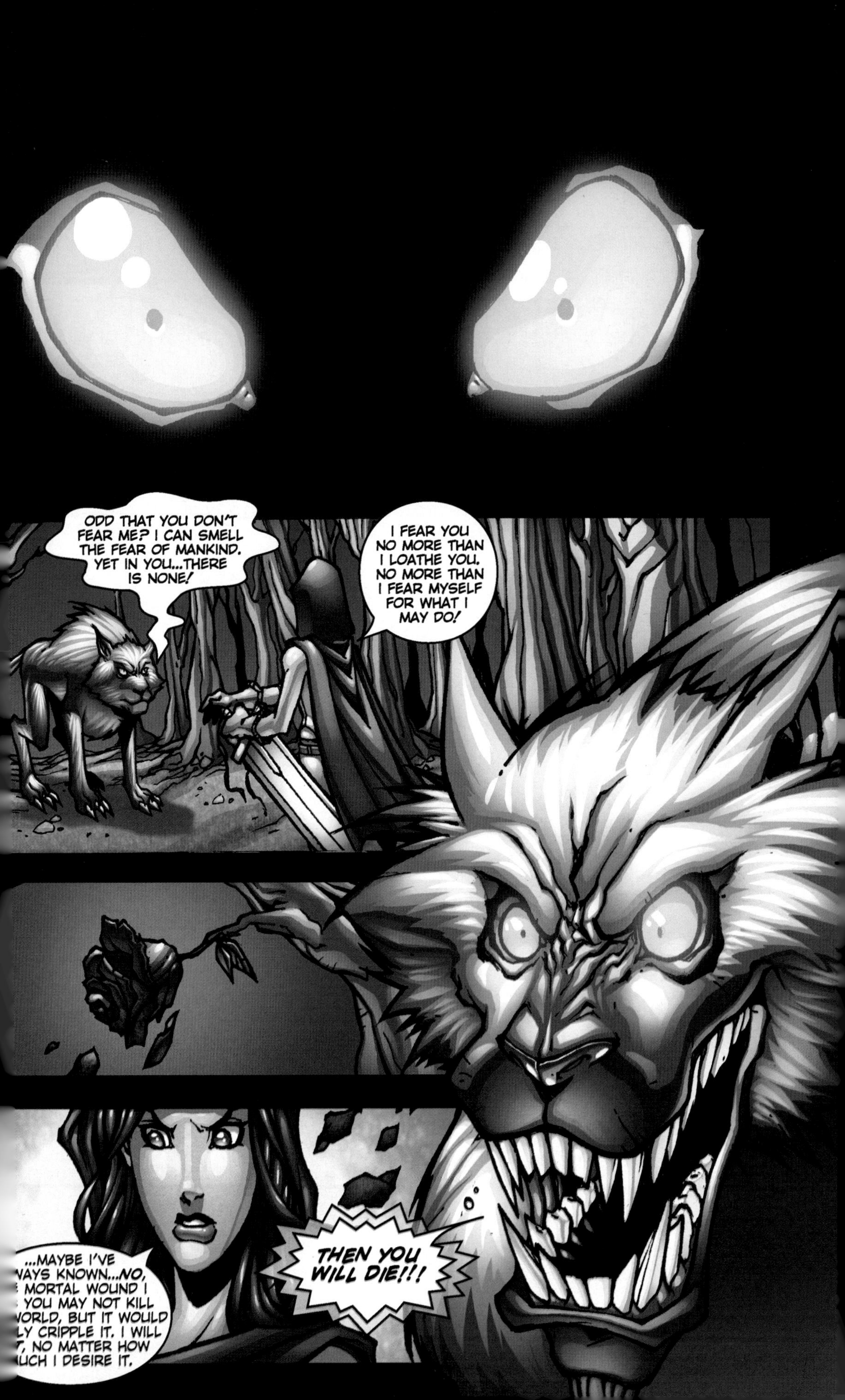
ODD THAT YOU DON'T FEAR ME? I CAN SMELL THE FEAR OF MANKIND. YET IN YOU...THERE IS NONE!
I FEAR YOU NO MORE THAN I LOATHE YOU. NO MORE THAN I FEAR MYSELF FOR WHAT I MAY DO!
...MAYBE I'VE VAYS KNOWN...NO, MORTAL WOUND I YOU MAY NOT KILL VORLD, BUT IT WOULD LY CRIPPLE IT. I WILL , NO MATTER HOW UCH I DESIRE IT.
THEN YOU WILL DIE!!!

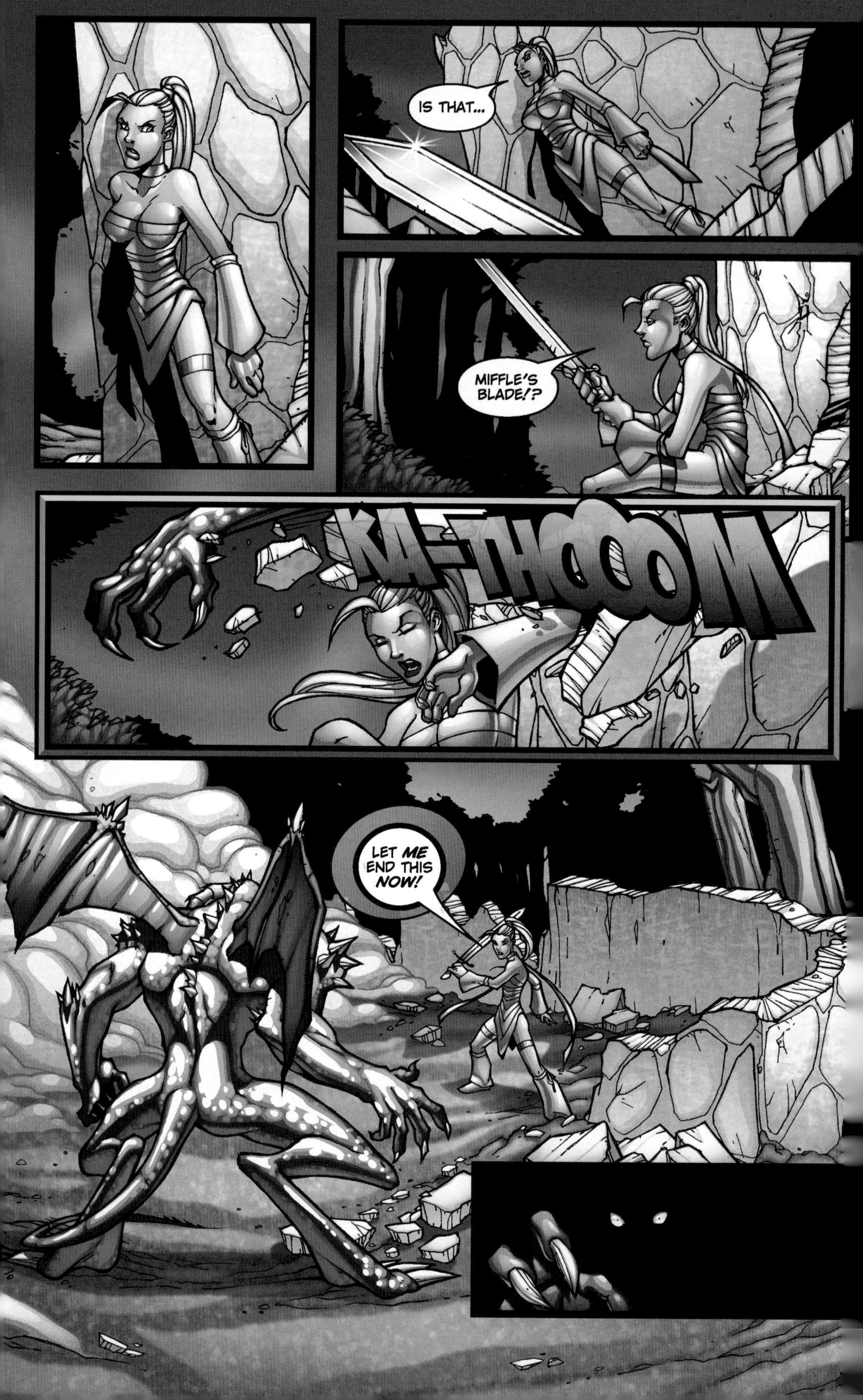
IS THAT...
MIFFLE'S BLADE!?
KA-THOOOM
LET ME END THIS NOW!

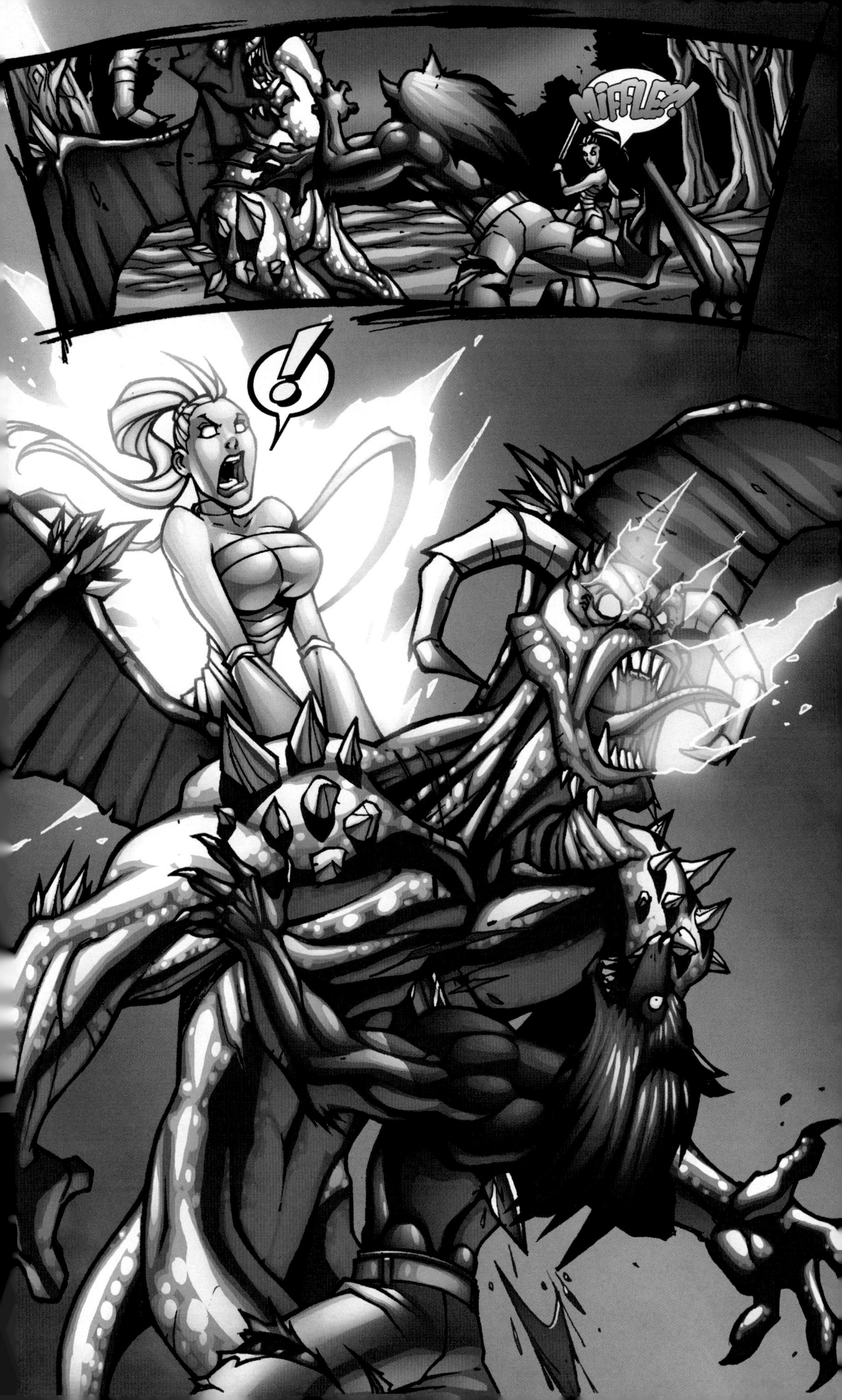
MIFFLE?!
!

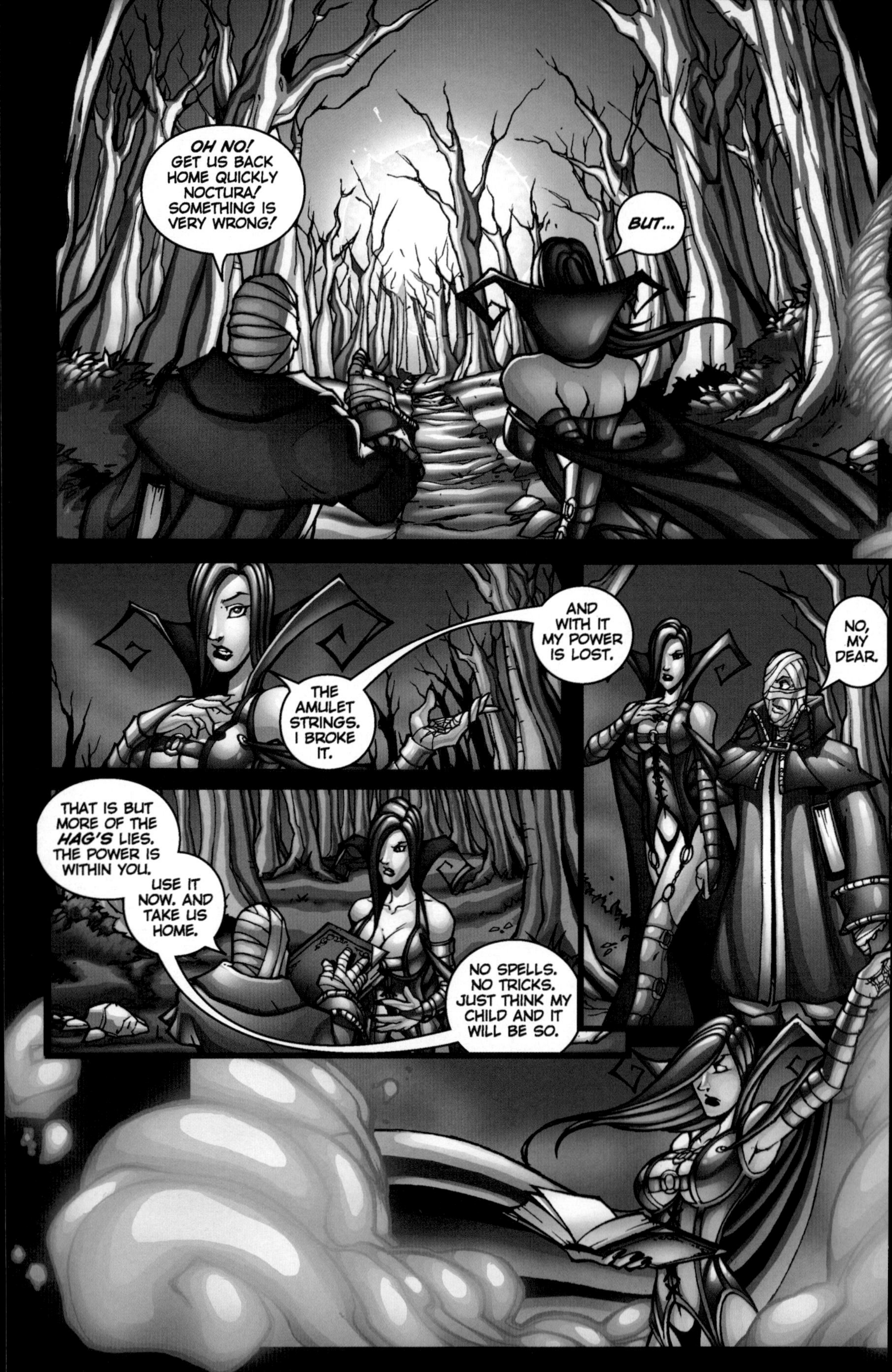

OH NO! GET US BACK HOME QUICKLY NOCTURA! SOMETHING IS VERY WRONG!
BUT...
THE AMULET STRINGS. I BROKE IT.
AND WITH IT MY POWER IS LOST.
NO, MY DEAR.
THAT IS BUT MORE OF THE *HAG'S* LIES. THE POWER IS WITHIN YOU.
USE IT NOW. AND TAKE US HOME.
NO SPELLS. NO TRICKS. JUST THINK MY CHILD AND IT WILL BE SO.

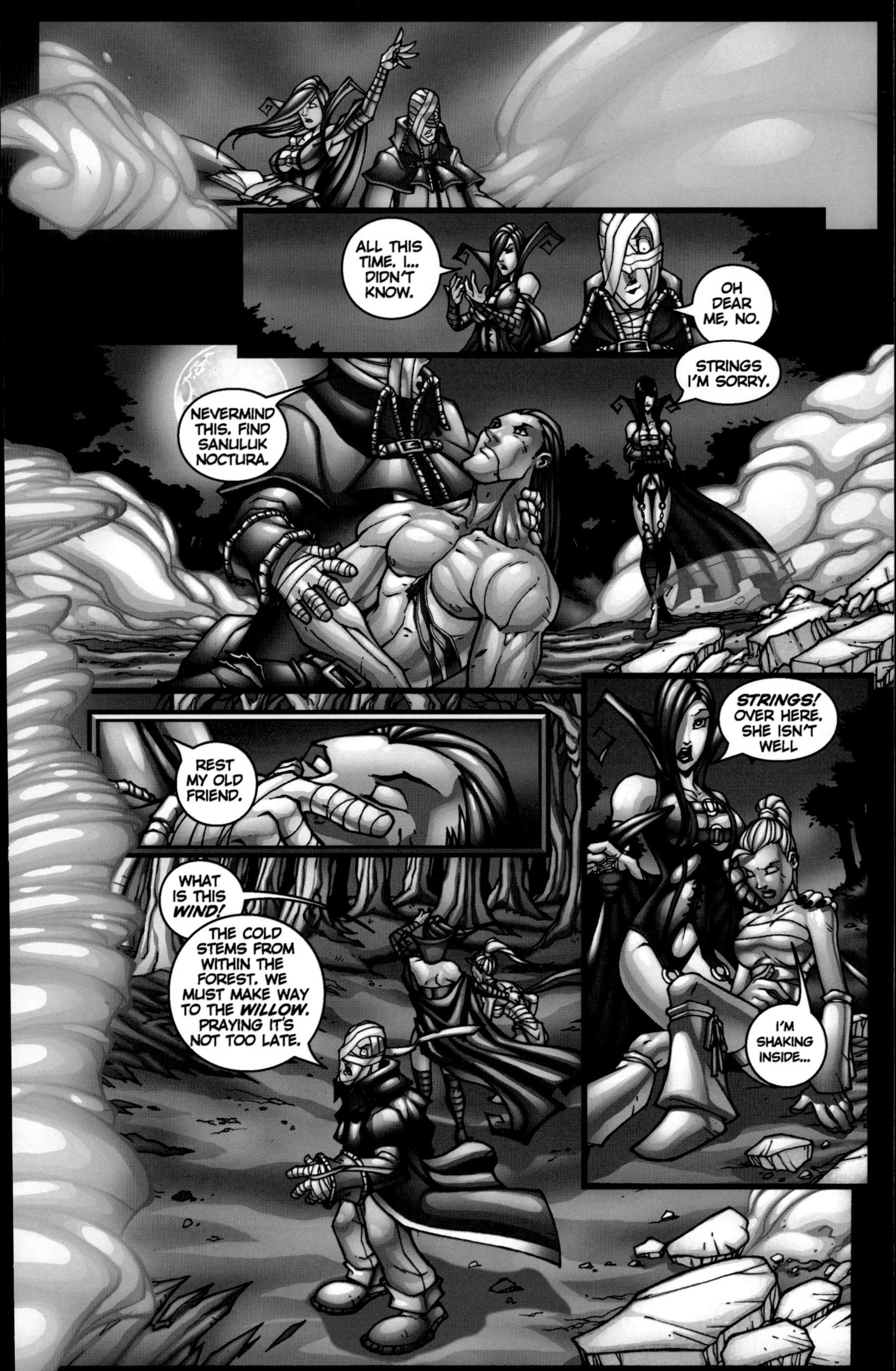
ALL THIS TIME. I... DIDN'T KNOW.
OH DEAR ME, NO.
STRINGS I'M SORRY.
NEVERMIND THIS. FIND SANULUK NOCTURA.
REST MY OLD FRIEND.
STRINGS! OVER HERE. SHE ISN'T WELL
I'M SHAKING INSIDE...
WHAT IS THIS WIND!
THE COLD STEMS FROM WITHIN THE FOREST. WE MUST MAKE WAY TO THE WILLOW. PRAYING IT'S NOT TOO LATE.

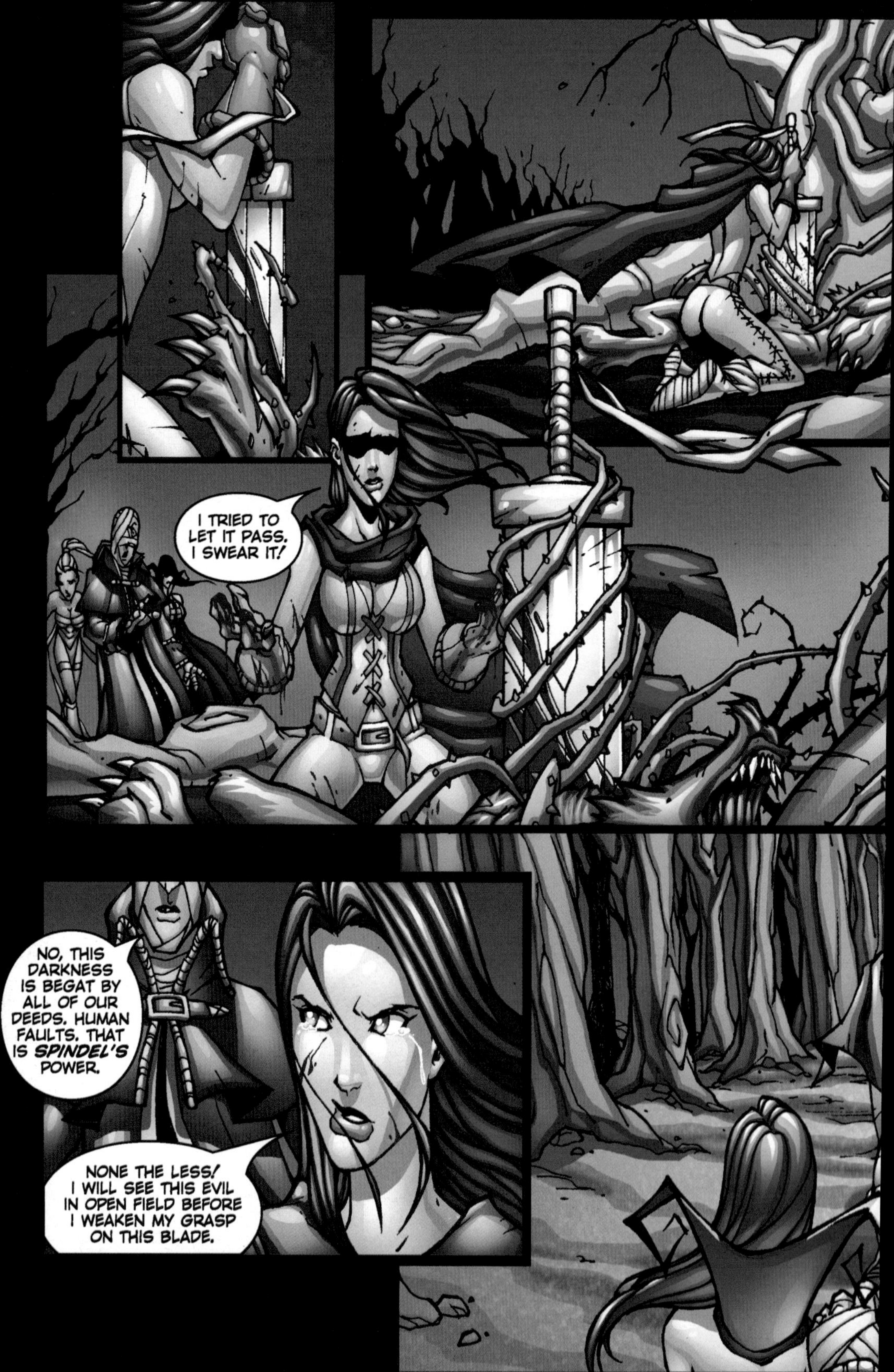
I TRIED TO LET IT PASS. I SWEAR IT!
NO, THIS DARKNESS IS BEGAT BY ALL OF OUR DEEDS. HUMAN FAULTS. THAT IS SPINDEL'S POWER.
NONE THE LESS! I WILL SEE THIS EVIL IN OPEN FIELD BEFORE I WEAKEN MY GRASP ON THIS BLADE.

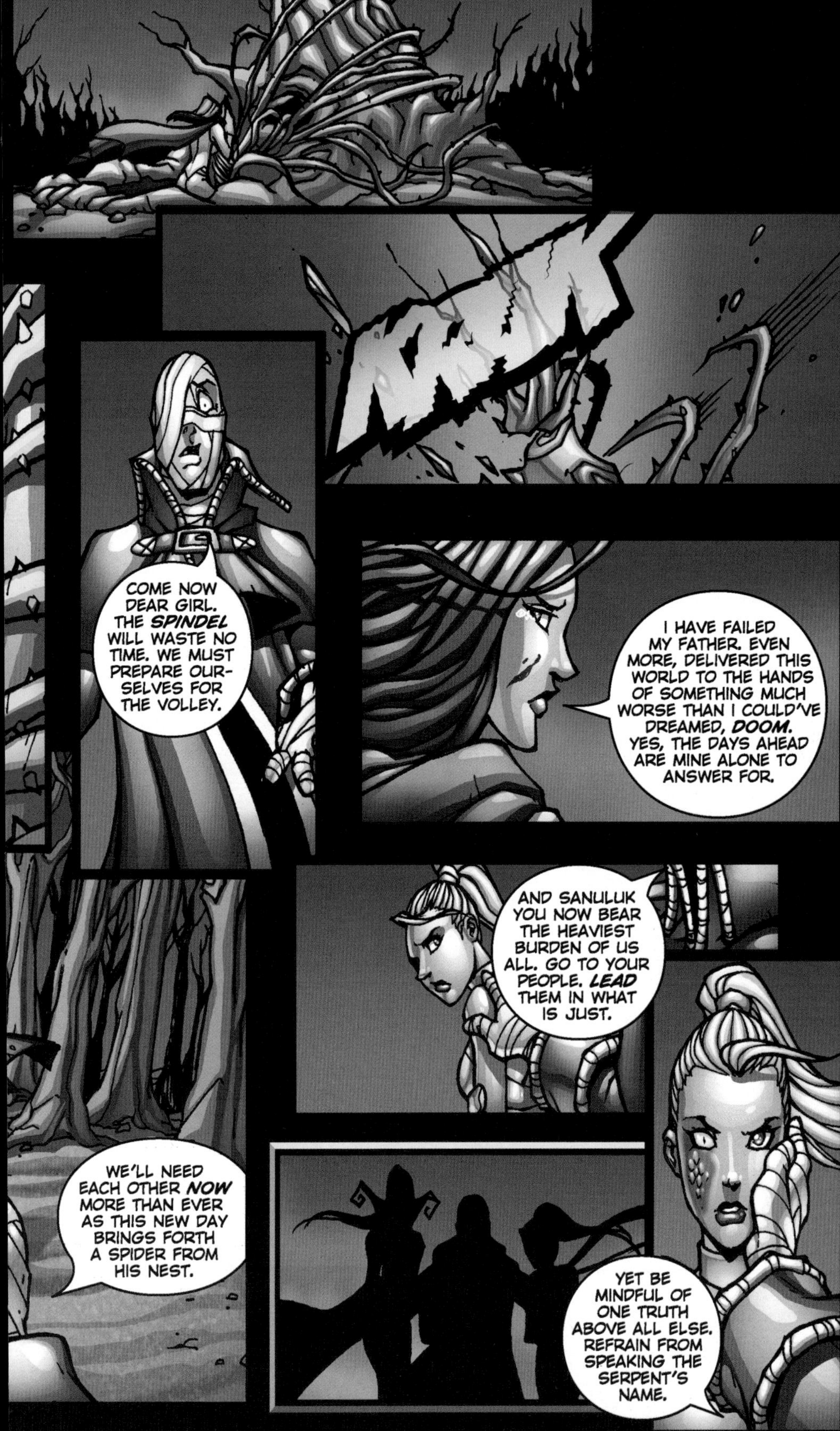
COME NOW DEAR GIRL. THE SPINDEL WILL WASTE NO TIME. WE MUST PREPARE OUR-SELVES FOR THE VOLLEY.
I HAVE FAILED MY FATHER. EVEN MORE, DELIVERED THIS WORLD TO THE HANDS OF SOMETHING MUCH WORSE THAN I COULD'VE DREAMED, DOOM. YES, THE DAYS AHEAD ARE MINE ALONE TO ANSWER FOR.
AND SANULUK YOU NOW BEAR THE HEAVIEST BURDEN OF US ALL. GO TO YOUR PEOPLE. LEAD THEM IN WHAT IS JUST.
WE'LL NEED EACH OTHER NOW MORE THAN EVER AS THIS NEW DAY BRINGS FORTH A SPIDER FROM HIS NEST.
YET BE MINDFUL OF ONE TRUTH ABOVE ALL ELSE. REFRAIN FROM SPEAKING THE SERPENT'S NAME.

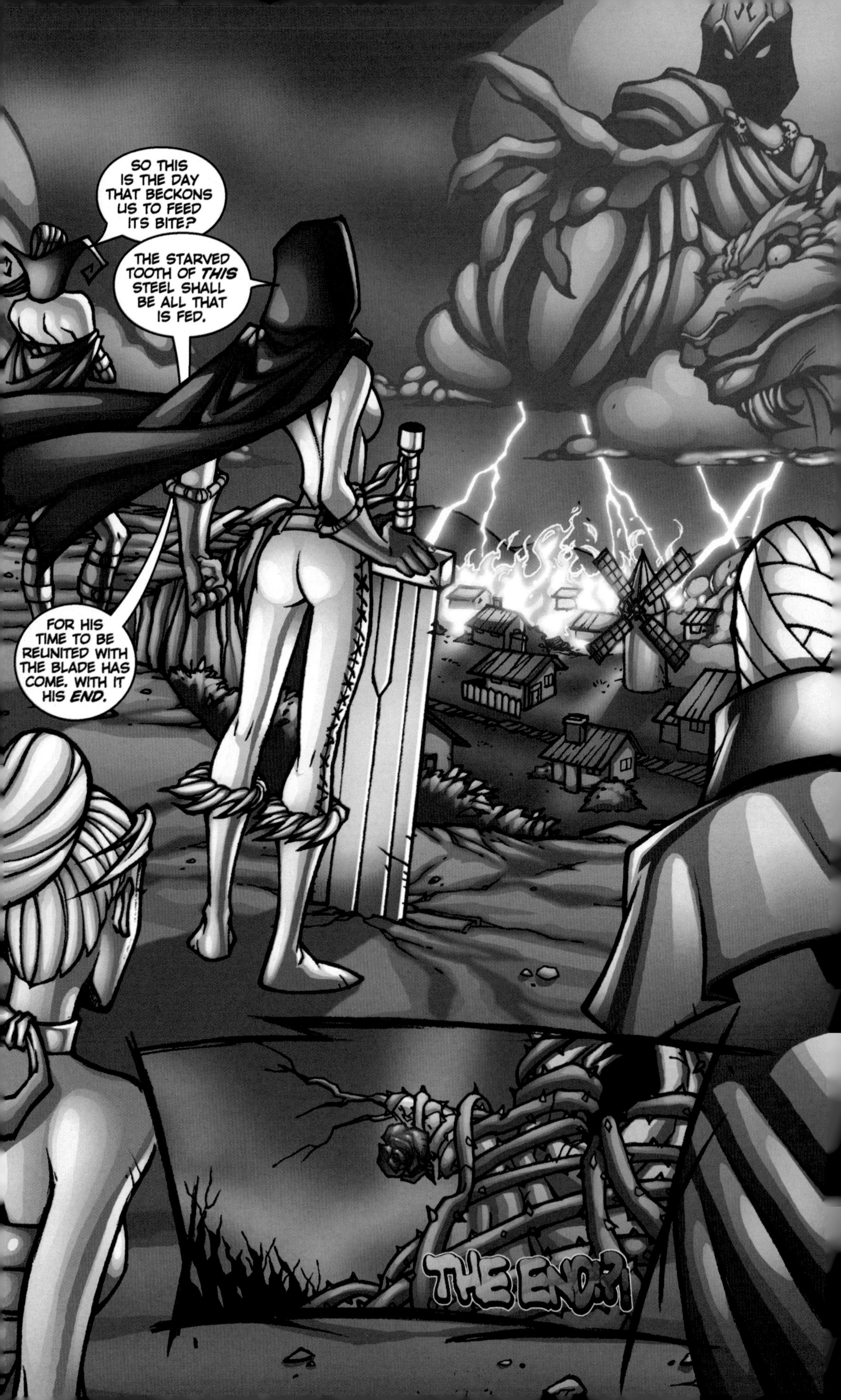
SO THIS IS THE DAY THAT BECKONS US TO FEED ITS BITE?
THE STARVED TOOTH OF *THIS* STEEL SHALL BE ALL THAT IS FED.
FOR HIS TIME TO BE REUNITED WITH THE BLADE HAS COME. WITH IT HIS *END*.
THE END?!

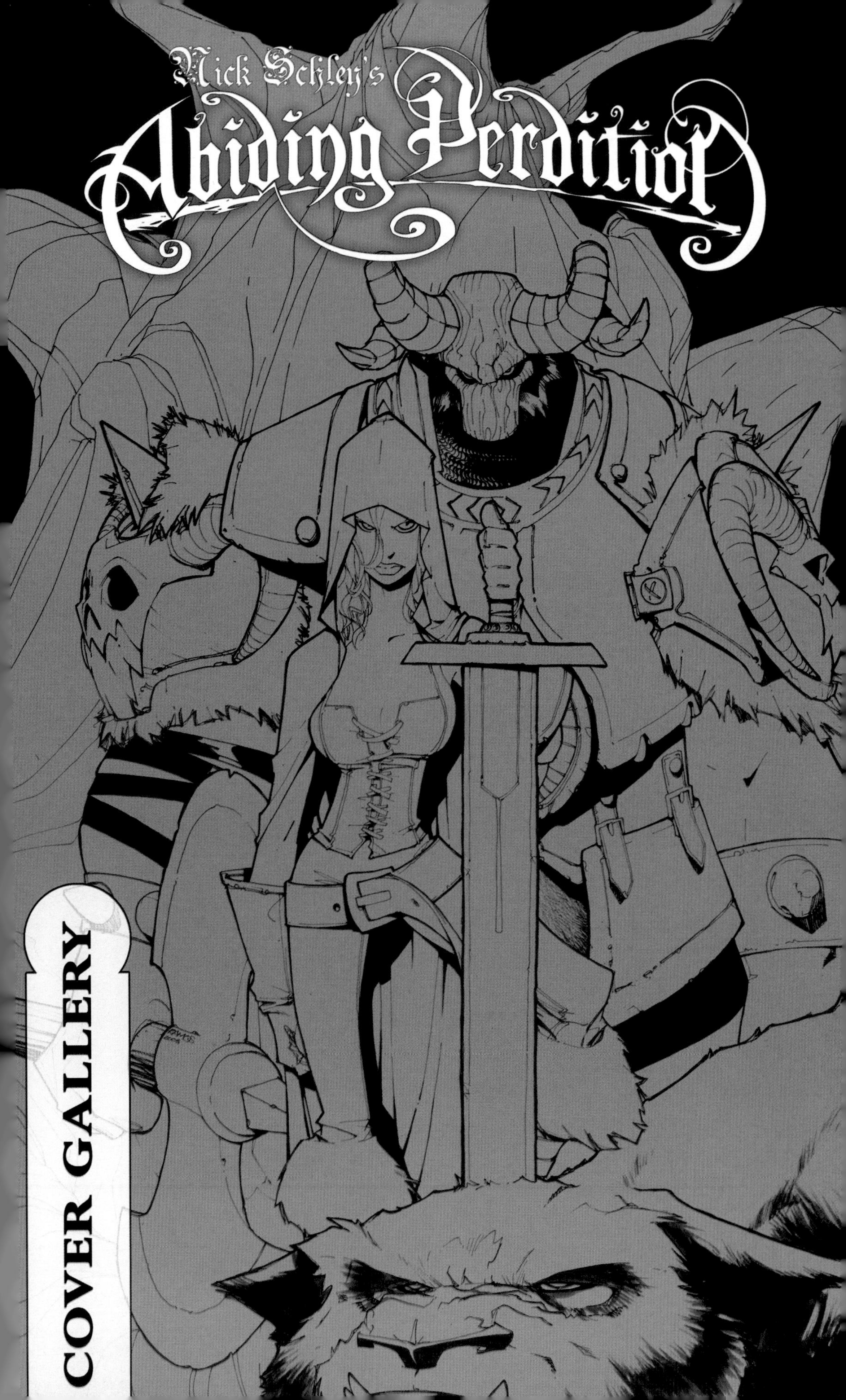
Nick Sekley's
Abiding Perdition
COVER GALLERY

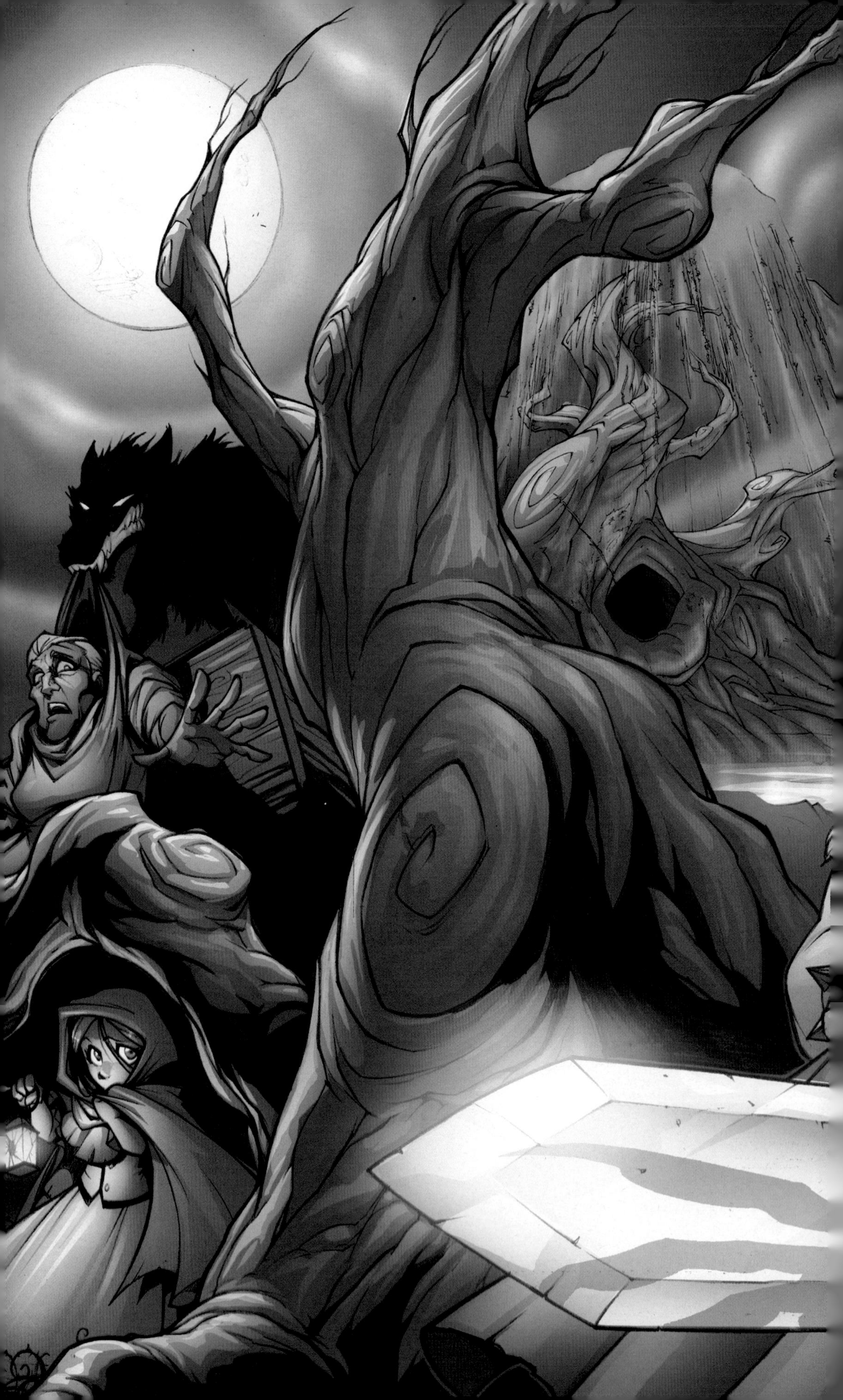

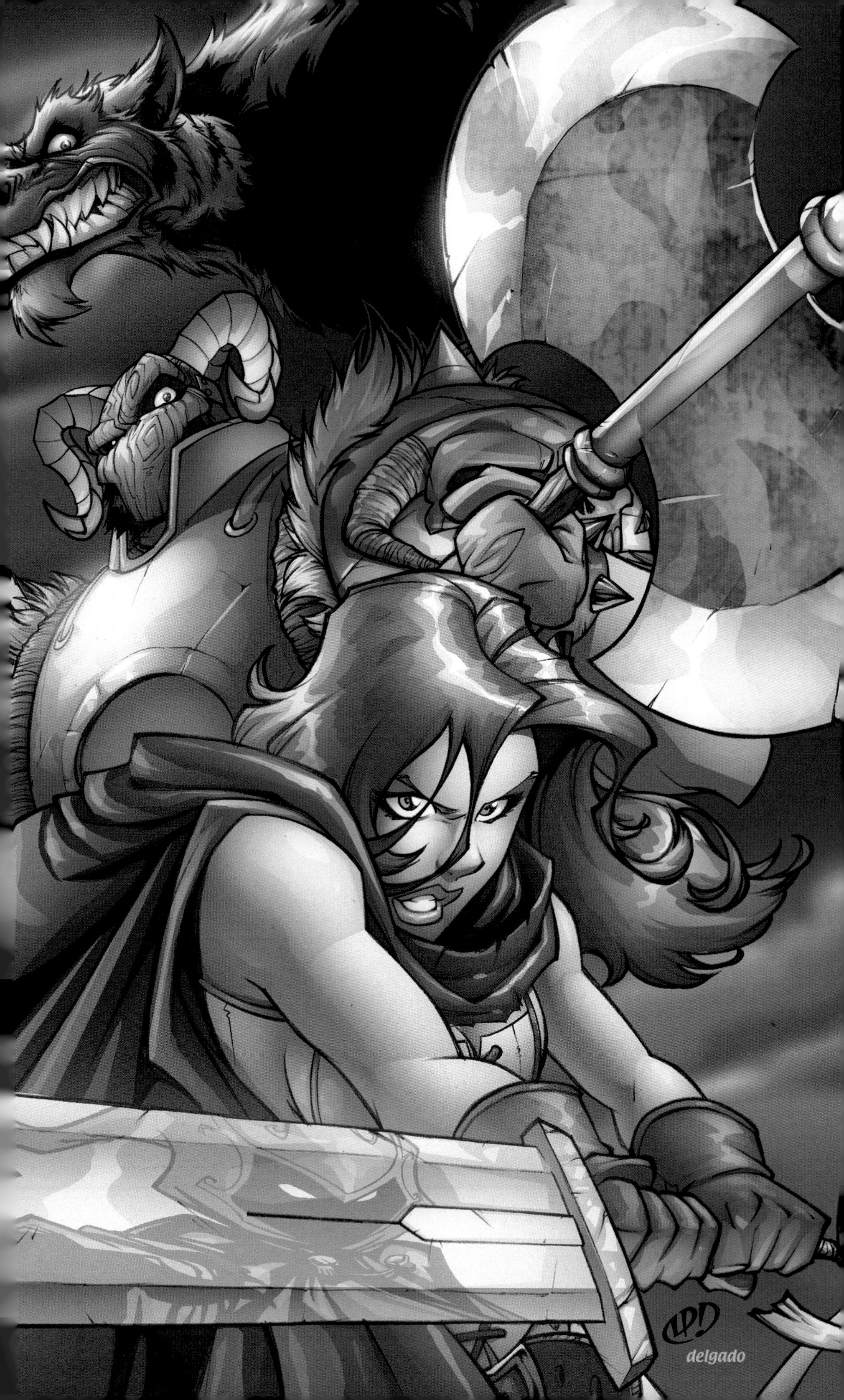
delgado

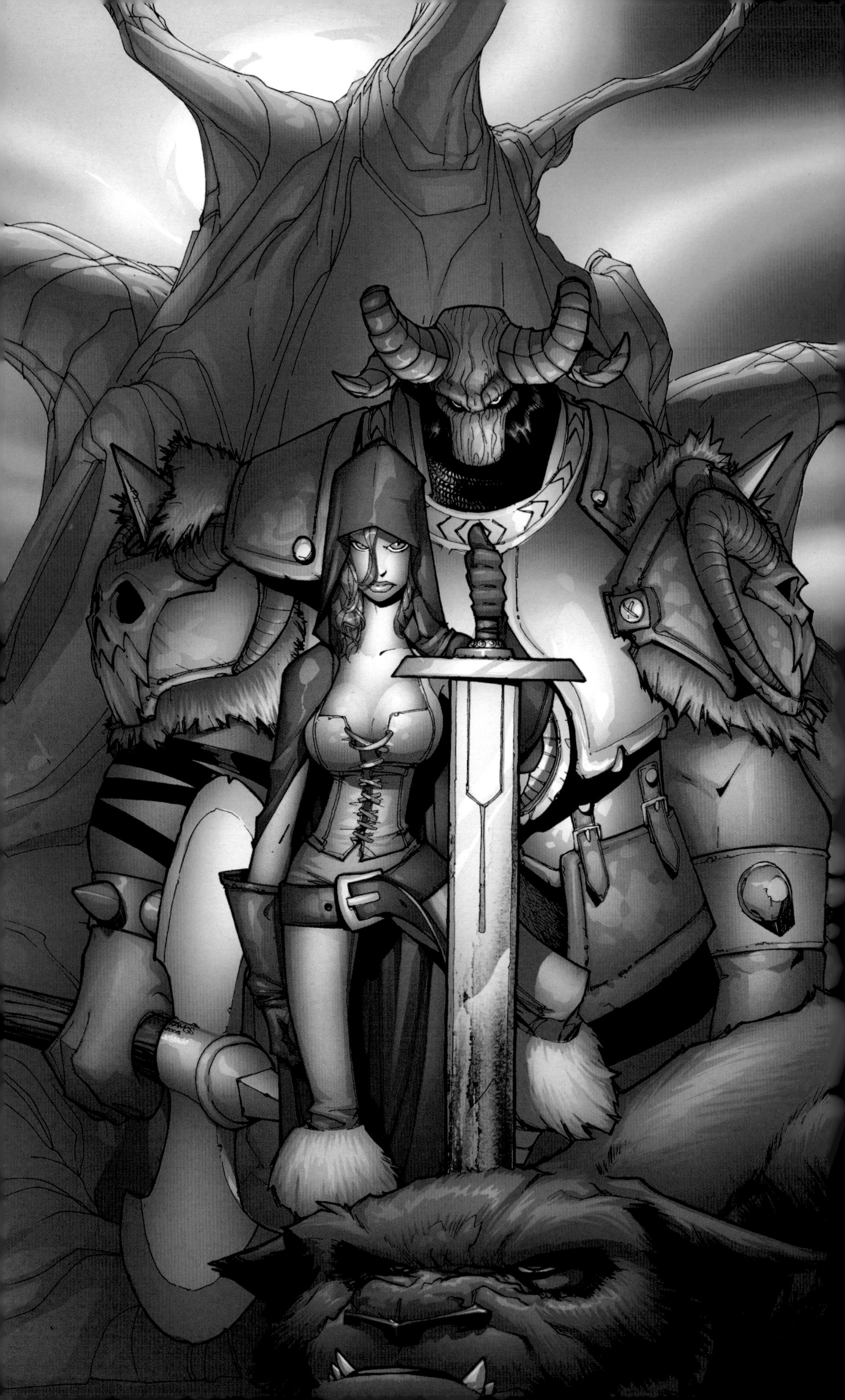

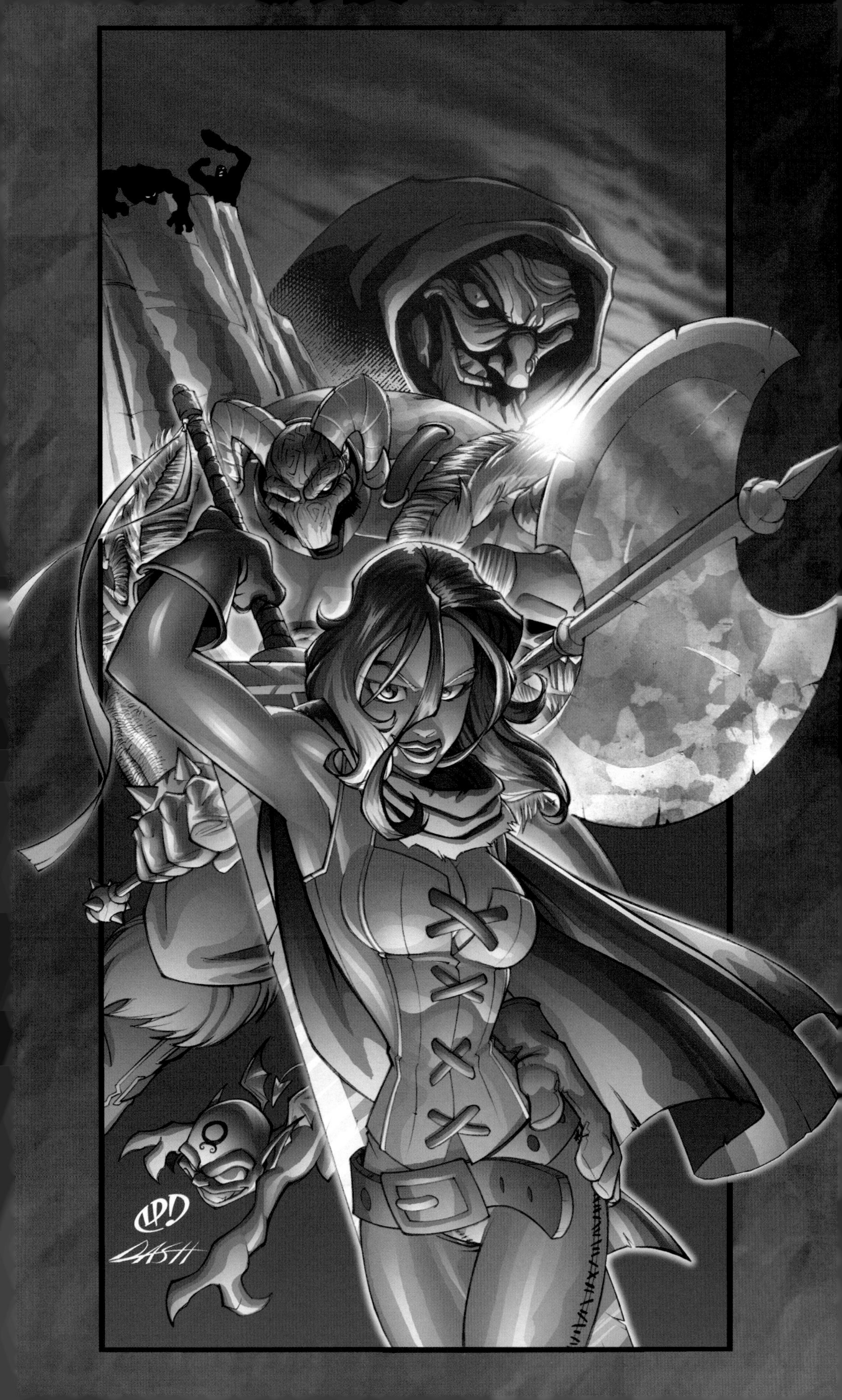

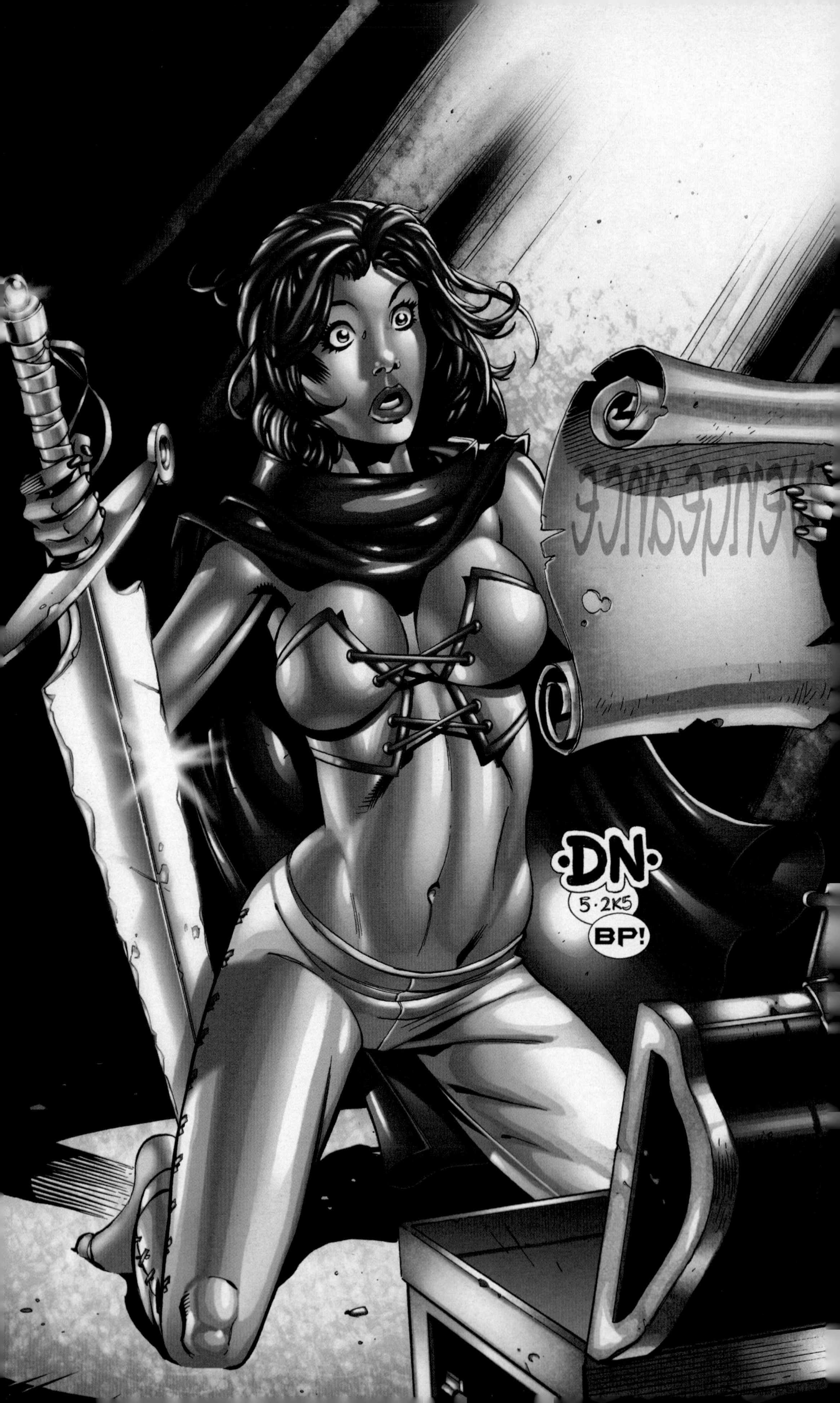
·DN·
5·2K5
BP!

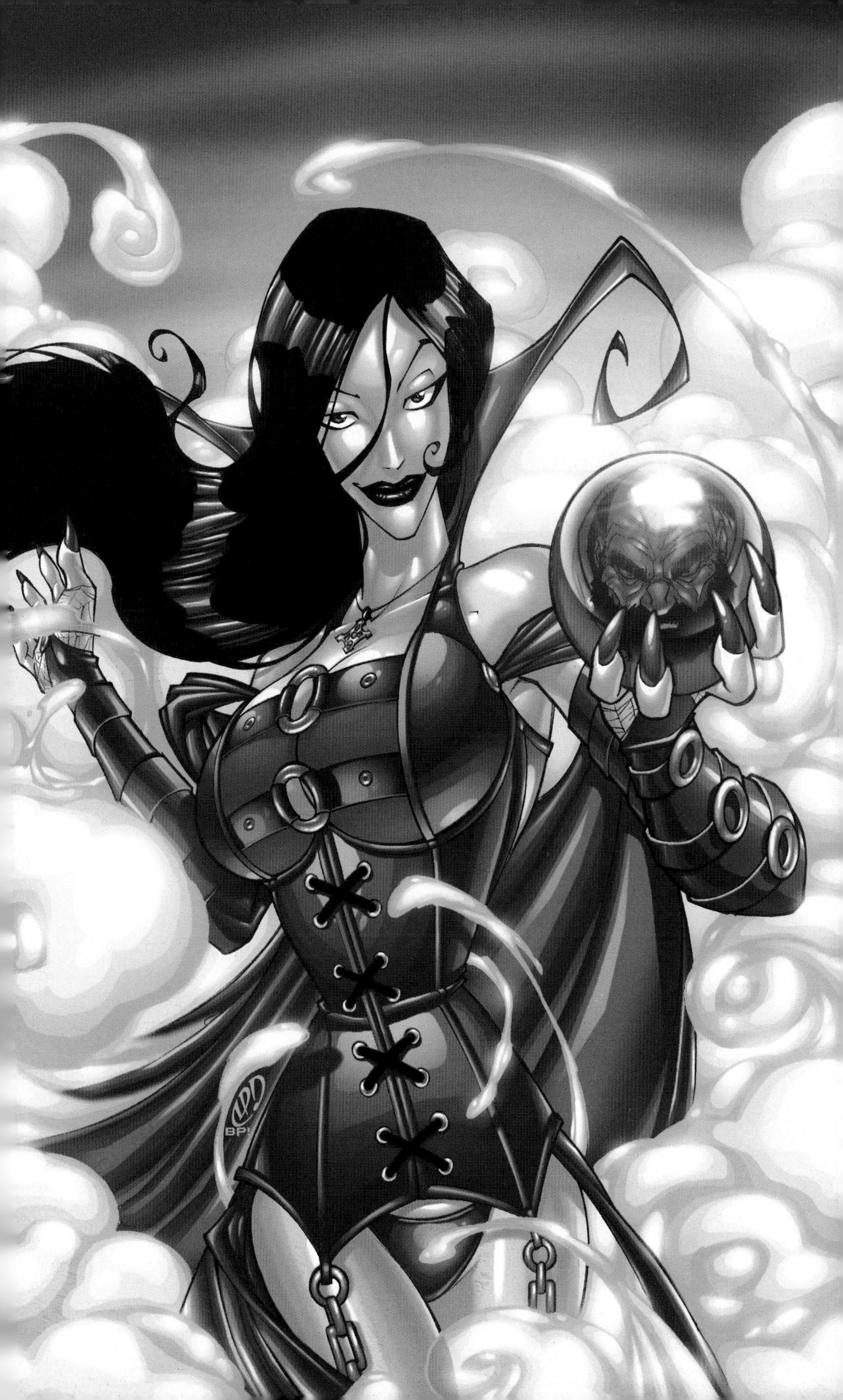
BP!

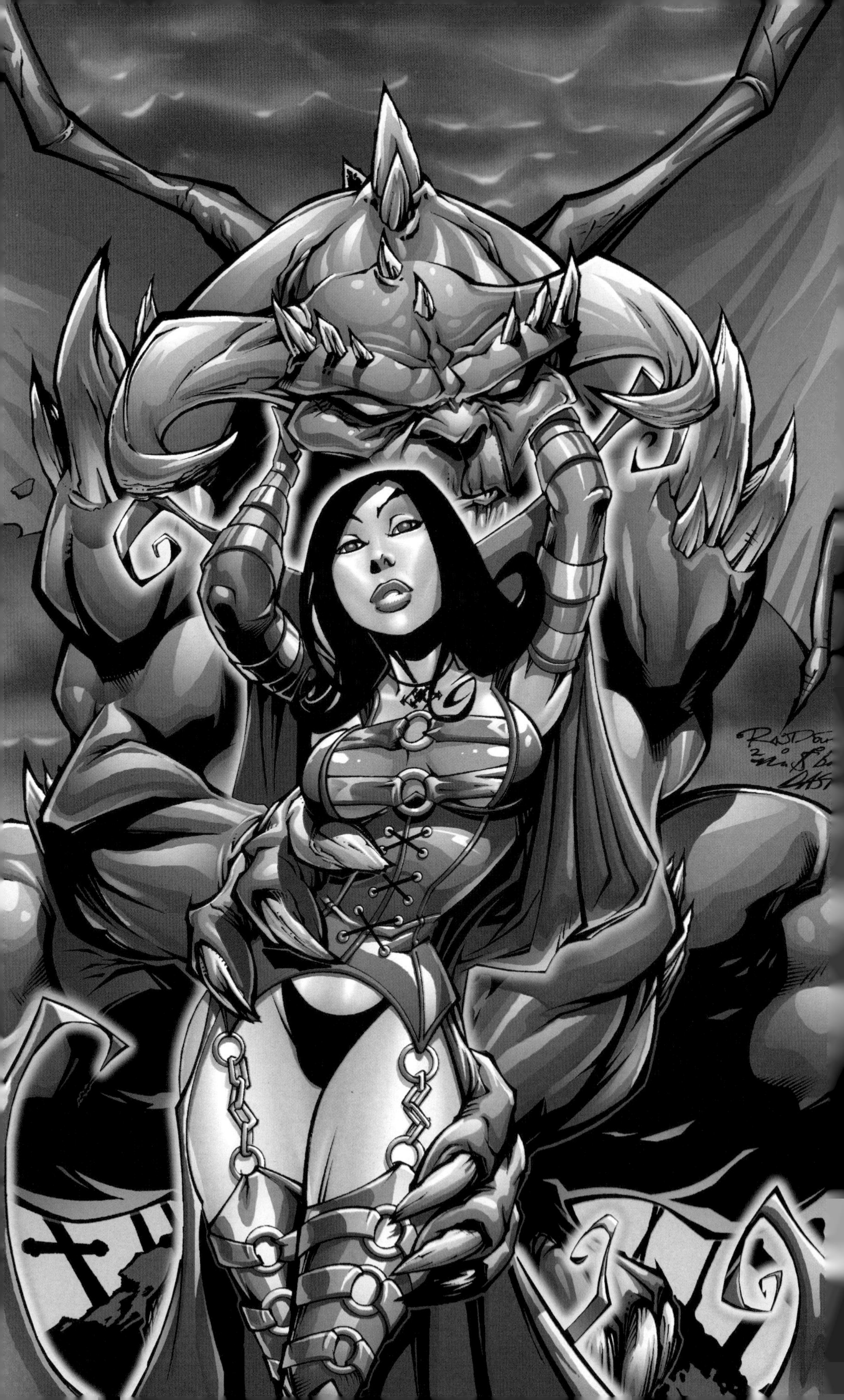

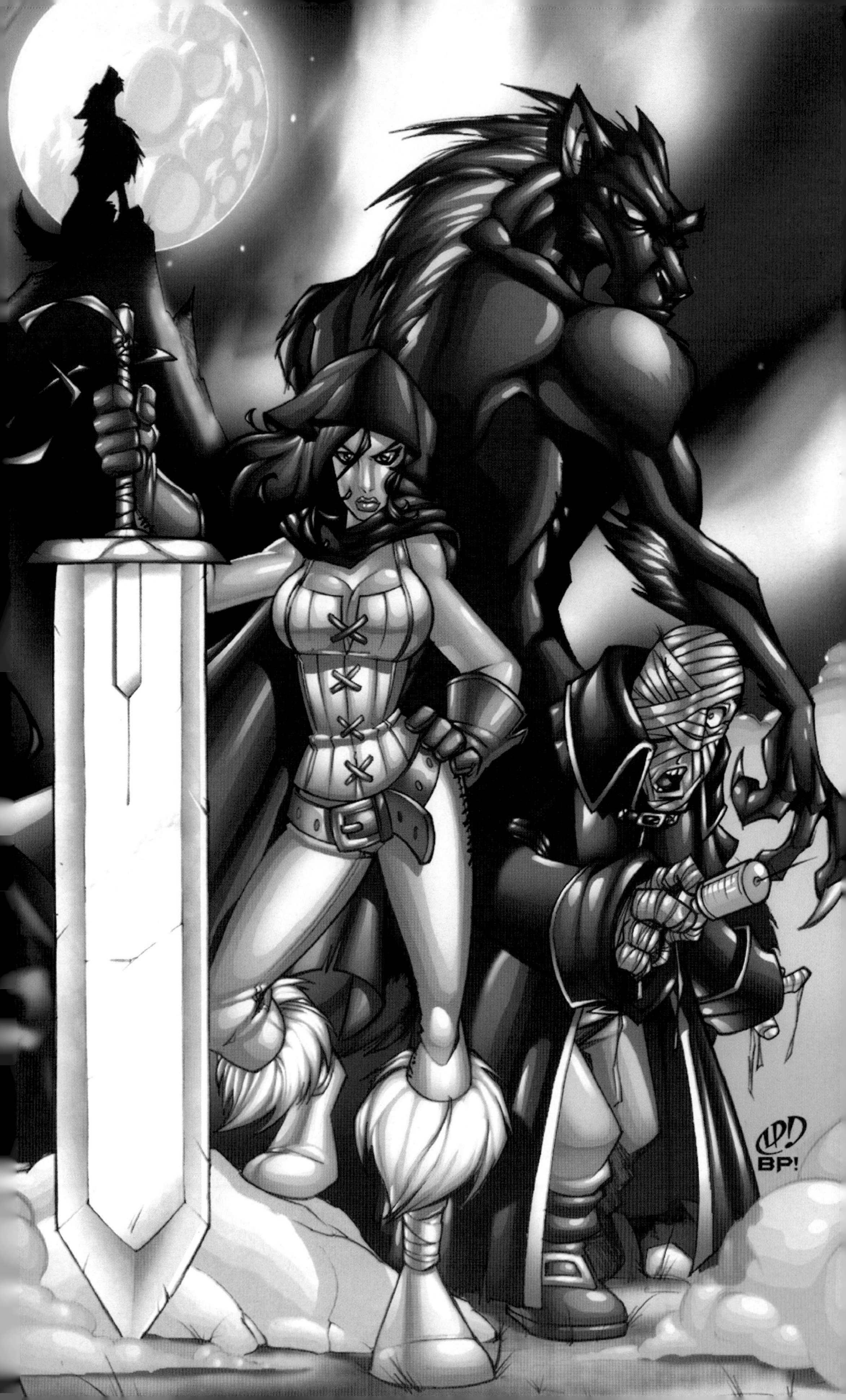
BP!

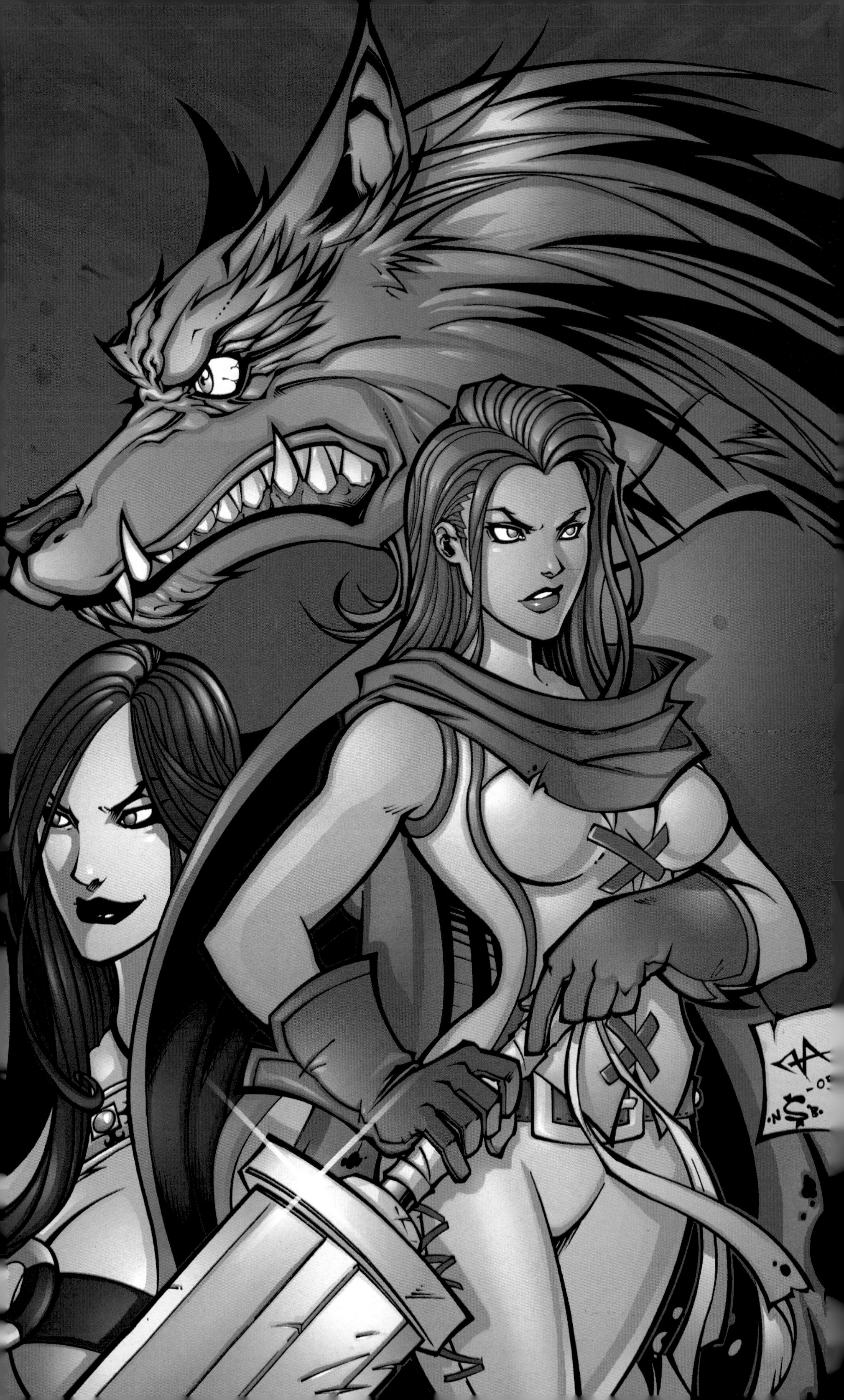

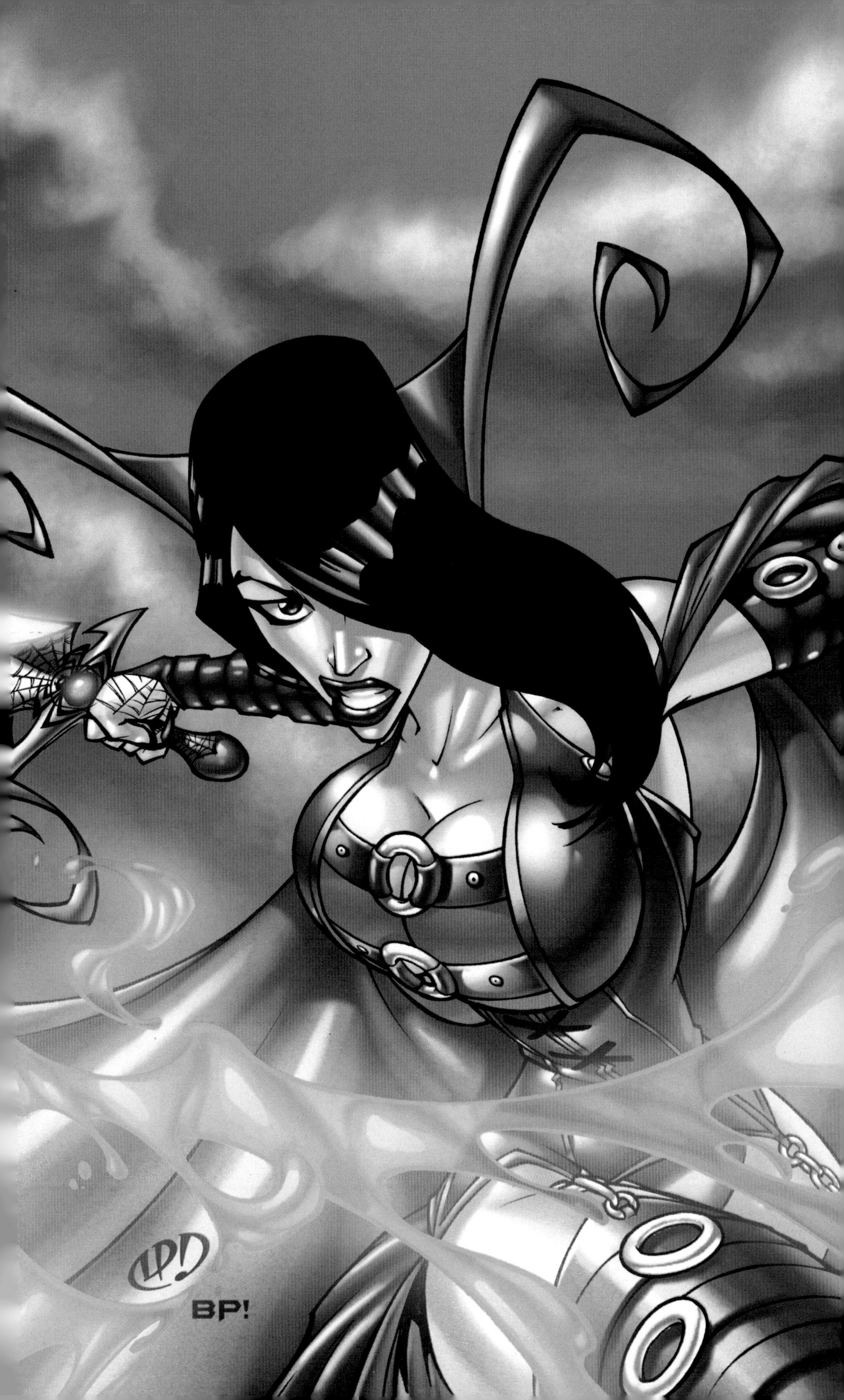
BP!

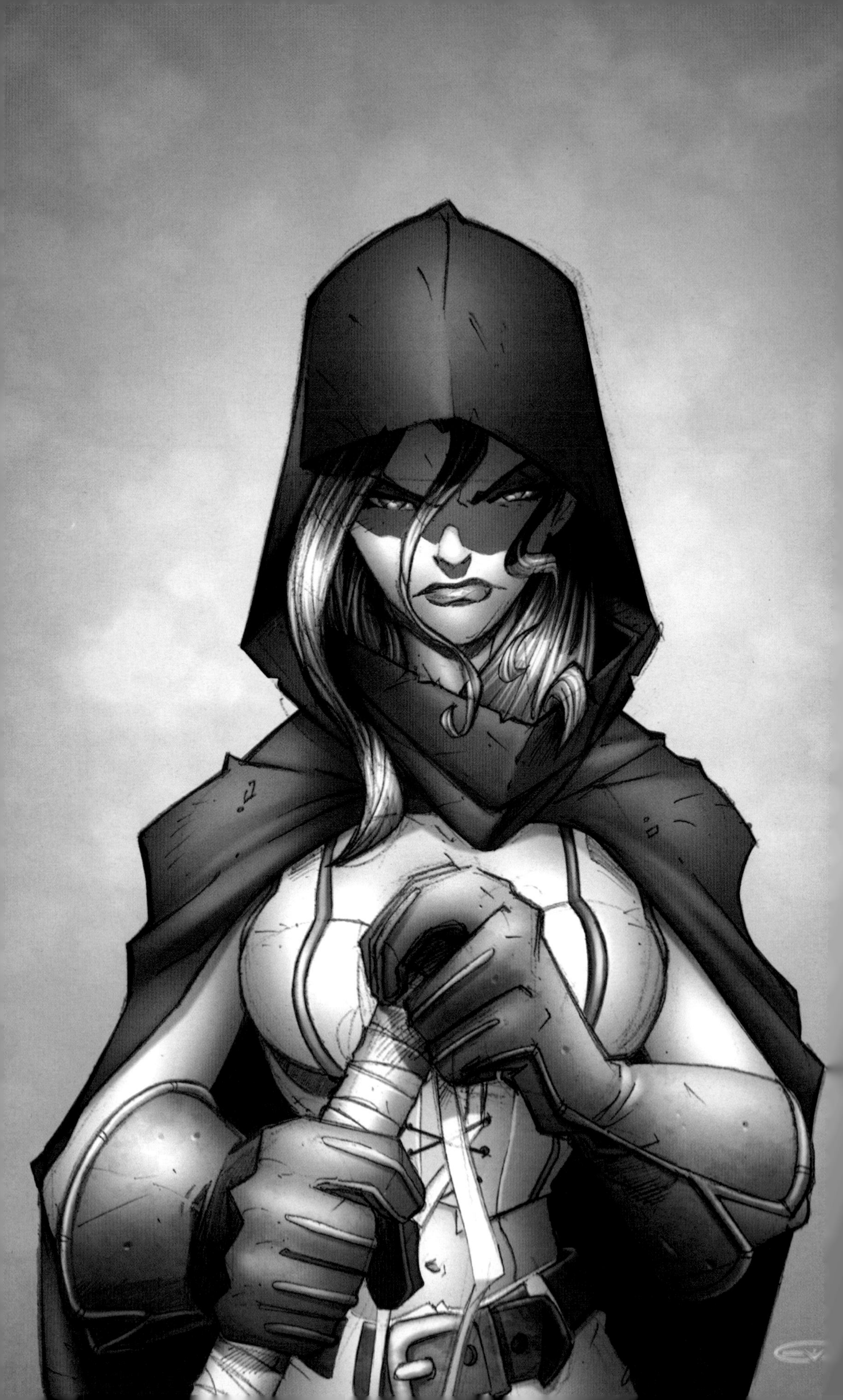

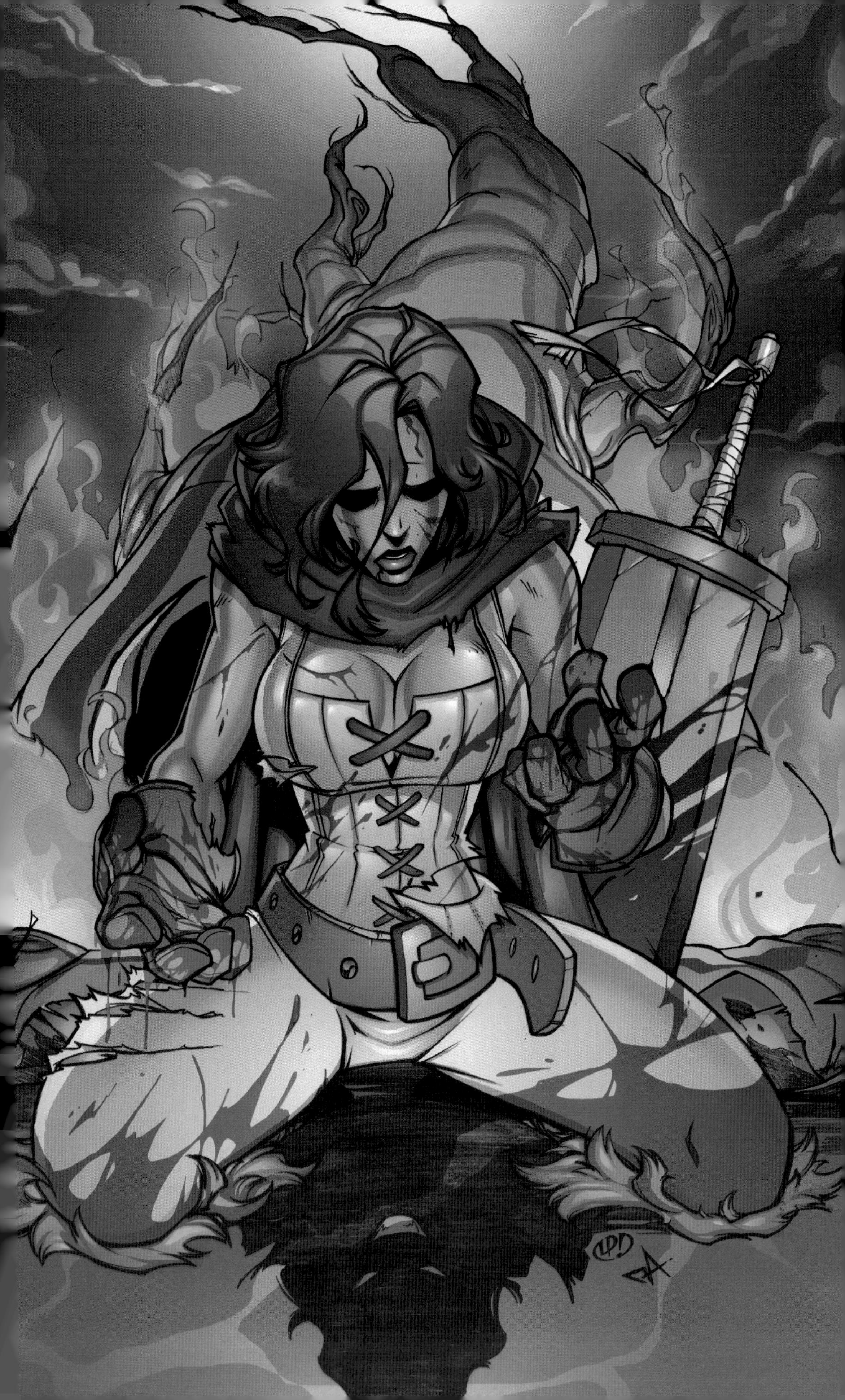

IN LOVING MEMORY OF

JESSE C. BOWLING SR.

1ST LT. US AIR CORPS. 4.6.1921-7.19.200

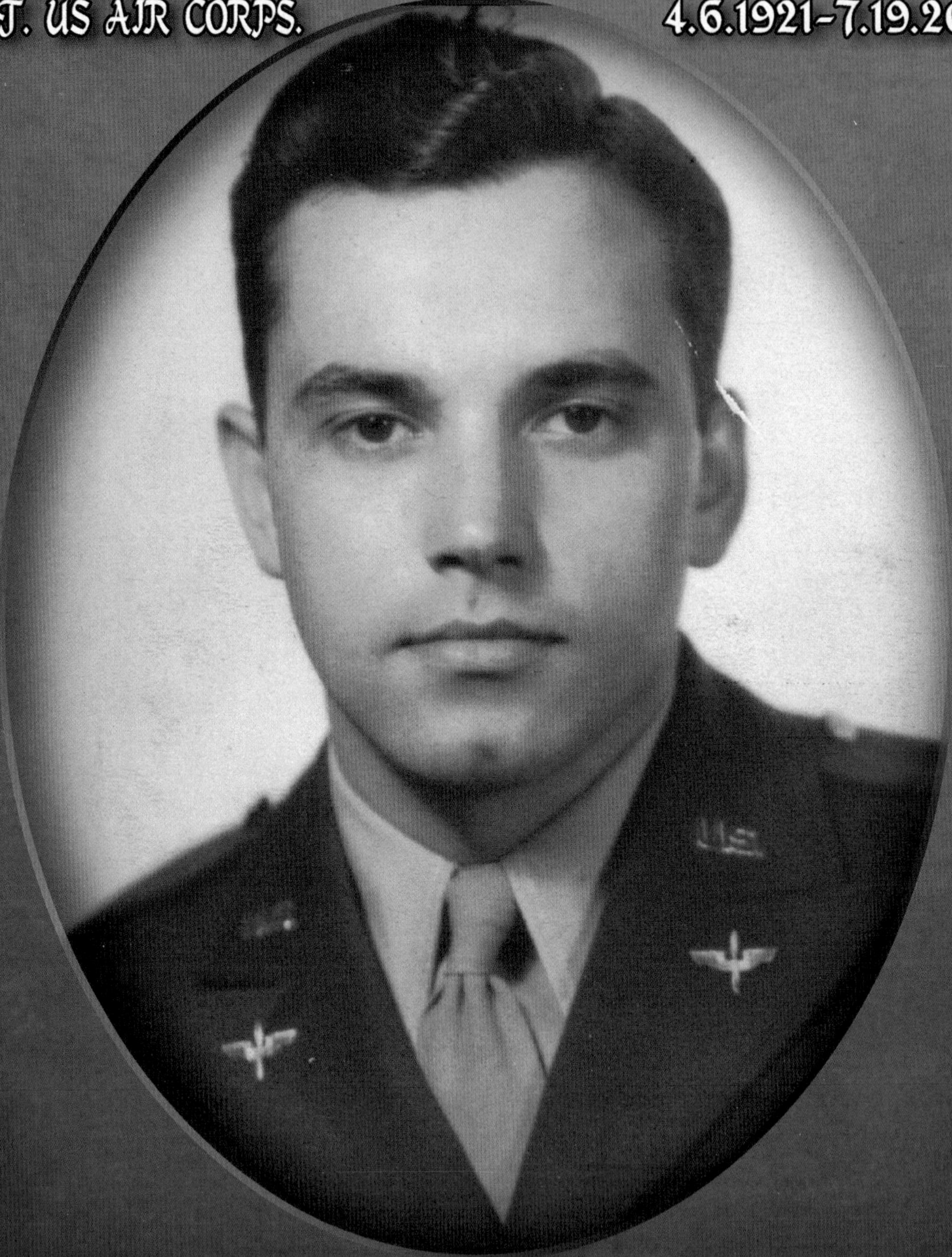

A MAN WHO WAS ADMIRED BY MOST HE MET AND LOVED BY ALL HE KNEW. HE IS SADLY MISSED BY HIS FAMILY WHOM HE SERVED AS A GLOWING EXAMPLE OF HOW TO LIVE.